D1055527

GREAT PREACHING ON

HELL

GREAT PREACHING ON

HELL

COMPILED BY
CURTIS HUTSON

SWORD of the LORD
PUBLISHERS
P.O.BOX 1099, MURFREESBORO, TN 37133

Printed and Bound in the United States of America

Preface

The greatest Hell preacher of all times was the Lord Jesus. While on earth He spoke only once in describing Heaven—in John 14: "In my Father's house are many mansions"; but He spoke no less than fourteen distinct times in the Bible describing Hell.

God did what He could to warn us of death, judgment and Hell. And in view of such warnings, it is disturbing that so few preachers today preach on these terrible truths.

There are 260 chapters in the New Testament, and Hell and judgment are either referred to or described some 234 times.

If we were on a highway 260 miles long and on that highway there were 234 signs warning of danger, surely we would have brains enough to seek out another road.

And we remind you that men are not only **loved** into Heaven; they are **warned** into it. "Noah . . . moved with fear, prepared an ark. . . ."

Dr. Bob Jones, Sr., once said, "What America needs most is about six months of red-hot preaching on Hell by men who are half-mad when they preach it. Love alone won't get the job done."

Once during a Christian fellowship meeting on the campus of a fine university, when some 80 brilliant law, medical or engineering students were asked, "How many of you gave your hearts to Christ simply through your great love for God?" not a single, solitary hand went up. But when asked, "How many of you gave your hearts to Christ because you knew there was an awful Hell from which to flee and that without a Sin-bearer you would be eternally lost?" every hand in the 80 went up.

We are living in a day when many preachers no longer believe in Hell, so, of course, do not preach it from their pulpits. But Hell is a fact. To dodge it will not annihilate it. To ignore it will not erase it. To deny it will not destroy it.

Lost—lost—lost! Damned—damned—damned! There to suffer the untold agonies forever and ever! We would not be so careless, so unconcerned, if we had fresh in mind what a horrible future awaits the Christ-rejecting sinner!

We went through some fifty years (or 1,100 issues) of THE SWORD OF THE LORD and chose for this volume the best sermons on Hell we ever printed, by fifteen Hellfire-and-brimstone preachers, who preached to great congregations, including lost people, and saw scores walk the aisles after hearing these warnings. Many of these messages are directed to the unsaved; others have a definite appeal to Christians to go after lost loved ones.

Our prayer is that you will heed what you hear, and go after the lost and warn them of the final abode of Christ-rejectors!

Sword of the Lord Publishers

Table of Contents

JOHN R. RICE
1895-1980

ABOUT THE MAN:

Preacher. . . evangelist. . . revivalist. . . editor. . . counselor to thousands. . . friend to millions—that was Dr. John R. Rice, whose accomplishments were nothing short of miraculous. Known as "America's Dean of Evangelists," Dr. Rice made a mighty impact upon the nation's religious life for some sixty years, in great citywide campaigns and in Sword of the Lord Conferences.

At age nine, after hearing a sermon on "The Prodigal Son," John went forward to claim Christ as Saviour. In 1916, with only $9.35 in his pocket, he rode off on his cowpony toward Decatur Baptist College. He was now on the road to becoming a world-renowned evangelist, although he was then totally unaware of God's will for his life.

There was many a twist and turn before Rice rode through the open door into full-time preaching—the army, marriage, graduate work, more seminary, assistant pastor, pastor—then FINALLY, where God planned to use him most—in full-time evangelism.

Dr. Rice and his ministry were always colorful (born in Cooke county, in Texas, December 11, 1895, and often called "Will Rogers of the Pulpit" because of their likeness and mannerisms)—and controversial. CONTROVERSIAL—and correctly so—because of his intense stand against modernism and infidelity and his fight for the Fundamentals.

Dr. Rice lived and died a man of convictions—intense convictions. But, like many other strong fighters for the Faith, Rice was also marked with a sincere spirit of compassion. Those who knew him best knew a man who loved them. In preaching, in prayer, and in personal life, Rice wept over sinners and with saints. But there is more. . .

Less than seventy-one hours before the dawning of 1981, one of the most prolific pens in all Christendom was stilled. Dr. John R. Rice left behind a legacy in writing of more than 200 titles, with a combined circulation of over 61 million copies. And through October of 1981, a total of 24,058 precious souls reported trusting Christ through his ministries, not counting those saved in his crusades nor in foreign countries where his literature has been translated.

And who but God knows the influence of THE SWORD OF THE LORD magazine which he started and edited for forty-six years!

And while "Twentieth Century's Mightiest Pen"—and man—has been stilled, thank God, the fruit remains! Though dead, he continues to speak.

I.

Hell — What the Bible Says About It

JOHN R. RICE

HOW CAN WE KNOW ABOUT HELL?

"19. There was a certain rich man, which was clothed in purple and fine linen, and fared sumptuously every day:

20. And there was a certain beggar named Lazarus, which was laid at his gate, full of sores,

21. And desiring to be fed with the crumbs which fell from the rich man's table: moreover the dogs came and licked his sores.

22. And it came to pass, that the beggar died, and was carried by the angels into Abraham's bosom: the rich man also died, and was buried;

23. And in hell he lift up his eyes, being in torments, and seeth Abraham afar off, and Lazarus in his bosom.

24. And he cried and said, Father Abraham, have mercy on me, and send Lazarus, that he may dip the tip of his finger in water, and cool my tongue; for I am tormented in this flame.

25. But Abraham said, Son, remember that thou in thy lifetime receivedst thy good things, and likewise Lazarus evil things: but now he is comforted, and thou art tormented.

26. And beside all this, between us and you there is a great gulf fixed: so that they which would pass from hence to you cannot; neither can they pass to us, that would come from thence.

27. Then he said, I pray thee therefore, father, that thou wouldest send him to my father's house:

28. For I have five brethren; that he may testify unto them, lest they also come into this place of torment.

29. Abraham saith unto him, They have Moses and the prophets; let them hear them.

30. And he said, Nay, father Abraham: but if one went unto them from the dead, they will repent.

31. And he said unto him, If they hear not Moses and the prophets, neither will they be persuaded, though one rose from the dead." — Jesus, in Luke 16:19-31.

Hell, What a Horrible Thought!

If there is a place of eternal torment where damned souls cry in vain for water amid the flames they cannot escape forever, it is the most terrible and alarming fact in this universe! The very possibility that such a doom may await the sinner is so shocking that nothing else can compare with it in importance. How can today's feasting or hunger, clothing or nakedness, honor or infamy, pleasure or pain compare in importance with a million years of pain, torment of body, mind and conscience? I beg every sinner to consider how worthwhile it is to know what God says about Hell.

And, fellow Christian, if one loved one of yours is in danger of the fire of Hell, how alarmed and anxious you ought to be! How earnest ought to be your entreaties, how fervent your prayers, how sleepless your efforts to save him from the DOOM OF LOST SOULS! Yes, if people are going to such a Hell that is so terrible, bonds of kinship and family ought not be the limit of our prayers and efforts. If there is one on this earth, even a total stranger, or an unknown savage, who may go to Hell, then everyone who has yet any of the milk of human kindness, any care for neighbor, any love for his fellowman, ought to have a consuming passion to rescue that poor soul!

To saints and sinners alike, the question of Hell becomes one of alarming importance. We ought to learn all we can about Hell in order to escape it ourselves and to rescue others from it.

Bible Our Only Source of Information About Hell

The only place we can learn about Hell is from the Bible. Science knows nothing beyond death. Human experience does not reach beyond the grave. If those on earth are ever to know what is beyond this life, they must learn it from God. Heaven, Hell, rewards and punishments, happiness and sorrow beyond the grave are matters about which the

Word of God is the only authority; so I will show what the Bible says about Hell.

Luke 16:19-31 is what Jesus Himself said about Hell, and much more, recorded in many other places in the New Testament. Jesus was the greatest Preacher on Hell of all Bible preachers. People often speak of Jesus as "the lowly Nazarene" or "the meek and lowly Jesus." But actually, though Jesus is the very essence of God's love made manifest in human form, His message of warning against the terrible consequences of sin was the plainest and sharpest in all the Bible.

Consider the following Scriptures, every one statements of the Lord Jesus about Hell. "But. . . whosoever shall say, Thou fool, shall be in danger of hell fire" (Matt. 5:22).

"And fear not them which kill the body, but are not able to kill the soul: but rather fear him which is able to destroy both soul and body in hell." —Matt. 10:28.

"As therefore the tares are gathered and burned in the fire; so shall it be in the end of this world. The Son of man shall send forth his angels, and they shall gather out of his kingdom all things that offend, and them which do iniquity; And shall cast them into a furnace of fire: there shall be wailing and gnashing of teeth." —Matt. 13:40-42.

"So shall it be at the end of the world: the angels shall come forth, and sever the wicked from among the just, And shall cast them into the furnace of fire: there shall be wailing and gnashing of teeth." — Matt. 13:49, 50.

"Ye serpents, ye generation of vipers, how can ye escape the damnation of hell?" —Matt. 23:33.

"Then shall he say also unto them on the left hand, Depart from me, ye cursed, into everlasting fire, prepared for the devil and his angels." — Matt. 25:41.

"And these shall go away into everlasting punishment: but the righteous into life eternal." —Matt. 25:46.

"And if thy hand offend thee, cut it off: it is better for thee to enter into life maimed, than having two hands to go into hell, into the fire that never shall be quenched: Where their worm dieth not, and the fire is not quenched. And if thy foot offend thee, cut it off: it is better for thee to enter halt into life, than having two feet to be cast into hell, into the fire that never shall be quenched: Where their worm dieth not, and

the fire is not quenched. And if thine eye offend thee, pluck it out: it is better for thee to enter into the kingdom of God with one eye, than having two eyes to be cast into hell fire: Where their worm dieth not, and the fire is not quenched. For every one shall be salted with fire, and every sacrifice shall be salted with salt."—Mark 9:43-49.

These Scriptures are in the words of the Lord Jesus Himself. Jesus was a "Hell-fire preacher." To Him, Hell was a horrible fact but a necessary one. With holy indignation He preached against sin and with solemn warning He urged men to flee from the wrath to come. Preachers who follow the Lord Jesus Christ must preach about Hell.

I call your attention again to the passage in Luke 16:19-31. Jesus gave it as solemnly as ever He uttered words in the presence of men.

The Bible does not call it a parable. It does not have the marks of a parable. Abraham, a historical character, is mentioned by name. Lazarus' name is given. These are not imaginary characters. This is not an illustration, a story, a fairy tale. This is literal fact, told in the most solemn language. No doubt the name of the lost man, too, would have been given, but the tender heart of the Saviour would not give offense to loved ones who may have heard the true account of the rich man who died and went to Hell because he did not repent.

If I do not believe this passage, I do not believe Jesus Christ. If this Scripture about Hell is not absolutely trustworthy, if it cannot be accepted as absolute truth, then I must reject the Bible as the Word of God and Jesus as the Son of God.

If I could not believe what the Bible says about Hell, I could not believe what it says about Heaven, about God, about Christ, about salvation, or about right or wrong. If the Bible is proved inaccurate and unreliable on one point, then it is a human book, and the Christian religion is no better than any other manmade religion. But if the Bible is true, then I must believe what it says about Hell.

The Deity of Christ at Stake

The story of the rich man in Hell is given in the words of Christ Himself. Jesus said more about Hell than did Moses, David, Isaiah, Paul, Peter, John or any other Bible character. Jesus is an authority. We are compelled to take what Jesus said.

We dare not take away one word concerning the torments of a doomed soul in Hell. We cannot add one comforting fact to what Jesus said here. To tamper with this account means straightout infidelity. If I prove any part of this teaching untrue, I have proved Jesus a human imposter and the Bible a human book. If we are not to believe this story of the rich man in Hell, there is nothing we can believe about the Bible, and nothing is left to the Christian religion. We must believe and we must take at face value what Jesus said about Hell. If we trifle at this point, we shall earn the curse of those who died unsaved and unwarned.

Why the Devil Deceives People About Hell

From the Garden of Eden until now, the Devil has been busy leading men to rebel against God and to sin. The best argument he can bring to get men to sin is to say that God does not punish sin.

To Eve in the Garden of Eden when God had said, "In the day that thou eatest thereof thou shalt surely die," the Devil answered, "Ye shall not surely die."

He made Israel believe in the days of Malachi, "It is vain to serve God," because they said, "They that work wickedness are set up; yea, they that tempt God are even delivered," and, "Every one that doeth evil is good in the sight of the Lord, and he delighteth in them" (Mal. 3:14, 15; 2:17).

It is the business of the Devil to make men believe that sin will not be punished. If he can get men to believe that there is no Hell, or that Hell is the grave, or that Hell is only figurative, or that men in Hell will be burned up at once without much pain, or that they will have another chance to be saved, or that after all, God is too good to send folks to Hell, then he accomplishes his purpose and gets men to continue in sin.

After all, the modern ideas about Hell are just a part of the modernism which denies that man is inherently wicked, denies the deity of Christ, the blood atonement, the inspiration of the Bible. Instead of direct creation of man, his fall in the Garden of Eden, and the depraved hearts of all mankind, the modernist believes that man is a product of evolution and is getting better all the time.

Instead of salvation by the blood of Christ, an atonement made by the Son of God for sinful men, the modernist teaches salvation by man's works and good character. Instead of a verbally inspired Word of God picturing man as a great sinner doomed to an awful Hell, with salvation offered free by a great Saviour, the modernist follows traditions of men and theories of science and reason.

Hell is an unpopular subject. J. M. Dawson said in the *Homiletic*

Review that 'the old idea about Hell has faded out and pastors of cultured churches refuse to revive it.'

But a man of God who believes the Bible must preach the terrible truth or he will be the cause of the ruin of those who lift their fruitless cries in a Hell of which they were not warned! A man who believes the Bible and seeks to please God must preach a literal Hell.

HELL, A LITERAL PLACE OF TORMENT

Is Hell Just the Grave?

Those who encourage men to reject Christ sometimes say that Hell is only the grave. How foolish that is when you hear the rich man cry out in Hell, "I am tormented in this flame"!

He was not simply in the grave! He wanted his brothers to repent "lest they also come to this place of torment." Repenting would not have kept his brothers from the grave; it would keep them from Hell.

Jesus spoke about Hell as a place "Where their worm dieth not, and the fire is not quenched" (Mark 9:48). Hell is "a lake of fire burning with brimstone" (Rev. 19:20). And, "The smoke of their torment ascendeth up for ever and ever: and they have no rest day nor night, who worship the beast and his image, and whosoever receiveth the mark of his name" (Rev. 14:11).

The Scriptures about Hell are so definite that anyone who says Hell is the grave is either an ignoramus or a deliberate deceiver.

I could talk very learnedly of *sheol*, of *hades*, of *Tartarus*, of *Gehenna*, Bible words in Hebrew and Greek for "Hell." The Hebrew word *sheol* and the Greek word *hades*, the latter used in Luke 16:23 in the passage about the rich man in Hell—I could show that these two words might often be translated simply "the unseen state." But Hell never means just the grave, and the way the Lord used the word in this passage proves that certainly to Him *hades* means what we mean by that old-fashioned word "Hell"—the place of the damned.

Hell Is a Place

The rich man in Hell knew that he was not just in some spiritual state. He wanted his brothers warned "lest they also come into this PLACE of torment." Hell is literally a "PLACE of torment."

Hell is not a state; it is a place. Throughout this book we spell "Hell" with a capital H, as names of other places are capitalized. If Chicago or America begin with a capital letter, so should that city of the damned, that country of lost souls. Hell is a place!

No Stops Between Death and Hell

Do not be deceived into thinking that a sinner will be given another chance to repent after death.

"And it came to pass, that the beggar died, and was carried by the angels into Abraham's bosom: the rich man also died, and was buried; And in hell he lift up his eyes, being in torments." —Luke 16:22, 23.

Lazarus died and immediately was carried by the angels to Paradise and found himself with the beloved ancestor, Abraham. There was no delay, no soul sleeping, no probation period for Lazarus. A Christian who dies goes immediately to the happy presence of God. When the thief on the cross died, he went with Jesus to Paradise (Luke 23:43).

My mother died when I was a six-year-old boy. She was conscious and happy to the last. She talked to us one by one about the Lord and Heaven, then she smiled and said, "I can see Jesus and my baby now."

When a Christian dies, he goes without delay to be with God.

So with the sinner on the road to Hell. The rich man died, was buried, "And in hell he lift up his eyes, being in torments." There is no evidence here of any delay in punishment. The torment of the rich man took place during the lifetime of his brothers, not in the far-distant future. When a lost man dies, he goes immediately to Hell and torment, says the Word of God.

Catholic Teaching About Limbo or Purgatory Unscriptural

Our Roman Catholic friends have invented the doctrine of purgatory, or limbo, an intermediate place between death and Hell. They say that after one suffers in purgatory for a time, he may then be allowed to go into Heaven. Catholic priests often teach their people that prayers, good deeds, or money paid to the priest will secure the release of loved ones from purgatory.

This teaching has not one verse of Scripture to back it up. The Bible does not even mention limbo, purgatory, nor any such place. Jesus never hinted that a man who died unsaved would have another chance.

Poor lost soul, do not depend upon any mercy or hope or opportunity for salvation after death. The rich man also died and was buried and in Hell he lifted up his eyes in torments. That was not purgatory but Hell.

The rich man would have been glad to learn that there was hope of release, hope that he could be prayed out of Hell. If he could have gotten out for good behavior, or if he could have paid his debt for sin and then passed on to Paradise with Abraham and Lazarus, that would have made the fire easier to bear. He may have had such hope. He thought one could pass between Heaven and Hell.

"He cried and said, Father Abraham, have mercy on me, and send Lazarus, that he may dip the tip of his finger in water, and cool my tongue; for I am tormented in this flame."—Vs. 24.

But it was a sad answer he got, an answer which proves that no one can ever pass from Heaven to Hell or from Hell to Heaven! Abraham answered:

"And beside all this, between us and you there is a great gulf fixed: so that they which would pass from hence to you cannot; neither can they pass to us, that would come from thence."—Vs. 26.

That great gulf between Hell and Paradise (or Heaven) is fixed. NO ONE CAN EVER PASS FROM ONE TO THE OTHER! There is no limbo, no purgatory, no middle ground! Beyond this life there remains only a Hell and a Heaven, and they are eternally separated!

Hell, a Place of Unutterable Suffering

The torment in Hell is evidently the principal point in this Scripture. Read again what Jesus said:

"And in hell he lift up his eyes, being in torments, and seeth Abraham afar off, and Lazarus in his bosom. And he cried and said, Father Abraham, have mercy on me, and send Lazarus, that he may dip the tip of his finger in water, and cool my tongue; for I am tormented in this flame."—Vss. 23, 24.

Notice the words "being in *torments*," and the rich man saying, "I am *tormented* in this flame" and Abraham's answer, from Heaven, "Thou art *tormented*."

This is the only glance that God has given us into Hell. How terrible the suffering! Here is a man who had had all that heart could desire; now he has nothing but torment. The beggar who laid at his gate full of sores while on earth is now happy in Heaven while the rich man is tormented in the flames of Hell.

Conscious Pain in Hell

This man is the same person he was on earth. He has the same kind of mind. He recognized Lazarus. He remembers his brothers. He remembers that he did not repent. He has the same bodily desires and longs for one drop of water to cool his tongue! He did not yet have his body in Hell, but he certainly retained bodily senses.

When the kind voice of Abraham answered from Heaven, "Son, remember," we can see that remembering will be one of the torments of Hell. Supposing that that rich man died and went to Hell during the lifetime of Jesus; then he has been "remembering" in Hell nearly 2,000 years.

He may remember every sin he committed. He may remember his base ingratitude to God. He may remember every opportunity he had but would not take. He may remember every sweet song, every mother's prayer, every wife's tear that urged him to seek the Lord. He may remember, now, one by one, the sins he was too busy to think of while he was clothed with purple and fine linen, faring sumptuously every day on this earth.

Hell is a place where men are conscious, in possession of their faculties of mind, memory and conscience.

There is no indication that this rich man in Hell loved God or wanted to do right any more now than when he died. He loved his brothers as he did on earth. His nature was not changed when he died. His soul did not sleep. There is conscious suffering and torment in Hell.

Physical Bodies Will Go to Hell

Jesus said that the rich man was buried and lifted up his eyes in Hell. Though his body at that time was in the grave, it would not prevent his having all the senses or asking for a drop of water to cool his tongue.

But the time is coming when that rich man will have his physical body in Hell. In Revelation 20:11-15 God gives a picture when the unsaved dead will come out of Hell, get their resurrection bodies from the graves on earth or from the waters of the sea, will stand before God for condemnation, then be cast forever into the lake of fire.

"And I saw a great white throne, and him that sat on it, from whose

*face the earth and the heaven fled away; and there was found no place
for them. And I saw the dead, small and great, stand before God; and
the books were opened: and another book was opened, which is the
book of life: and the dead were judged out of those things which were
written in the books, according to their works. And the sea gave up
the dead which were in it; and death and hell delivered up the dead
which were in them: and they were judged every man according to their
works. And death and hell were cast into the lake of fire. This is the
second death. And whosoever was not found written in the book of
life was cast into the lake of fire."*

The Hell where men are now is a Hell of lost souls where people
are conscious and suffer while their bodies remain in the graves on earth.
But at this future judgment of all the unsaved, we read that "the sea
gave up the dead which were in it; and death and hell delivered up
the dead which were in them."

The bodies come from death to life so that men stand before God.
Hell gives up the spirit dead while the earth gives up the physical dead,
and the bodies and souls of lost men come together again. This is the
time of which God speaks:

*"That at the name of Jesus every knee should bow, of things in
heaven, and things in earth, and things under the earth; And that every
tongue should confess that Jesus Christ is Lord, to the glory of God
the Father."*—Phil. 2:10, 11.

Literal knees will bow and literal tongues will be compelled to confess their sins before Christ and the assembled multitude; then these,
in literal bodies, will be cast into the lake of fire.

"Fear Him Which Is Able to Destroy Both Soul and Body in Hell"

It was this terrible, physical Hell where men will be tormented in body
as well as mind of which Jesus spoke when He said:

*"Wherefore if thy hand or thy foot offend thee, cut them off, and
cast them from thee: it is better for thee to enter into life halt or maimed,
rather than having two hands or two feet to be cast into everlasting fire.
And if thine eye offend thee, pluck it out, and cast it from thee: it is
better for thee to enter into life with one eye, rather than having two
eyes to be cast into hell fire."*—Matt. 18:8, 9.

Jesus spoke of physical bodies in Hell when He said: "And fear not them which kill the body, but are not able to kill the soul: but rather fear him which is able to destroy BOTH SOUL AND BODY IN HELL" (Matt. 10:28).

The Devil has deceived people into believing that Hell is some indefinite, ghostly place where there might be some discomfort but no actual personality, no conscious suffering, no physical torment.

May God help us to see that these tortures await the doomed and damned and ruined souls who reject Christ and go to Hell!

Is There Literal Fire in Hell?

Already we have seen that Hell is a literal place where physical bodies will dwell. The question arises: Is there literal fire in Hell? The answer of the rich man in Hell is, "I am tormented in this flame."

Again and again we are told of the fire of Hell.

Jesus said in Matthew 5:22 that one who says, "Thou fool," shall be in danger of Hell fire.

In Matthew 18:9 we are warned of the possibility that people having two eyes might "be cast into hell fire," and the same statement is given in Mark 9:47, 48 where Jesus spoke of "hell fire, Where their worm dieth not, and the fire is not quenched."

In Revelation 20:14, 15, Hell is called "the lake of fire," and there it is said that Hell (*hades*, the spirit Hell) is to be "cast into the lake of fire," the second death.

If we believe the Word of God, then we must believe that when physical bodies leave the Great White Throne Judgment, they must go into a place of fire.

HELL IS ETERNAL PUNISHMENT

If after rejecting Christ on earth a condemned soul were to die and then simply cease to be, that would be terrible punishment. When a sinner dies without Christ, he misses all the glories of Heaven, the reign of Christ on earth, and eternal happiness in the presence of God. If Hell meant only to pass out of existence and miss the joy that God has prepared for those that love Him, that would be an eternal loss that no sinner could afford to risk.

Or if a sinner might stay in Hell until his suffering passed beyond endurance, then mercifully cease to know, cease to feel, cease to suffer and be no more, that would be a terrible Hell. Ten minutes of Hell would be so horrible that anyone with any sense would want to miss it at any cost.

But the Hell spoken of in the Bible is an eternal Hell. Not only is the place itself eternal but souls will be tormented forever. No other honest construction can be put upon the many Scriptures that talk about Hell.

The rich man is still in Hell, just as Lazarus is still in Heaven. Abraham said to the rich man, "Now he is comforted, and thou art tormented." The time element in the two cases is evidently the same. There is a great gulf fixed between the two places, meaning no one can get out of Hell. Clearly the rich man is still there.

Sinners Must Stay in Hell at Least Until the Judgment

Besides, God pledged Himself that every sinner shall come to judgment. He promised that dead bodies shall rise again. "And many of them that sleep in the dust of the earth shall awake, some to everlasting life, and some to shame and everlasting contempt" (Dan. 12:2).

Lost people will be resurrected just as surely as the saved.

The same thing is taught in John 5:28, 29: "Marvel not at this: for the hour is coming, in the which all that are in the graves shall hear his voice, And shall come forth; they that have done good, unto the resurrection of life; and they that have done evil, unto the resurrection of damnation."

Lost people in the graves will hear His voice and come forth to the resurrection of damnation! The rich man was buried and in Hell he lifted up his eyes, being in torments. As long as his body is in the grave, the rich man will stay in Hell. The millions in Hell cannot be brought out, cannot cease to be, for God has promised to bring them back to their bodies when the lost in the graves hear the voice of Jesus and come forth!

Revelation, chapter 20, verses 11 to 15, tells when this resurrection of lost people from the grave will take place. After the thousand years' reign of Christ on earth is over, sinners shall come out of Hell; their bodies will be gathered from the sea and from the land; and in their bodies men shall stand before Christ to receive their eternal condemnation!

"And I saw a great white throne, and him that sat on it, from whose face the earth and the heaven fled away; and there was found no place for them. And I saw the dead, small and great, stand before God; and

the books were opened: and another book was opened, which is the book of life: and the dead were judged out of those things which were written in the books, according to their works. And the sea gave up the dead which were in it; and death and hell delivered up the dead which were in them: and they were judged every man according to their works. And death and hell were cast into the lake of fire. This is the second death. And whosoever was not found written in the book of life was cast into the lake of fire."

The rich man, then, along with all the other millions in Hell, must stay there, tormented in flames, remembering, remembering, remembering, until he faces Jesus at the Great White Throne Judgment. As long as you can find a skull in a museum, a skeleton in a doctor's office; as long as human bodies are yet decaying in the cemeteries; so long the souls of lost men are tormented in Hell, awaiting the resurrection of their bodies at the last great judgment day! Then the rich man's ashes will reassemble and his soul will come out of Hell to face Jesus so that his knee can bow before Christ and his tongue can confess that Christ is Lord! At the very least, sinners cannot cease to suffer in Hell until that day.

Physical Torment Continues Forever Beyond the Judgment

If every sinner would have to suffer in Hell a few score years, or hundreds of years, or thousands of years, until the Great White Throne Judgment, that would be terrible enough, God knows! Every sinner could then come out of Hell, get his resurrection body, and appear before that awful court for sentencing. If then he could drop into the lake of fire and his poor wicked personality be snuffed out in a moment's flame, that would be bad enough. But the Bible carefully teaches that sinners must live on in torment forever beyond the judgment.

The terms used in the Bible about Hell and the condemnation of lost people are not words of temporary meaning. They indicate an eternity of suffering and shame. Daniel 12:2 says that some shall awake "to shame and everlasting contempt." EVERLASTING contempt! In Mark 3:29 Jesus warned against the "danger of ETERNAL damnation."

The future blessedness of a Christian and the doom of a lost man are many times contrasted in the Bible, but the inference everywhere is that the one lasts as long as the other. To the one is promised "everlasting life," to the other, "everlasting contempt." Abraham said to the rich man concerning Lazarus, "Now he is comforted and thou art tormented." Lazarus was being continually comforted; the rich man was being continually tormented.

"The Smoke of Their Torment Ascendeth Up For Ever and Ever"

In Revelation 14:10, 11 God gives us a vivid and fearful picture of the torment of the lost, proving that people will remain in an eternal Hell of torment.

"The same shall drink of the wine of the wrath of God, which is poured out without mixture into the cup of his indignation; and he shall be tormented with fire and brimstone in the presence of the holy angels, and in the presence of the Lamb: AND THE SMOKE OF THEIR TORMENT ASCENDETH UP FOR EVER AND EVER: AND THEY HAVE NO REST DAY NOR NIGHT, who worship the beast and his image, and whosoever receiveth the mark of his name."

The smoke of their torment continues to rise day after day, forever and ever. If that were all, one might hope that after a sinner had been consumed with the fires of Hell and had ceased to be, the smoke should go on up and up and higher up forever. But the rest of the verse makes it clear that sinners continue to suffer there forever: "And they have no rest day nor night"! The night brings no rest from the torture of the day, and the dawn of a new day after a night of horror only promises more torment to those in that restless place, those who rejected Christ and would not have His mercy!

This is the kind of Hell Jesus talked about when He said, "Where their worm dieth not, and the fire is not quenched."

I do not know all that this Scripture means. I know that in this present world all the aches and pains of body are caused by sin. The infections of germs, the plagues of parasites which infest the human body, the decay of cancer—all are the result of sin. They could not have happened to a perfect Adam in the Garden of Eden.

It may well be that a thousand such unspeakable horrors of bodily suffering await the sinner in Hell beyond the resurrection of the unsaved dead and the last judgment day. When Jesus said, "Their worm dieth not, and the fire is not quenched," He certainly meant continuous suffering.

Example of Antichrist and False Prophet
Prove Torment of Hell Eternal

As if given to prove this very point, the Bible tells of two men—human beings like ourselves—who will be in the lake of fire with their physical bodies a thousand years. Then at the end of the thousand years, they are still to be in Hell.

In Revelation 19:11-21 we are told of the return of Christ in glory and the Battle of Armageddon, and how the beast (the Antichrist) and the false prophet with him will be cast alive into the lake of fire. Though John sees these events in Revelation as if past, it is clearly a prophecy of the future.

"And the beast was taken, and with him the false prophet that wrought miracles before him, with which he deceived them that had received the mark of the beast, and them that worshipped his image. These both were cast alive into a lake of fire burning with brimstone."—Rev. 19:20.

The Hell into which these two men will be cast alive is a physical Hell, the lake of fire. They will be "both soul and body in hell" as Jesus said men would be (Matt. 10:28). Read on through the twentieth chapter of Revelation and learn how that old serpent, the Devil and Satan, is shackled a thousand years and shut up in a bottomless pit; how the saints will reign with Christ on the earth a thousand years; how, when the thousand years are finished, Satan shall be loosed for a little season and cause the last great rebellion. Then in Revelation 20:10 the Devil himself is seized at the end of the thousand years' reign and cast into Hell. The "beast" and the false prophet, after a thousand years in the lake of fire, are still there. "And the devil that deceived them was cast into the lake of fire and brimstone, WHERE THE BEAST AND THE FALSE PROPHET ARE, and shall be tormented day and night for ever and ever."

After a thousand years in the lake of fire with both soul and body, people will still be there, "And shall be tormented day and night for ever and ever." It is evident that that is the fate of all sinners who go to Hell, as well as the fate of the Devil himself.

Sinner, do not let Satan deceive you about this matter. As sure as the Bible is God's Word, then just that sure there is an eternal Hell, a place of everlasting torment for the sinner who rejects Christ.

How Do Bodies Stay Alive in Hell?

If you were to ask me how a human body could long endure the pain of the fires of Hell, my answer would be: I do not know. Indeed I do not know how God keeps us alive day by day. Before the Flood men lived often nearly a thousand years. God shut Adam and Eve away from the tree of life lest they should eat of it and live on forever, even though they were sinners. After all, death is more a mercy than a punishment. It is sufficient that God's Word teaches that those with physical bodies will be cast into Hell and have no rest day nor night. There are scores of things in the Bible which I cannot understand, but I can believe them and that is all God requires.

Now a few moments of fire will usually destroy a body. But we may be sure God has other laws which are not the laws of nature as we now know them. God is a God of miracles. His ways are not our ways, nor are His thoughts our thoughts. What He has said, He will bring to pass. It would take no more of a miracle for one to stay alive in the fires of Hell than that a body should be reassembled from the dust of the earth or gathered out of the waters of the sea, yet He has promised to do just that. Christ says these bodies will be tormented forever in Hell.

Fire will usually destroy life in a human body, but three Hebrew young men, Shadrach, Meshach and Abednego, walked in a furnace of fire unharmed, and even their garments did not receive the smell of smoke. One like the Son of God came and walked with them in the furnace. It is as easy to believe there will be physical bodies in the lake of fire as to believe that God kept the Hebrew children in the fire unharmed.

WILL A LOVING GOD SEND A SINNER TO HELL?

Infidels say that—that weak and sinful men would not send their children to a place like Hell, and that if God loves His children, He would not condemn them to go to Hell.

I answer back that no one is a child of God until he has been born again. Jesus said to the Pharisees in John 8:44, "Ye are of your father the devil." Only the children of the Devil go to Hell.

Hell is the result of sin. Men go to Hell because they ought to, not because God hates them.

The Wages of Sin Is Death

Sin is a hateful subject to those who do not like the Bible teaching about Hell. But sin is the cause of Hell. The wages of sin is death. When God said to Adam in the Garden of Eden, "In the day that thou eatest thereof thou shalt surely die," He had reference to the death of the soul, not primarily to physical death. When Adam sinned, he began to die physically; but he immediately died spiritually. But for the mercy of God, he would have gone to Hell. The second death is caused, like the first, by sin. Unless God changes all His laws when we come to the next world, there will have to be a place where sin is punished.

In This World Sin Brings Suffering; Why Not in Hell?

Sin brings pain and suffering, tragedy and ruin. I saw the other day a man shuffling down the street, with legs partially paralyzed—"Jake-leg-paralysis!" He suffers for his sin. Is God to blame for that?

A blind man came to me for prayer and help, led by his nine-year-old daughter. Though it was wintertime, the sad-faced child was dressed in a gingham garment and without a coat. This father, a slave to drink, told me how he had lost his job and how finally wood alcohol had turned him blind, how his wife took in washing, and how he then sometimes stole the money to spend for bootleg whiskey. Sin brought him trouble. Was God to blame for that?

I went to the Tarrant County jail to see a young man who was convicted of murder and was already sentenced to the electric chair. He was taken out of solitary confinement and given time to shave. When he came out of the cell to see me (in the presence of a burly jailer), this young man, hardly more than a boy, had a hand as palsied as a man of eighty. His young wife and his mother day and night were besieging the governor for a pardon.

He wept as he told me the story of what sin had done to his home and life and heart. He was beginning to reap what he sowed. His sin had found him out.

When I found pity arising in my heart for him, I could not help remembering that other manly young fellow, shot down on the street by this hijacker's gun, according to the decision of twelve jurors.

Sin brought stalking tragedy; sin brought broken hearts; sin brought unease of mind and conscience; sin brought death. Was God to blame for that?

Earn Their Own Hell

Anyone who cannot believe in Hell is not intelligent. He does not face the facts. He will not examine the evidence that God puts on every side of him. You who say you "cannot believe a loving God would send a sinner to Hell," let me ask you some questions.

Do you believe a loving God will allow sin to put a man in the hospital with a diseased body?

Do you believe God will allow sin to put a man in jail, with his liberty taken away for months or years or even for life?

Do you believe God does allow sinners to go to the electric chair to pay for murder?

Doesn't God allow sin to break homes, to bring disease, death and misery?

Doesn't God allow sin to bring war to the nations that forget God, and death to millions?

And if the same God is running things just the other side of the thin veil we call death, then you may be sure that in the next world the sinner will reap what he sows and will get his honest wages. And every Christ-rejecting, Hell-deserving sinner will come to the place of torment, reserved for those who will not repent and be saved.

The one who does not believe in Hell is a willful fool who does not want to believe what his eyes see.

"The wages of sin is death."—Rom. 6:23.

"Be sure your sin will find you out."—Num. 32:23.

"Be not deceived; God is not mocked: for whatsoever a man soweth, that shall he also reap."—Gal. 6:7.

When you see the ruin wrought by man's sin, tell me—is God to blame for that? In this world, trouble, tragedy, heartache, ruin and death are the fruits of sin. We may be sure that in the next world God's laws about sin have not changed. People go to Hell because they are sinners. The torments of Hell are the fruits of their sin. People go to Hell because they ought to go. Hell is the place for sinners.

Punishment in Hell Differs "According to Their Works"

Some people are more wicked than others, so they deserve more punishment. Those who had greater opportunities and turned them down ought to be held more strictly accountable, and the Bible teaches that they will be. Hell is hotter for some people than for others.

Revelation 20:12, 13 says the unsaved dead will be judged according to their works:

"And I saw the dead, small and great, stand before God; and the books were opened: and another book was opened, which is the book of life: AND THE DEAD WERE JUDGED OUT OF THOSE THINGS WHICH WERE WRITTEN IN THE BOOKS, ACCORDING TO THEIR WORKS. And the sea gave up the dead which were in it; and death and hell delivered up the dead which were in them: AND THEY WERE JUDGED EVERY MAN ACCORDING TO THEIR WORKS."

Judgment will be on the basis of what men deserve. People go to Hell because they deserve to go. Some will have a worse Hell because they deserve a worse Hell. They will be judged accurately according to God's records of their works and punished in Hell accordingly.

That Hell will be more bearable for some than for others is found elsewhere in the Bible. Jesus said that Sodom, Tyre and Sidon will find it more tolerable in the judgment than Chorazin, Bethsaida, Capernaum, or other cities that rejected the Gospel after much enlightenment (Luke 10:10-15). The greater the enlightenment and opportunity which a sinner has, the greater his punishment if he rejects it.

"And that servant, which knew his lord's will, and prepared not himself, neither did according to his will, shall be beaten with many stripes. But he that knew not, and did commit things worthy of stripes, shall be beaten with few stripes. For unto whomsoever much is given, of him shall be much required: and to whom men have committed much, of him they will ask the more." —Luke 12:47, 48.

Hell will certainly be hotter for some than for others. God always does right. A man who rejects Christ fifty years and with great enlightenment still resists God, will be punished more than a younger person. One who is reared in this enlightened land and hears the Gospel all his life, then dies without Christ, will find Hell more terrible than a heathen savage who had only the enlightenment of the law written in his heart, that is, his conscience, and the evidence of nature around about him that there is a God.

Hell is the result of men's sins. Greater sin makes a more terrible Hell for the sinner.

Sin Continues in Hell

The torments of Hell seem to be so terrible! Would a short life of sin here earn an eternity of torment? Is God fair to keep a man forever in Hell for the sins of his life? An intelligent question and there is an intelligent answer. The reason sinners must stay in Hell is that they are sinners still. Hell is not only a place of punishment for sin, but it is a place where sin continues.

When the rich man died and was buried and in Hell lifted up his eyes, being in torments, he was still the same sinner, unchanged in character and heart, as when he lived on earth in plenty and did not repent. In Luke 16, the rich man uttered no word of sorrow for his sin. He asked Abraham for mercy, but not God. As a lost Jew, he revered the memory of the founder of the Hebrew race, but he did not love God. He asked for water to cool his tongue, but not that his sins be forgiven. He knew he was in Hell because he did not repent, yet in Hell he still did not repent! The unsaved rich man while on earth loved his brothers and wished them well; when he died and went to Hell, he loved them still with a natural human love, but he did not love God. This sinner on earth remained a sinner in Hell.

In fact, there is every reason to believe that in Hell there will be an abandonment to wickedness such as is not possible on this earth. On earth there are many restraining influences, many holy and blessed impulses which will never affect any man in Hell.

Here there are Christians on every side to restrain and warn the sinner. There he will be forever in the presence of those who hate God. There he will never hear a gospel sermon. In Hell one will never hear a sacred song. There the influence of respectability will even be lacking and people in Hell will give themselves over to unbridled sin forever.

How freely men will be permitted to indulge their sinful appetites, we do not know, but that their wicked hearts will grow even more wicked through the years seems almost certain. Even the Holy Spirit, it appears, will call no longer at the heart door of those in Hell.

The most terrible thing about Hell is that it is a place of sinning as well as sinners. Sinners themselves continue to make Hell what it is.

Men Will Be Without Honor, Women Without Virtue, in Hell

Thousands go to Hell who in this world call themselves honest men. Remember that paying grocery bills does not make one a Christian. "Marvel not that I said unto thee, Ye must be born again." But we may be sure no man in Hell would remain honest very long when every motive for virtue and honesty is gone.

Multitudes of virtuous women, chaste wives and mothers it may be, will be in Hell. Human virtues are not enough to save the soul: ". . . there is no difference: For all have sinned, and come short of the glory of God." Christ is the only way of salvation. But we may well believe that virtuous women will not remain virtuous and chaste in Hell. Hell will be given over to the unsaved, and the leading spirits there "are dogs, and sorcerers, and whoremongers, and murderers, and idolaters, and whosoever loveth and maketh a lie" (Rev. 22:15). When every restraining influence of respectability, example, the Holy Spirit and good advice is gone, there will be no virtue in Hell, no honesty, no goodness.

Preachers Have Misrepresented Hell

Some preachers—good men—picture sinners in Hell repenting, loving God, begging for forgiveness, and picture God as laughing and mocking at their torment.

That is not the Bible teaching about the people in Hell nor about God. The rich man in Hell was sorry to reap what he had sown. He wanted mercy for his body, but he did not seek forgiveness of his sins. On the other hand, Abraham, speaking for God, did not laugh at the rich man's torment nor mock his cries. Instead, he said with tender sadness, "Son, remember."

When evil catches up with the sinner, then wisdom, even his own common sense, laughs at his calamity and mocks when his fear comes (Prov. 1:20-27). We may be sure that this is true about sinners in Hell. But God does not rejoice over their torment; and the reason sinners are left in Hell is that they have the same rebellion, the same wickedness, the same unbelief they had here on earth, but intensified by the environment of Hell and unrestrained by not a single godly influence.

Can you see why sinners who reject Christ and deliberately choose evil instead of good, then when they go to Hell, continue in sin? Can you see why they should continue to be punished? Sinners in Hell make their own Hell. People go to Hell because they deserve it, and they stay there for the same reason. Punishment continues because sin continues in Hell.

Sinners Would Be Miserable in Heaven

Suppose sinners should go to Heaven or should come back to the glorified new earth where Christ and God the Father will reign forever with the saved. There all the millions of angels and the redeemed will be praising Christ; but these despise Christ, some of them crucified Him, and all of them turned Him down saying, "We will not have this man to reign over us."

In the heavenly world there would be no room for lust or drunkenness or covetousness or lies; all these wicked went to Hell because they loved such things. Sinners would be miserable in the presence of a God whom they did not love, living according to rules which only the good would enjoy. Heaven would be Hell to the sinner.

Sinners Would Ruin Heaven for Others

In fact, sinners would make Heaven a hell for everybody else. Sinners, let out of Hell, would covet the golden paving of the heavenly Jerusalem, the pearls which make her gates, and the precious stones which are the foundations of her walls. For their own greed they would destroy the Paradise of God if they could.

Sinners, let out of Hell with their vile hearts still unchanged, would lust after the angels as did the men of Sodom. Remember that the men of Sodom are in Hell and that Sodom was destroyed for such sin. Such sinners would defile and taint Heaven. They would make the new Heaven and the new earth like the old ones.

If There Were No Hell—

One blessed day I am going to Heaven. My, what a happy time I anticipate there! Colored people down South sometimes sing,

> **I'm gonna lay down my burden**
> **Down by the riverside,**
> **Down by the riverside,**
> **Down by the riverside;**
> **I'm gonna lay down my burden**
> **Down by the riverside,**
> **And study war no more!**

That longing to lay down the sword, to have the fight ended, to earn victory at last, I have expected to be fulfilled in Heaven. Suppose one fine day I wake up in Heaven, with all my loved ones. As I settle down to enjoy my heavenly mansion, there is a ring on the doorbell. The Angel Gabriel is waiting for me.

"John, get your Bible. The Lord wants you out on an evangelistic tour," he tells me.

"Well," I say hesitantly, "I was hoping now to get rest and be with my family. I thought the fight was over. But bless God, I will preach for Him a million years if He wants that." So I take my Bible and get ready to leave with the Angel Gabriel.

Meantime he explains, "Well, as you know, all the sinners are up here in Heaven. God was too good to send any of them to Hell, so they need some preaching mighty bad."

As I go out the front door with the angel and with my Bible under my arm, ready for an evangelistic tour, Gabriel turns and warns me sharply, "Don't leave your door unlocked! Remember, every thief, every bum, every crook and burglar who lived on earth is up here in Heaven now, so lock your door!"

Rather startled, I lock the door. Gabriel continues, "And don't you have some lovely daughters?"

"Yes—and you ought to see my six girls with their long, lovely hair and winsome smiles!"

"Well, don't ever let them go out at night unescorted. They must be watched very carefully. Remember that Heaven is now full of criminals. God was too good to send any sinner to Hell, and so all those wicked Sodomites who would have raped the angels are now on our streets up here, and every lustful man who ever betrayed and seduced an innocent girl is here; so take good care of your girls, and warn them of the danger."

By this time my eyes are misty and I am feeling the keenest disappointment. This is not the kind of Heaven I was looking forward to! But bravely, taking my Bible, I start down the street. But we are interrupted by a funeral procession; for since there are sinners in Heaven, there will be death. Policemen are on every corner because with all the unregenerates who hate God and would not turn to Christ, of course Heaven will have crime unless carefully policed.

As we walk on, we pass a large jail, for where sinners are, there must be jails.

Soon I hear the cry of a newsboy:

ALL ABOUT THE WAR! HITLER'S WAR IN HEAVEN, TOWNS WIPED OUT AND NOW IN FLAMES. THOUSANDS HOMELESS, MILLIONS UNDER ARMS, OTHER MILLIONS DEAD.

Oh, yes, of course. If God were too good to send sinners to Hell,

then Hitler would be in Heaven and with him would be war, murder
and misery.

God in Heaven, is that possible! No! That is a false picture. I am sorry
that sinners reject Christ and sorry that they must go to Hell, but with
all my soul I thank God that one day there will be a place where every
wicked, Christ-rejecting sinner will be shut out, and those that love God
can at long last be free of worry and can enjoy peace, sweet peace!

If God did not send sinners to Hell, then there could be no real Heaven
for God, or saints, or angels.

But there is a Heaven and so there must be a Hell. And the only
way Heaven can be a place of joy, peace and rest is to have a Hell
to confine sinners.

What does God say about the blessed home of the saints in eternity?
We are told by the beloved John: ". . . God shall wipe away all tears
from their eyes; and there shall be no more death, neither sorrow, nor
crying, neither shall there be any more pain: for the former things are
passed away" (Rev. 21:4).

That could only be so in a world without sin. Isaiah 35:5-10 pictures
the blessedness which could never be possible if sinful men were present and had their way:

*"Then the eyes of the blind shall be opened, and the ears of the deaf
shall be unstopped. Then shall the lame man leap as an hart, and the
tongue of the dumb sing: for in the wilderness shall waters break out,
and streams in the desert. And the parched ground shall become a pool,
and the thirsty land springs of water: in the habitation of dragons, where
each lay, shall be grass with reeds and rushes. And an highway shall
be there, and a way, and it shall be called The way of holiness; the
unclean shall not pass over it; but it shall be for those: the wayfaring
men, though fools, shall not err therein. No lion shall be there, nor any
ravenous beast shall go up thereon, it shall not be found there; but the
redeemed shall walk there: And the ransomed of the Lord shall return,
and come to Zion with songs and everlasting joy upon their heads: they
shall obtain joy and gladness, and sorrow and sighing shall flee away."*

The perfection of a redeemed earth as told in Revelation, chapters
21 and 22, would not be possible if sinners were there! An earth cursed
by sin must bring forth thorns and thistles; it would be infested with
ravenous beasts, germs of decay and disease.

There must be no sinners on the new earth, no sinners to contaminate the holiness of the presence of God and to take the joy from the hearts of Christians. Don't you see why sinners must go somewhere else besides Heaven?

There, thank God, we will be done with sin! If God should empty Hell into Heaven, there would be no more Heaven. That world, like this, would be a vale of tears. If sinners were in Heaven, we would need locks on the doors. If sinners were in Heaven, there would needs be courts, jails and penitentiaries. If there were sinners there, there would be sickness and suffering; so there we would need doctors and hospitals for those in beds of pain. If sinners were there, then Heaven would be a place of broken hearts.

If we would not have Heaven a place of lies, deceit, envy, strife, hatred, covetousness, drunkenness and lust, then a good God must keep sinners out.

It is the providence of a good God that one day those who hate Him and love sin, those who will not be born again, those who follow darkness instead of light, rebels against the Father and haters of His Son, will be taken away and will no more tempt the children of God nor bring them grief and pain.

Matthew 13:41-43 says:

"The Son of man shall send forth his angels, and they shall gather out of his kingdom all things that offend, and them which do iniquity; And shall cast them into a furnace of fire: there shall be wailing and gnashing of teeth. Then shall the righteous shine forth as the sun in the kingdom of their Father. Who hath ears to hear, let him hear."

It is the providence of a wise and good God that those who will not themselves enter into everlasting joy and peace may be segregated in the madhouse of Hell. If they will not have a Saviour from sin, at least God must see that they do not make hell for a whole universe by their sin.

Hell, a Madhouse

Once I was entertained at a ranch home in west Texas. The hospitality was of that cordial and sincere warmth that is proverbial among ranch people. Yet in the case of this Christian man and wife, a reserved soberness hinted at some secret sorrow. When I inquired, their pastor told me the story.

They had a son, the youngest (now grown) whom they loved as you love your baby boy. He was their pride and joy. In the midst of a summer harvest, he lost his mind. With unfailing love they tended him day by day like a baby. His poor, unbalanced mind conceived a hate for his mother. He fancied that all the family had conspired against him to take his life. They guarded him and waited on him. After the mother had worn herself out in a few short months caring for him, the poor, demented lad seized a knife one day and would have killed her had he not been restrained.

The family physician pressed on them their inescapable duty. "You cannot make the boy happy here. You cannot give him back his mind. You cannot even give him the proper care. The only place for him is a padded cell, where he can be watched by trained keepers and given every attention, until death eases his sufferings. There is no hope that he will ever be better." Turning to the father the physician said, "You had better do it now before he kills his mother."

They saw the wisdom of the doctor's advice and followed it with broken hearts.

The arrangements were made, and the sheriff took the insane boy to a madhouse. The father and mother did not love him any less by doing so. They didn't send him there because they hated him, for they were inconsolable in their loss. They did the only right thing, which was made necessary by hopeless insanity. The boy is no more miserable, for anywhere with him would be a madhouse. It was the only way the home could be made safe and enjoy some measure of peace.

God is like that father; He has no choice. To do right, He must provide for the safety of His own in Heaven. Incurably wicked sinners who rejected every offer of mercy, trampled under foot the blood of Christ, scorned the Holy Spirit and hardened their hearts—sinners who will not let God change their hearts—such must be put in the madhouse of Hell. A loving God gave His Son in order to keep people out of this place of doom. If men will not be saved, they must be lost. Those who will not go to Heaven must go to Hell. Sinner, do not blame God if you land in Hell!

KEEPING PEOPLE OUT OF HELL: THE SOUL-WINNING MOTIVE

How profoundly moved a Christian ought to be who thinks of the millions who go to Hell! Little wonder that modern Christians have gotten away from the burden and passion for the salvation of sinners. They have forgotten the Bible teaching on Hell. Preachers have explained away the torments of the damned!

What a compelling motive we have for prayer, for preaching, for soul winning, when we actually realize that every responsible being who leaves this world without a definite change in heart immediately lifts his eyes in Hell, tormented in flame!

The motive of saving sinners from Hell moved Paul the apostle. So troubled was he because his kinsmen, the Jews, were in danger of Hell, that he could honestly say:

"I say the truth in Christ, I lie not, my conscience also bearing me witness in the Holy Ghost, That I have great heaviness and continual sorrow in my heart. For I could wish that myself were accursed from Christ for my brethren, my kinsmen according to the flesh." — Rom. 9:1-3.

The burden of his heart was so great that after leaving Ephesus he called together the preachers of the city—most of them doubtlessly converted under his ministry—reminding them: "Therefore watch, and remember, that by the space of three years I ceased not to warn every one night and day with tears" (Acts 20:31).

He realized the doom of a soul; it never left him! Day after day he toiled, working far into the night to teach people to repent, all the while with tears rolling down his face! Paul did not have any different Gospel from what we have; he just had a deeper concern for the salvation of sinners. With him it was a holy passion, practically the only concern of his life. To see sinners saved from Hell was almost, to Paul, worth being himself accursed from Christ.

Jude 23 tells the duty of Christians toward sinners: "And others save with fear, pulling them out of the fire; hating even the garment spotted by the flesh."

May God grant that this book may imprint on the hearts of you Christians a holy fear concerning Hell so that you will snatch your loved ones out of the fire itself!

Soul Worth More Than Body; the Boy Who Fell in a Well

A good many years ago men were digging an oil well near Electra, Texas, eighteen miles north of my boyhood home. They had drilled the hole down into the earth 180 feet with a twelve-inch bit and had stopped for a little while. Children played about the uncovered hole in the earth. A five-year-old boy slipped on the derrick floor and fell down, down into the earth, feet first. The hole was tight and the boy went down slowly so the fall did not kill him immediately. If only he could be rescued in time!

Attracted by the screams of the children, men began to gather. The word spread like wildfire until from nearby towns and cities the people thronged to the well. The father said, "My God, don't tell his mother! We'll get him out some way!"

A rope was put around the father's body so he could be let down in the well, but his broad shoulders stuck in the twelve-inch hole. Again and again they tried to loop a rope over the shoulders of the child, but in the darkness he fought it off.

Salt water was slowly rising in the hole; the baby boy cried again and again, "Daddy, get me out!"

Every device the frenzied oil men could think of was used as the boy's cries grew weaker and weaker. When at last the cry stopped and it was certain the little fellow was dead, they let down the grabhooks and brought the little body to the surface, chilled and strangled. The rough and profane oil field workers, having done their best to save the child, sat down and in helpless grief, cried like children. Well they might, for one little child's life was worth all the effort they had put forth.

But in the same grief-stricken crowd, estimated at 5,000 gathered around that derrick, probably hundreds were unsaved, without any hope but that they too soon would die, be buried, and like the rich man, lift their eyes in Hell! The little boy was, we may be sure, safe in the arms of Jesus. He who took the little children in His arms and blessed them, takes unaccountable children to His bosom when they die. How strange that people care so much about this life and so little about eternity!

If a ship founders at sea, millions of dollars' worth of equipment are rushed into service to save the physical lives of those on board. To save a life these days, all of modern science, doctors, nurses, hospitals, money—all are used without thought of the expense involved. In times of depression, billions of dollars are spent to see that children have shoes, or that men and women have food and a cover at night.

We ought to "remember the poor," as the Scripture tells us to do, but a million times more important is one soul. Let us save souls from Hell first, then make men as comfortable as we can.

Man's Duty to Man

Lay aside for a moment every consideration of duty to God. Forget, if you will, every command of God's Word to win souls. Even yet it remains that if you love your fellowman, you ought to work to save their souls from an eternal Hell.

No excuses are any good here. You would not wait to be formally introduced to someone before you would put up a ladder to a burning building where they were held captive at an upper window. Good men would not leave to paid lifeguards the throwing of a rope to the drowning. To leave saving souls to the preachers is not only heartless but it is inexcusably wicked. God pity us! We preachers ourselves are all too guilty! We are too much concerned with a hundred details to shed a tear and put forth an effort for sinners!

How Jesus Valued a Soul

Jesus said: "For what shall it profit a man, if he shall gain the whole world, and lose his own soul? Or what shall a man give in exchange for his soul?" (Mark 8:36, 37).

My soul is worth more than the world! And the soul of any sinner is worth to him just as much as mine is to me. Sinners, everything is lost if your soul is lost. That is one way Jesus had of measuring the value of a soul.

But the best measure of how Jesus felt is that He died for sinners. If you ever doubt that there is a real, a terrible, a burning and eternal Hell, just go back and read again the story of Christ in the garden of Gethsemane and on Calvary's cross. If there is not a Hell, then the bloody sweat in the garden was wasted. If there is not a Hell, then the shame, the spitting, the plucking out of His beard, the crown of thorns, the cat-o'-nine-tails upon His back, were worse than useless! If there were not an awful Hell to save sinners from, then the horrible death that Jesus died after hours of agony on the cross was not worthwhile.

Jesus knew the torments of Hell, and that is what makes His death for sinners logical and reasonable. Knowing the doom of condemned sinners, no wonder Jesus interrupted His sleep to win Nicodemus, did without food to win the people of Samaria, yea, even stopped His agonizing death long enough to save the thief!

Dear Christian, if you have any kinship to the Saviour, any concern about those things which move His heart, then help keep sinners out of Hell!

How Can You Eat or Sleep With
Loved Ones Unsaved?

In a revival service at Shamrock, Texas, a young woman arose and between sobs told how her husband was unsaved. "When I want other things, I go after them," she said, "and I have decided this morning that I want my husband saved more than anything else in the world."

The next day I went to the home of the young couple for lunch. After the meal, "Miss Jessie," as she was commonly known, brought the Bible and said in the presence of her husband, "Brother Rice, Charles is not a Christian. I want you to read and pray with him now that he will be saved."

We read the Scriptures and I prayed for the young man, urging upon him his duty and danger, but he would not trust the Lord.

As we arose from the table and the young husband prepared to take his wife to the store where she worked and to go to his own labor, Miss Jessie said, "Charles, I am not going to work this afternoon. Tell Mr. Forbis that I will not be there."

Puzzled, and very grave, the young man went to his job. As I departed, the wife said with tears, "Brother Rice, how can I stand behind a counter, measure goods, sell hose, ribbons or gloves, knowing that my husband is lost and may die at any moment and go to Hell? I must get hold of God today. My husband must be saved!"

That night when Charles came home Miss Jessie called him to supper. Only one plate was on the table. Somewhat disturbed, the young husband asked no questions. When he wanted to rest in the evening, Miss Jessie said, "No, Charles, you must go with me to church." And he did.

That night I preached the best I could. Others were saved, the last pleading verse of the invitation was sung, but Charles did not come! We stood about afterward and talked and prayed. Finally all went home but a few. Big Jeff Mankins stood ready to pull the light switch in the tabernacle. The janitor was ready to lock the door. But Miss Jessie stood in the center of the floor weeping. When Charles suggested, "Honey, we had better go," she shook her head and sobbed the more. He walked about here and yonder, distressed and troubled. Finally when I laid my hand on his arm, he burst into tears. I will never forget how he came up behind his young wife, put his arms around her and said, "Jessie, I will settle it tonight!"

She won her husband because she put it first. She realized a little of the terrible danger and condemnation of a lost soul. Millions go to Hell because fathers, mothers, brothers, sisters, wives, husbands, neighbors, care little and do nothing about their eternal destiny.

May God lay this on your heart today. If there is someone you might keep out of Hell, work at it today.

> **Rescue the perishing, care for the dying,**
>   **Snatch them in pity from sin and the grave;**
> **Weep o'er the erring one, lift up the fallen,**
>   **Tell them of Jesus the mighty to save.**

WHO GOES TO HELL AND HOW TO MISS IT

More People Lost Than Saved

Do many people go to Hell? Yes, Jesus teaches that far more people die unsaved and go to Hell than Christians who go to Heaven.

"Enter ye in at the strait gate: for wide is the gate, and broad is the way, that leadeth to destruction, and many there be which go in thereat: Because strait is the gate, and narrow is the way, which leadeth unto life, and few there be that find it."—Matt. 7:13, 14.

The gate to Hell is wide, the road is broad, and many go in thereat! The gate to life is straight, that is, tight, and the way is narrow, and Jesus says there are few that find it! You who read this ought to be all the more alarmed and make the more certain that you do not go unawares into Hell.

Surprised to Wake Up in Hell

Most of those in Hell did not expect to go there. Certainly the rich man did not. He thought Lazarus ought still to be his servant. He was startled to find himself in flames!

Jesus told about some who expect to be saved but who will be condemned:

"Many will say to me in that day, Lord, Lord, have we not prophesied in thy name? and in thy name have cast out devils? and in thy name done many wonderful works? And then will I profess unto them, I never knew you: depart from me, ye that work iniquity."—Matt. 7:22, 23.

The Bible tells where tares are mixed with wheat, where good fish are with bad, where lost people mix with Christians and even deceive

themselves. The Pharisee who went into the Temple to pray, thanking
God that he was better than the publican, was doubtless surprised when
he went to Hell. He thought he was good! Did he not fast two days
a week? Was he not a leader in public prayer? Was he not a churchgoer?
Was he not an honest men, paying all his debts? He even tithed all
his income, as he reminded the Lord! Yet he was lost and unless this
Pharisee repented before he died, he is now in Hell!

It becomes very clear, then, from God's Word, that multitudes go
to Hell who did not expect to. Friends, do not let yourselves be deceived by Satan. Do not face the terrible surprise of waking up in Hell.

Incurable, Awful Wickedness of Unregenerate Hearts; Cannot Escape Without Change

Men are not willing to believe that unsaved people are always
wicked, but the Bible constantly affirms that it is so.

The wife may believe that her lost husband is "such a good man."
God alone sees his heart, and He says in Jeremiah 17:9, "The heart
is deceitful above all things, and desperately wicked: who can know it?"

In doting blindness the fond father and mother may speak of their
"dear innocent child." Many a mother has said to me about her boy,
"Why, Brother Rice, he never did anything wrong in his life!" That is
a direct contradiction of the Word of God.

"There is NONE righteous, no, not one."—Rom. 3:10.

"For ALL have sinned, and come short of the glory of God."—Rom.
3:23.

*"All we like sheep have gone astray; we have turned EVERY ONE
to his own way; and the Lord hath laid on him the iniquity of us all."*—
Isa. 53:6.

The rich man, a sinner, deserved to go to Hell. Outwardly he may
have been moral, upright, intelligent and lovable, but in his heart, where
God alone could see, he was a deliberate, malicious, willful, continual,
unrepentant sinner.

Remember they were refined, educated, cultured, religious, praying
men who condemned Christ to be crucified, "wolves in sheep's clothing."
What Jesus said about them in Matthew 23:27, 28 perfectly describes
the heart of the best "moral man" that ever lived who has not trusted
Christ:

"Woe unto you, scribes and Pharisees, hypocrites! for ye are like unto whited sepulchres, which indeed appear beautiful outward, but are within full of dead men's bones, and of all uncleanness. Even so ye also outwardly appear righteous unto men, but within ye are full of hypocrisy and iniquity."

Those who have not had a change of heart may appear to be moral or clean or good, but they are only so outwardly. The One who knows the hearts of all men pictures to us the unsaved heart.

It was for this reason that Jesus said to Nicodemus in John 3:3, "Verily, verily, I say unto thee, Except a man be born again, he cannot see the kingdom of God."

So that there could be no misunderstanding, Jesus repeated twice more in the same conversation the requirements that all must be born again to ever see the kingdom of God!

The Lost Love Darkness, Hate Light, Choose Sin, Reject Christ

Jesus gave a very clear picture of why sinners must turn and believe in Christ or be forever condemned:

"And this is the condemnation, that light is come into the world, and men loved darkness rather than light, because their deeds were evil. For every one that doeth evil hateth the light, neither cometh to the light, lest his deeds should be reproved."—John 3:19, 20.

The best proof of any man's wicked heart is that he has not turned to Christ. The only honest reason any man could ever give for not coming to Jesus is that he loves his sin and will not come to THE LIGHT lest his sin should be reproved. Those without God may be cultured, pleasant, courteous and refined, but certainly they are bad by choice. The lost heart is deliberately wicked, wicked enough to hate Christ, the Light. Men reject Christ purposely, loving sin better than salvation. Without being converted, such wicked sinners must go to Hell.

Let me press on your heart another saying of Jesus concerning the wickedness of men, in Matthew 6:24: "No man can serve two masters: for either he will hate the one, and love the other; or else he will hold to the one, and despise the other. Ye cannot serve God and mammon."

The man who does not love Christ hates Him. The man who does not hold to Christ despises Him. Few anywhere would admit that they hate or despise Christ, but God's Word tells us that all who are unsaved and therefore holding to Satan and serving him, are the bitter enemies of the Son of God! They have taken sides with the murderers, the crucifiers of God's Son.

By nature and choice men are enemies of God, children of wrath and headed toward Hell. Then they must turn to Christ for mercy and pardon and a new heart if they are to escape the fires of Hell.

"Moral" People Go to Hell

Jesus did not say that the morals of the rich man were worse than others. All that is said about the rich man's life on earth is this: "There was a certain rich man, which was clothed in purple and fine linen, and fared sumptuously every day" (Luke 16:19).

That does not say that he was any more covetous than others. It is not said that he mistreated or refused to aid the beggar. The Scripture does not say that the rich man committed adultery, or murder, that he gambled, or drank, or swore. His trouble was *inside*. Like all the unsaved everywhere his wicked heart was against God.

Many go to Hell who outwardly are moral and upright.

Be sure to remember, too, that the rich man did not go to Hell because he was rich. Hell contains more poor than rich men, we may be sure; and the Bible says Abraham, David and many other rich people will be in Heaven.

In Hell Because He Did Not Repent

The rich man knew why he went to Hell. He pled for Abraham to send Lazarus to testify to his five brothers, "Lest they also come into this place of torment." In the conversation he said, "If one went unto them from the dead, they will REPENT"! The rich man knew that if his brothers were to escape Hell, they must repent. He went to Hell because he did not repent.

What was true of this rich man and his brothers, is true of everyone, for Jesus says twice, in Luke 13:3 and Luke 13:5: "I tell you, Nay: but, except ye repent, ye shall all likewise perish."

It is repent or perish for every sinner. Sinners, turn or burn!

How Shall I Repent?

Repentance means to change your mind, to turn from sin toward

Christ. To repent includes trusting Christ. Trusting Christ includes re-pentance. You could not truly turn from sin in the heart without turn-ing toward Christ, without trusting Him. The rich man had a wicked heart; so does every person ever born. He loved his sin and did not turn from it toward Christ. That is why he went to Hell.

All who read this may be sure that unless you have turned to Christ, trusting Him to change your heart and forgive your sins, you are con-demned to Hell. Oh, turn now, before you find yourself with the rich man—tormented in flames.

You Need Not Be Lost

My own heart has been deeply stirred and burdened as I have talked to you about Hell. But one blessed fact comes back to my mind again and again: nobody need go to Hell! The heart of God is concerned about sinners. He does not want a single soul to be lost. He said, "For God sent not his Son into the world to condemn the world; but that the world through him might be saved" (John 3:17).

In II Peter 3:9 we are told why the Saviour has not returned to bring judgment on the earth: "The Lord is not slack concerning his promise, as some men count slackness; but is longsuffering to us-ward, NOT WILLING THAT ANY SHOULD PERISH, BUT THAT ALL SHOULD COME TO REPENTANCE."

The appealing cry of God, not only to Israel, but to all mankind, is: "Say unto them, As I live, saith the Lord God, I have no pleasure in the death of the wicked; but that the wicked turn from his way and live: turn ye, turn ye from your evil ways; for why will ye die . . .?" (Ezek. 33:11).

The bloody sweat of Jesus in the garden of Gethsemane calls sin-ners. His tears as He wept over Jerusalem showed His love for all mankind. His brokenhearted cry on the cross, "Father, forgive them; for they know not what they do," shows God's heart toward sinners.

Sinner, you need not go to Hell; God wants you saved. Let us look again and find new meaning in that "little Gospel," John 3:16: "For God so loved the world, that he gave his only begotten Son, that whosoever believeth in him should not perish, but have everlasting life."

God's love means more when we realize what He paid to keep peo-ple out of Hell.

II.

Eternal Punishment

ROBERT MURRAY MC CHEYNE

(Famous Scotch Preacher)

"Where their worm dieth not, and the fire is not quenched."—Mark 9:44.

I. THOSE IN THE BIBLE WHO SPOKE ABOUT HELL

DAVID. David was a man after God's own heart, yet he speaks of Hell. The sweet psalmist of Israel, he who was filled with love to men and to God—hear what he says about Hell.

"The sorrows of death compassed me, and the pains of hell gat hold upon me: I found trouble and sorrow."—Ps. 116:3.

Then hear of his deliverance:

". . . thou hast delivered my soul from the lowest hell."—Ps. 86:13.

He tells us also of the fate of the ungodly who will not accept Christ:

"The wicked shall be turned into hell, and all the nations that forget God."—Ps. 9:17.

"Upon the wicked he shall rain snares, fire and brimstone, and an horrible tempest: this shall be the portion of their cup."—Ps. 11:6.

PAUL. Paul was filled with the love of Christ, and great love had he for sinners. Surely that love wherewith God loved Jesus was in Paul. He loved his enemies.

Notice what his feelings were when he stood before Agrippa:

"I would to God, that not only thou, but also all that hear me this day, were both almost, and altogether such as I am, except these bonds."—Acts 26:29.

He wished them to have the same love—the same joy—the same peace—the same hope of Glory.

Now Paul never mentions the word *Hell*. It seems as if it were too awful a word for him to mention. Yet hear what he says:

"For many walk, of whom I have told you often, and now tell you even weeping, that they are the enemies of the cross of Christ: Whose end is destruction. . . . "—Phil. 3:18,19.

"For when they shall say, Peace and safety; then sudden destruction cometh upon them. . . . "—I Thess. 5:3.

". . . the Lord Jesus shall be revealed from heaven with his mighty angels, In flaming fire taking vengeance on them that know not God, and that obey not the gospel of our Lord Jesus Christ: Who shall be punished with everlasting destruction from the presence of the Lord, and from the glory of his power."—II Thess. 1:7-9.

JOHN THE BELOVED DISCIPLE. He had leaned on Jesus' bosom at the Last Supper and drawn love out of His bosom. His character was love. You will notice how affectionately his epistles are written. He addresses them, "Beloved," "Little children." Yet he speaks of Hell, calling it seven times over "the bottomless pit"—the pit where sinners shall sink through all eternity. He calls it "the great winepress of the wrath of God" (Rev. 14:19).

But John had another name for Hell—"the lake of fire" (Rev. 20:14). It had often been called "hell," but it was left for John, the beloved disciple, to call it "the lake of fire."

THE LORD JESUS HIMSELF. Although He came from God, and "God is love"; although He came to pluck brands from the burning, yet He speaks of Hell. Though His mouth was most sweet and His lips like lilies dropping sweet-smelling myrrh; though the Lord God had given Him the tongue of the learned that He should know how to speak a word in season to him who is weary; though He spake as never man spake—yet He spoke of Hell. Hear what He says:

". . . whosoever shall say, Thou fool, shall be in danger of hell fire."—Matt. 5:22.

But the most awful words that ever came from His lips were:

"Ye serpents, ye generation of vipers, how can ye escape the damnation of hell?"—Matt. 23:33.

Again,

"Depart from me, ye cursed, into everlasting fire, prepared for the devil and his angels."—Matt. 25:41.

And He speaks of it in some of His parables, too:

". . . the angels shall come forth, and sever the wicked from among the just, And shall cast them into the furnace of fire: there shall be wailing and gnashing of teeth."—Matt. 13:49,50.

And He repeats the words of our text three times over. And could anything be plainer than the words in Mark:

"He that believeth not shall be damned"?

II. CONSIDER WHY THESE SPOKE SO PLAINLY OF HELL

1. Because it is all true. Christ is the faithful and true Witness. Once He said, "If it were not so, I would have told you." Once He said to Pilate, "Every one that is of the truth heareth my voice."
He Himself is "the truth." "It is impossible for God to lie."
When Jesus appeared on earth, He came with love; He came to tell sinners of Hell and of a Saviour to save them from Hell; and how could He keep it back? He saw into Hell, so how could He not speak of it? He was the faithful Witness.
So it was with David, Paul and John. Paul said he had kept nothing back—he had not shunned to declare all the counsel of God. How could he have said that if he had not spoken of Hell as he did?
So must ministers.
Suppose I were never to mention Hell again; would that make it more tolerable? Oh, it is true! It is true! It is true! And we cannot but mention it.
2. Because they were so full of love to sinners. They are the best friends who do not flatter us.
You know, beloved, that Christ's bosom flowed with love. Out of love He had not where to lay His head. Out of love He came to die. Out of love, with tears He said,

"O Jerusalem, Jerusalem, thou that killest the prophets, and stonest them which are sent unto thee, how often would I have gathered thy children together, even as a hen gathereth her chickens under her wings, and ye would not!"—Matt. 23:37.

And with the same breath He said,

"How can ye escape the damnation of hell?"

So it was with Paul:

"Knowing therefore the terror of the Lord, we persuade men."—II Cor. 5:11.

Paul could weep over sinners:

"I ceased not to warn every one night and day with tears."—Acts 20:31.

3. That they might be free from blood-guiltiness. Jesus did not want your blood laid at His door; therefore, He spoke of the "furnace of fire" and of "the worm that dieth not." He says, 'How often would I have gathered you, but you would not!' God would not have blood-guiltiness laid to His charge. He says:

"As I live, saith the Lord God, I have no pleasure in the death of the wicked; but that the wicked turn from his way and live: turn ye, turn ye from your evil ways; for why will ye die. . . ?"—Ezek. 33:11.

So it was with David:

"Deliver me from bloodguiltiness, O God."—Ps. 51:14.

It was fear of blood-guiltiness that made David speak so plainly. So it was with Paul. He says,

"Wherefore I take you to record this day, that I am pure from the blood of all men."—Acts 20:26.

So it is with ministers. We must acquit our conscience. If you, sinner, go to the judgment seat unpardoned, unsaved, your blood will be on your own head, not on ours.

As I was walking in the fields yesterday, the thought came with overwhelming power into my mind, that every one I preached to will soon be sent either to Heaven or Hell. Therefore, brethren, I must warn you, I must tell you about Hell.

III. NAMES GIVEN TO HELL IN THE WORD OF GOD

The first is fire, taken from an earthly element suited to our capacity, as Christ takes to Himself a name to suit us, such as a shepherd, a door, a way, a rock, an apple tree, etc.

So when God speaks of Heaven, He calls it Paradise, a city which hath foundations, golden streets, pearly gates. And when He speaks of Hell, He calls it "a furnace of fire," "a bottomless pit," "perdition," etc.

Now, one of these names will not do; but take them all together, and we may conceive something of what Hell is.

On the southern side of Mount Zion is a valley covered over with vines—the Valley of Hinnom where Manasseh made his children pass through the fire to Moloch.

Now this is the name by which Christ calls Hell—"a valley of fire." And again He calls it "a furnace of fire." The walls will be fire, it will be fire above and below, and fire all around about.

Again, Hell is something like "a furnace of fire." It will be enclosed with burning mountains of brass. There will be no breath of wind to pass over their faces. It will be flames of fire forever and forever. It is called "devouring fire": "Who among us shall dwell with the devouring fire?" (Isa. 33:14). Compare this with Hebrews 12:29, "For our God is a consuming fire." It is the nature of fire to consume; so it is with the fire of Hell; but it will never annihilate the damned. It is a fire that shall never be quenched.

Another name given to Hell in the Word of God is "the prison." The multitudes who perished at the Flood are shut up in this prison. Ah, sinner! If you are shut up in it, you will never come out until you have paid the uttermost farthing, and that you can never do—the bars are the justice and holiness of God.

Another name given to Hell is "the pit." It is the bottomless pit where the unsaved will sink forever and forever. It will be a continual sinking deeper and deeper every day.

Sinner, is it not time to cry, "Deliver me out of the mire, and let me not sink. Let not the deep swallow me up, and let not the pit shut her mouth upon me"?

Another name given to Hell in the Word of God is "a falling into the hands of God":

"It is a fearful thing to fall into the hands of the living God."—Heb. 10:31.

"Can thine heart endure, or can thine hands be strong, in the days that I shall deal with thee?"—Ezek. 22:14.

God will be your irreconcilable enemy, sinner. God, who takes no pleasure in the death of the sinner, but rather that he should live—that

God, I say, will be your eternal enemy if you die Christless—if you will not believe—if you will not be saved. Oh, what will you do, poor sinner, when His wrath is kindled!

Another name given to Hell is "the second death":

"And death and hell were cast into the lake of fire. This is the second death."—Rev. 20:14.

This is the meaning of God's threatening to Adam:

". . . of the tree of the knowledge of good and evil, thou shalt not eat of it: for in the day that thou eatest thereof thou shalt surely die."— Gen. 2:17.

Perhaps you may have stood by the bed of a dying sinner and seen how he gasped for breath—his teeth clenched—his hands clasped the bedclothes—his breath became fainter and fainter, until it finally died away.

Ah! this is the first death; and it is like the second death. The man would try to resist, but he finds it is in vain; he finds eternal Hell begun and God dealing with him, and he sinks into gloom and dark despair. This is the death sinners are to die, yet never die.

Another name given to Hell is "outer darkness." Christ calls it outer darkness:

"But the children of the kingdom shall be cast out into outer darkness: there shall be weeping and gnashing of teeth."—Matt. 8:12.

"Then said the king to the servants, Bind him hand and foot, and take him away, and cast him into outer darkness; there shall be weeping and gnashing of teeth."—Matt. 22:13.

You will see it also in II Peter 2:4:

". . . God spared not the angels that sinned, but cast them down to hell, and delivered them into chains of darkness. . . ."

Again in Jude, verse 13:

"Raging waves of the sea, foaming out their own shame; wandering stars, to whom is reserved the blackness of darkness for ever."

Oh, my friends, this is Hell—"the blackness of darkness"—"outer darkness"—"the chains of darkness"!

IV. THE HELL OF THE BIBLE IS NOT ANNIHILATION

Some think that, though they are not saved, they will be annihilated. Oh, it is a lie! I will show you that.

1. It will be no annihilation, when we read of the cries of the damned.

"And he cried and said, Father Abraham, have mercy on me. . . for I am tormented in this flame."—Luke 16:24.

Again, look at the words in Matthew 22:13,

". . . there shall be weeping and gnashing of teeth."

These plainly show us that it is no annihilation.

2. Hell will be no annihilation, when we consider that there will be different degrees of suffering.

"It shall be more tolerable for Tyre and Sidon at the day of judgment, than for you."—Matt. 11:22.

And it is said the Pharisees would receive "greater damnation." Every man is to be judged according to his works.

3. It will be no annihilation, when we consider the fate of Judas.

". . . woe unto that man by whom the Son of man is betrayed! it had been good for that man if he had not been born."—Matt. 26:24.

Judas is wishing now that he had never been born. I have no doubt he wishes to die, but he will never be able to die.

So it will be with all who shall go to Hell—all unworthy communicants. I tell you, if you die Christless, you will wish you had never been born— you will wish you had never seen the green earth or the blue sky.

4. It will be no annihilation, for it is an eternal Hell.

Some weak and foolish men think and please their fancy with the thought that Hell will burn out and they will come to some place where they may bathe their weary souls. Ah! you try to make an agreement with Hell; but if ever there comes a time when the flame that torments your soul and body shall burn out, then God would be a liar, for three times He repeats the words of our text and says it shall never be quenched. It is eternal, for it is spoken of in words never used but to denote eternity.

"And the smoke of their torment ascendeth up for ever and ever...."—Rev. 14:11.

Again,

"And the devil that deceived them was cast into the lake of fire and brimstone, where the beast and the false prophet are, and shall be tormented day and night for ever and ever."—Rev. 20:10.

Compare this with Revelation 4:9,

"And when those beasts give glory and honour and thanks to him that sat on the throne, who liveth for ever and ever."

So you see, the torments of the damned are spoken of with the eternity of God. If ever there comes a time when God ceases to live, then they may cease to suffer.

Again, the eternity of Hell and the eternity of Heaven are spoken of in the very same language:

"And there shall be no night there; and they need no candle, neither light of the sun; for the Lord God giveth them light: and they shall reign for ever and ever."—Rev. 22:5.

The same words used for the eternity of the saints are used for the eternity of the damned.

V. NOW I APPLY THIS TRUTH

1. To you who are believers. All this Hell that I have described is what you and I justly deserved. We were over the lake of fire, but it was from this that Jesus saved us. He was in the prison for you and me. He drank every drop out of the cup of God's wrath for you and for me—He died, the Just for the unjust.

O beloved, how should we prize, love and adore Jesus for what He has done for us! We will never, never know, until safe across Jordan, how our Hell has been suffered for us—how our iniquity has been pardoned.

But, O beloved, think of Hell. Have you no unconverted friends who are treasuring up wrath against the day of wrath? Oh, have you no prayerless parent, no sister, no brother—have you no compassion for them—no mercy's voice to warn them?

2. To you who are seeking Christ anxiously. I know some of you are. Dear soul, what mercy that God would awaken you to flee from this fiery furnace! Oh, what a mercy to be awakened to flee! Your unconverted friends will tell you there is no need of being so anxious. Oh, is there a need for you to flee from the wrath to come? Learn, dear soul, just how precious Christ is. He is a hiding place from the wind, a covert from the tempest. All the things in the world are like a speck of dust, all is loss for Jesus. He is all and all.

He is free to you, beloved: take no rest until you can say, "He is mine!"

HENRY (HARRY) ALLEN IRONSIDE
1876-1951

ABOUT THE MAN:

Few preachers had more varied ministries than this man. He was a captain in the Salvation Army, an itinerant preacher with the Plymouth Brethren, pastor of the renowned Moody Memorial Church in Chicago, and conducted Bible conferences throughout the world. Sandwiched between those major ministries, Ironside preached the Gospel on street corners, in missions, in taverns, on Indian reservations, etc.

Never formally ordained and with no experience whatever as a pastor, Ironside took over the 4,000-seat Moody Memorial Church in Chicago and often filled it to capacity for 18½ years. A seminary president once said of him, *"He has the most unique ministry of any man living."* Although he had little formal education, his tremendous mental capacity and photographic memory caused him to be called the "Archbishop of Fundamentalism."

Preaching—warm, soul-saving preaching—was his forte. Special speakers in his great church often meant nothing; the crowds came when he was there. He traveled constantly; at his prime, he averaged 40 weeks in the year on the road—always returning to Moody Memorial for Sunday services.

His pen moved, too; he contributed regularly to various religious periodicals and journals in addition to publishing 80 books and pamphlets. His writings included addresses or commentaries on the entire New Testament, all of the prophetic books of the Old Testament, and a great many volumes on specific Bible themes and subjects.

In 1951, Dr. Ironside died in Cambridge, New Zealand, and was buried there at his own request.

III.

A Missionary-Minded Man in Hell

H. A. IRONSIDE

(Preached in 1943 at Moody Memorial Church, Chicago)

Tonight we turn to a very familiar Scripture, yet one that is not preached on as often today as in the days of our fathers. Some way people forget that the Bible has a great deal to say about eternal judgment as well as about the revelation of God in Christ.

I read from the 16th chapter of Luke, beginning with the 19th verse. Hear the words of our Lord Jesus Christ:

"There was a certain rich man, which was clothed in purple and fine linen, and fared sumptuously every day: And there was a certain beggar named Lazarus, which was laid at his gate, full of sores, And desiring to be fed with the crumbs which fell from the rich man's table: moreover the dogs came and licked his sores. And it came to pass, that the beggar died, and was carried by the angels into Abraham's bosom: the rich man also died, and was buried; And in hell he lift up his eyes, being in torments, and seeth Abraham afar off, and Lazarus in his bosom. And he cried and said, Father Abraham, have mercy on me, and send Lazarus, that he may dip the tip of his finger in water, and cool my tongue; for I am tormented in this flame. But Abraham said, Son, remember that thou in thy lifetime receivedst thy good things, and likewise Lazarus evil things: but now he is comforted, and thou art tormented. And beside all this, between us and you there is a great gulf fixed: so that they which would pass from hence to you cannot; neither can they pass to us, that would come from thence. Then he said, I pray thee therefore, father, that thou wouldest send him to my father's house: For I have five brethren; that he may testify unto them, lest they also come into this place of torment. Abraham saith unto him,

They have Moses and the prophets; let them hear them. And he said, Nay, father Abraham: but if one went unto them from the dead, they will repent. And he said unto him, If they hear not Moses and the prophets, neither will they be persuaded, though one rose from the dead."

The first thing I would like to emphasize before attempting to go into the exposition of these words is that they were spoken by the tenderest, the most gracious, loving Man who ever walked this earth—our Lord Jesus Christ. He was truly Man and yet truly God; therefore, He could draw aside the curtain of the other world and picture things as they are over there. He knew what was on the other side. He had come from the other side of the veil into this world to reveal God to us and to die on the cross for our sins. In this story that He relates, He gives us some reasons why we ought to be tremendously concerned about preparing for what comes after death.

I emphasize that Jesus said these things, because so often when we talk to people about eternal verities, particularly when we deal with the subject of eternal judgment, they say, "That is just the theory of some man."

Some even forget that the apostles of the Lord Jesus were divinely inspired. They say, "It is Paul," or, "It is Peter" or somebody like that who speaks of Hell and judgment and of torment after death for those who die in their sins.

But, dear friends, it is not Peter who speaks here. It is not Paul who speaks here. It is not one of the other apostles. It is Jesus, He who is the Way, the Truth and the Life, who never uttered one word that was not absolutely the truth. So when you read this story, you are reading a truthful record spoken by the Son of God.

Not a Parable

I know some people are very fond of speaking of this as though it were just a parable. I am willing to admit that in a certain sense it is a parable, because a parable is a story told to illustrate a spiritual reality, and this story is told for that purpose. But when men say it is only a parable, evidently they mean by that that it has no foundation in fact. That is not the case. Our Lord Jesus spoke of this as an incident with which He was well acquainted. There is not the slightest evidence here that He was making up a fanciful story, or that this was just an illustration of something altogether different from what it purported to be.

There are a group of people today who tell us that this could not reveal unto us life after death because, they say, when people die, they become absolutely unconscious until the day of judgment. These who call themselves Jehovah's Witnesses tell you that. Sometimes very well-meaning but misguided people called Seventh-day Adventists will tell you that. Those called Christodelphians will tell you the same thing. But there is absolutely nothing here that would even suggest that it is simply a fanciful story.

If it is just a parable, what does it mean? Men have racked their brains to try to think up some meaning or another. Jehovah's Witnesses, so-called, will tell you this. They say the rich man here represents the Jew, who was a man with special privileges in the old dispensation. To them, the beggar lying at his gate represents the Gentile nations outside, strangers to the covenants of promise. Their death means a change from one dispensation to another. The Jew lost his place of privilege, and now the Gentile is in Abraham's bosom and he has the place of privilege.

All that sounds very good. It sounds as if it might be a logical explanation of the meaning of this story if it were only a parable. But the trouble is, it doesn't go far enough.

Try to carry that explanation a little further, and you are right up a tree. You cannot carry it through, because you know if you take the rich man as representing the Jew who is now on the outside and does not enjoy the blessing that once was his, then you have to go a little further. The rich man cries for help and Abraham says, "It is too late." He says, "There is a great gulf fixed between you and us so that they that would come from you to us, cannot; and those that would go from us to you are unable to do so." That is not true as applied to representative positions of Jew and Gentile.

If I wished to desert Christianity, I could go over to a Jewish synagogue and I could become a Jew, as many Gentiles have done. And on the other hand, doubtless many Hebrew Christians are here tonight who can tell you, "We once were Jews, rejecting Christ, but now we know Him as our Saviour."

When they became converted and when they began to enjoy the blessings that we Gentile Christians enjoy, they did not hear any voice saying to them, "There is a great gulf fixed and you cannot pass over. You cannot come from your place to the place of blessing the Gentiles enjoy." That explanation will not hold water. For any Jew may come into the full enjoyment of all the blessings that a Gentile Christian has found in Christ if he wills to do so. The gulf is not fixed in this world.

Now look at the story and take it just as you would a story any other faithful preacher is declaring. Suppose, for instance, I stand here and preach the Word. Now I want to illustrate something. I say, "A certain man I knew over in California," and go on to tell something about him without giving his name. At the close of my address, suppose you should remain and ask me about the man of whom I spoke, and I should say, "I didn't really mean that I knew any such person. I don't really know any man like that." I think you would look at me in amazement and say, "Do you mean to tell me that you deliberately stood up there and lied in order to try to illustrate what you were preaching? You said there was a certain man in California, and you talked as if you knew all about his circumstances. After all, you were only deceiving us."

No honorable preacher would do that, and I know Jesus would not. Jesus was talking to these people, preaching a sermon to Jews of the day, and in the course of the sermon He said, "There was a certain rich man . . . . " Was there, or was there not? He says there was. "There was a certain rich man." Now that would get attention from everyone there. Many would be asking, "Who was that rich man?" Jesus did not give us his name. We call him Dives, but Dives just means "rich man." It is just another way of giving his condition.

You know, several times in Luke's Gospel Jesus speaks that way. On another occasion He said, "There was a certain rich man which had a steward." The steward was said to have wasted his goods and was called to account. Do you believe that was not true? Jesus was evidently referring to some incident with which He was well acquainted.

On another occasion He said, "The ground of a certain rich man brought forth plentifully." He had a bountiful harvest. He said to himself, "What am I going to do? I haven't a place to bestow my goods. I know what I will do; I will pull down my barns and build greater. Then I will get in the fruits of my harvest, and I will say to my soul, 'Soul, thou hast much goods laid up for many years; take thine ease, eat, drink and be merry.' " But God said unto him, "Thou fool, this night thy soul shall be required of thee: then whose shall those things be, which thou hast provided?" Was Jesus making up a story? No, He was giving an actual fact concerning a certain rich man.

And He uses exactly the same expression here, "There was a certain rich man." He did not tell his name. This is just a simple story. It does not even say, as in many instances, "Jesus spake a parable." If it had said that, I could understand that He was simply using an illustration which may or may not have actually occurred, though I am inclined to think that, in practically every instance, even when Jesus used parables, they actually occurred, because He was absolutely the True One.

But here He tells us, "There was a certain rich man." Then He says he was clothed in purple and fine linen and fared sumptuously every day—not occasionally, not one day in the week, but every day. This man had everything his heart could desire, everything he might yearn for.

Then Jesus said—now notice the definiteness of it here: "There was a certain beggar named Lazarus." He tells us the name of the beggar. He knew that beggar well. You see, "He calleth his own sheep by name." He does not tell us the name of the rich man because he was not one of His sheep. But Lazarus was. The beggar was one of His, though his circumstances were so poor, so hard, so difficult. He was a son of Abraham, a man of faith, yet found in this desperate condition. "There was a certain beggar named Lazarus, which was laid at his gate, full of sores."

The Beggar Carried by Angels to Paradise

Notice this beggar did not come to the gate of the rich man begging alms. He did not come voluntarily. He did not walk there, for he could not walk. But his friends, such as they were, carried him instead of properly supporting him themselves, looking after him at home. It was an easier thing to take him and put him down at the gate of the rich man. Surely someone would give him something, some guest coming out, or the rich man himself will do something for him. So they laid him at the rich man's gate.

He was full of sores. Disease had laid hold of his poor body, and he was a helpless, dying man. The dogs had more pity than human kind, for "the dogs came and licked his sores."

Then we read, "And it came to pass, that the beggar died, and was carried by the angels into Abraham's bosom."

There is not a word about a funeral for the beggar. I do not suppose he had one. I have an idea that word was sent to the proper authorities that a poor dead beggar was lying there at the gate and that something had better be done about it. Probably they got his body and took it out and buried it in the potter's field. Perhaps they did not even do that. Perhaps they took it down into the Vale of Hinnom where the fire was continually burning and where the carcasses of dead animals were being consumed. I do not know what they did with it. The Bible does not say.

But it tells what became of the man's soul. His body died, but he himself, the real man, the man who lived in that poor stricken body, the man who had now left that earthly tabernacle so dilapidated, so disgusting in its outward appearance, the man who once lived there, moved out; and the moment he stepped out of that tabernacle, the hosts of Heaven were there to greet him. He was carried by the angels into Abraham's bosom. And Abraham was in Paradise.

In Hebrews we are told that Abraham looked for a city which hath foundations, whose builder and maker is God. And Abraham's spirit is among those spirits of just men made perfect, of whom we read in that same epistle. Abraham was there in Paradise with all the saints of past ages, with all those who had turned to God and trusted His Word. Abraham believed God, and it was counted to him for righteousness.

I do not know where some of my brethren get what seems to be a foolish idea, that Abraham's bosom was a certain place and that it was a part of Hades called by that name. Abraham's bosom was the bosom of Abraham. Abraham was a personality in Paradise, though dead as to this world.

How dare I call him a living being? Because my Lord called him that when He was talking to the Sadducees. The Sadducees did not believe in spirits; they did not believe anyone could live after death. They did not believe in the resurrection. The Lord Jesus said, "You do err. If you would read your Bible you would know better."

What did God say to Moses in the burning bush? "I am the God of Abraham, and the God of Isaac, and the God of Jacob." He did not say He was the God of Abraham and the God of Isaac and the God of Jacob, but, "I am the God of Abraham and of Isaac and of Jacob." And Jesus said He is not the God of the dead but the God of the living, for they all live unto Him. So Abraham, Isaac and Jacob are all alive, though their bodies are dead and they are in Paradise.

Now this poor beggar joined them there and Abraham, the father of the faithful—I think I see him rising to welcome this poor man who loved God, believed in Him and had had such a hard time on earth.

You say, "Well, if this man were really a man of faith, why did God allow him to suffer?" Peter tells why He allows a man of faith to suffer: "That the trial of your faith, being much more precious than of gold that perisheth, though it be tried with fire, might be found unto praise and honour and glory at the appearing of Jesus Christ."

God was going to make up to this man for all he suffered on earth. He trusted God under the most difficult circumstances, and thus glorified Him, and someday all would be made up to him.

What a wonderful thing it must have been to see that man carried by angels into Paradise and Abraham receiving him!

The Rich Man in Hell

Then we read, "The rich man also died. . . ." It does not say that any angels were waiting for him. It says, though, that he was buried: "The rich man also died, and was buried."

Oh, I fancy they had a great time when he died. All the lodges he belonged to would be there in their uniforms and the brass band to play the "Dead March" as they went on to the cemetery. I have an idea they had a wonderful soloist to sing some of these lovely things like "Beautiful Isle of Somewhere." I have an idea they had one or more distinguished rabbis of the city to preach a great sermon over him and talk about all the good he had done. He was probably one of the miserable idle rich who had not done any good to anybody but himself, and that turned out to be harm. But that is the way they send them off, you know, when they are rich. It is so different when they are poor. He would have a great funeral. I think the *Jerusalem Gazette* devoted a whole page to him and told about the wonderful things this man had done. And all the time—what about his poor soul?

Listen to what Jesus says, not what I say: "The rich man also died, and was buried; And in hell he lift up his eyes, being in torments."

Oh, but wait a minute, brother! Here is one of Jehovah's Witnesses. What is it he wants to tell me? Oh, I see, the word *Hell* there should be *Hades*. It does not mean Hell at all. That is what Judge Rutherford says. That is what all these annihilationists and soul-sleepers say—that the word *Hades* does not mean *Hell*. Why do they say that? In order to get away from the thought of suffering after death because of sins committed here, they tell us *Hades* is simply the grave.

Let's oblige them and let us do away with the word *Hell* and use the word *grave* instead. "The rich man also died and was buried and in the *grave* he lifted up his eyes, being in torment." Why, the poor man must have been buried alive! You see, we do not do away with torment because we change the word. Whatever we want to call it, it is there, and no honest man can fail to see that Jesus meant us to understand that there is something terrible after death for the man who dies in his sin. There is no getting away from that.

Somebody else says, "Well, I admit it isn't just the grave, but Hades is just the unseen world. I think the final Hell comes after the great white throne."

For the unsaved man, Hades refers to a place of suffering between death and resurrection. Just read it using the Greek word: "And in *Hades* he lifted up his eyes, being in torment." It refers here particularly to the departed spirits of the lost. I do not know what torment there will be there. He is referring here, of course, to one between death and the resurrection when he will have a real body. He is referring to one out of the body, though He uses physical terms so we can understand it. Between death and resurrection this man is now suffering in Hades.

Let me hasten on to say this: the rich man did not go to Hell because he was rich, and the poor man did not go to Paradise because he was poor. That is not it at all. I know that Jesus said, "It is easier for a camel to go through the eye of a needle, than for a rich man to enter into the kingdom of God." It is hard; and the disciples looked up in amazement and said, "Who then can be saved?" Jesus said, "What is impossible with men is possible with God." A man may be a rich man and yet be saved. One thing about it, if he is saved he will want to use his riches to the glory of God and for the alleviation of human misery, and he will not leave Lazarus lying outside his gate with no one but dogs to show any interest in him.

If that rich man had turned to God in repentance, if that rich man had been a man of faith, if he had received God's salvation, he would have been glad to use what God had trusted him with for the blessing of others and not simply for himself.

There is no sin in being rich unless one is selfishly rich and thinks only of using what he has for himself. Of course there is no virtue in being poor. One might be very, very poor and be very, very wicked. Many poor men are just as wicked as some very rich men.

But the point here is this: Lazarus was a child of faith. As a son of

Abraham, he believed God. As full of misery as he was, his heart was going out to the God of Heaven whom he had trusted for himself. The rich man ignored God and had no place for God in his thinking.

May I ask you, which one do you line up with? Does God have any place in your thinking? Are you much concerned about the will of God? Are you concerned about the revelation God has given of Himself in Christ? Does the Lord Jesus Christ mean anything to you? Oh, if He does not, your condition is just as serious and just as solemn as the condition of that rich man just before the hour of death struck him and he went out into a lost eternity.

Unending Torment in Hell

But now what I am concerned about is the change that took place in this man after he died. He was very selfish while he lived, never interested, apparently, in doing anything for other people. But you know a remarkable thing is, after he died he became a missionary-minded man. He began to think of other people and what could be done for them. Not immediately; at first, just as before, he was thinking of himself and cried to Abraham—he could see him afar off, and Lazarus in his bosom—and he said, "Father Abraham, have mercy on me, and send Lazarus, that he may dip the tip of his finger in water, and cool my tongue; for I am tormented in this flame."

Look at this: you have a praying man in Hell. But the trouble was, he began praying on the wrong side of the tomb. He went through life prayerless. The moment he got over on the other side, he began to pray.

What did he pray for? He did not ask for very much; only a drop of water on the tip of a beggar's finger. But even that was denied him. Living water, the water of life, might have been his. He had rejected it when grace was free. Now he had come to a place where living water was never known, where there was no relief from his misery.

Abraham said, "Son, remember." Oh, the awfulness of memory! Some of you here tonight would give everything you have to forget some events that have taken place in your life. You look back over the years, and things come back that haunt you and trouble you many times in the restless night. Oh, if you could only put it away, only forget it! Sometimes you are able to forget it for a little while.

My friend, if you die in your sin, you will never be able to forget the one sin committed; you will never be able to forget the grace you have despised; you will never be able to forget the gospel messages you have heard and refused to believe; you will never be able to forget the invitations to come to Jesus which fell upon your ears but you turned them down. One of the most awful thoughts that can ever come to a lost soul must be this: *Jesus died, yet I am in Hell. Jesus died and I knew all about it; I knew He died to save sinners like me, yet I am in Hell because I wouldn't trust Him when I might have done so. I wouldn't turn to Him in repentance when He waited to save me.*

Memory! "Son, remember that thou in thy lifetime receivedst thy good things, and likewise Lazarus evil things: but now he is comforted, and thou art tormented."

The comfort that came to Lazarus would be in large measure the answer to the suffering that he endured on earth. We read, "Our light affliction, which is but for a moment, worketh for us a far more exceeding and eternal weight of glory" (II Cor. 4:17). But all the bitter anguish that this man endured in eternity would only be accentuated as he looked back and thought of the luxury in which he once lived on earth when he was so careless of God.

Eternity—it is an awful thing to have to look back through all eternity on mercy rejected.

Then Abraham went on to say, "Beside all this, between us and you there is a great gulf fixed: so that they which would pass from hence to you cannot; neither can they pass to us, that would come from thence." There you have two things: the absolute denial of the annihilation of the wicked that lie on the wrong side of the fixed gulf forever; then the denial of universal salvation. The man who dies in sin will never get over to the other side of the gulf, just as the man who dies in Christ will never get over to the suffering side of the gulf. There is a great gulf fixed.

Thank God, it is not fixed yet. If you are here tonight unsaved, the cross of Christ is like a great bridge across that gulf. You may take Him as your Saviour and pass from one side to the other. If you die in your sins, it will be too late.

In Hell He Wanted Others Saved

Now we find how this man suddenly became awakened to the importance of missionary effort. I don't suppose he had ever given a half-shekel in his life for missions. Why should he? He was not saved himself, so why should he be interested in others? Now in Hell he suddenly becomes very missionary-minded. He said, "I pray thee therefore, father, that thou wouldest send him to my father's house: for I have five brethren."

What a family—six brothers, one in Hell, and five on the way! "I have five brethren that he may testify unto them, lest they also come into this place of torment."

I have heard unsaved men foolishly saying, "Oh, well, if I am lost there will be a lot of people in Hell to share with me."

My dear friend, that will be no comfort to you. Here is a lost man, and he says, "Abraham, can't you do something to keep my five brothers from sharing this fate with me? I don't want them here. I don't want them to suffer what I am suffering. Won't you send Lazarus to them? Let him go as a missionary to tell them the way out, to tell them to be saved while there is time. I don't want them to come here." He knew what it meant to be shut away from God for eternity, and he said, "I don't want my brothers to share it."

Abraham answered him, "They do not need Lazarus. They have Moses and the prophets; let them hear them." He meant they had the Old Testament, they had their Bibles; let them read them. This man says, "Oh, if one went unto them from the dead they would repent. If Lazarus came back to tell them what it is like over here and attempted to warn them, they would believe him; they would repent." But he was told, "Oh, no, they would not. If they would not believe the Bible, they would not believe a man who should rise from the dead." In other words, "They would think he had not been dead at all, just in a swoon, that he was crazy anyway, and they would not believe him, even though he professed to come back from the dead."

You may say, "Why doesn't God work a miracle to save me?" He worked a miracle when He gave His Son to die, then raised Him from the dead. God says, "Here is the record of it. You believe this and you will be saved. If you do not believe that, you will never be saved." God says, "He that believeth on him is not condemned: but he that believeth not is condemned already." Why? "Because he hath not believed in the name of the only begotten Son of God."

What about you? I am not trying to explain Hell to you. I cannot. I am not trying to tell you what any figures mean, if they are only figures. I do not know. I am just giving what Jesus said. And you will have to admit this: that the Word of God says if you die loving what God hates and hating what God loves, there is something terrible awaiting you after death. Do not try to wriggle out of that. Do not try to dispute that. It is perfectly plain in God's holy Word. Oh, think of going out into eternity without God!

> Eternity: Time soon will end,
>   Its fleeting moments pass away;
> O sinner, say, where wilt thou spend
>   Eternity's unchanging day?
> Shalt thou the hopeless horror see
>   Of Hell for all eternity?

JOHN LINTON
1888-1965

ABOUT THE MAN:

The story of John Linton is another of those sagas that shine with the wonder-working grace of God.

One of twelve children, this immigrant boy from Scotland gravitated to the life of a wastrel, a wanderer. This wicked youth seemed to be destined to a life of cheating, lying and stealing.

But God moved in when John was thirteen. He had left home, had lied to suspecting police, had hid in barns; then finally he was taken in by a Christian woman and mothered. Here John learned the sweet lesson of the Heavenly Father's patience, tenderness and forgiveness to an erring child. So he confessed Christ and claimed His forgiveness. This was the turning point in his life.

Shortly he emigrated to Canada. And at James Street Baptist Church, Hamilton, Ontario, John Linton heard God's call to preach the Gospel.

He attended Gordon Bible College in Boston. Under the consecrated teaching there, Linton "grew like a hothouse plant." His pastor persuaded him to go to a Baptist college in Woodstock, where he could finish high school work as well.

College life became a geographical game of musical chairs—Boston, Woodstock, Toronto, Manitoba. All the while he was preparing to be a "good preacher" he was busy "practicing preaching."

He graduated with a master's degree, married a childhood sweetheart and became a pastor. It was during his pastorate at High Park Baptist Church, Toronto, that he became vitally interested in revival and evangelism. Linton entered—and God blessed—across Canada, across America, until his decease in 1965.

John Linton is not normally listed among the elite of the evangelists in this century: Moody, Sunday, Bob Jones, Sr., Appelman, John Rice. But he was not some lesser light—God mightily moved through his ministry. He left a trail of converts to Christ as well as revived, restored, rejoicing churches.

His gospel soundness, his compelling delivery, his Scotch brogue and his devotion to our Lord made him widely acceptable. You cannot hear the inimitable Scotch brogue in his sermon, but you can enjoy its sweet and powerful message.

He died at age 77 in the pulpit while conducting evangelistic services.

IV.

Why Some Preachers Ought to Visit Hell

JOHN LINTON

"And in hell he lift up his eyes, being in torments."—Luke 16:23.

Can you imagine the surprise this man received who, safe and secure amid an abundance of wealth, petted and pampered by all who knew him, having everything on earth his heart could wish, peacefully closing his eyes in death, then, without a moment's interruption, found himself in torments?

He had heard about Hell during his lifetime, but had thought little of it as an actual fact. He had heard men argue that God was too loving to create such a place. He had joked about Hell, had often used the word as a swear word. He had told men in anger to go there. But that Hell was a real place and that he who had lived so securely, so voluptuously, on earth, should find himself forever in this place of awful torment—the thought crushed him with consternation and horror!

Our Lord describes in calm, measured words the revolutionary effect upon this man of the first five minutes in Hell. His whole attitude toward this life undergoes a radical change as the scales fall from his eyes and the terrible reality of Hell stands unveiled before him.

Before death, this man is lolling in wealth, eating and drinking, and so intent enjoying life he thinks of no one but himself. Revelling and feasting, he does not have God in his thoughts. In the next minute, according to Jesus Christ, he is a man on fire with desire to get men right with God, to get them to repent of their sins, to get them ready for the life beyond. Five minutes in the lost world makes this godless man want to be a soul winner, a preacher of the Gospel, an evangelist to his own family. Oh, how he prays for them! How he pleads their cause! How he cries out that his brothers might be saved from this place of awful torment!

Mind you—this man had never given the souls of his brothers a thought; but now all he can think of is, his brothers are lost and heading for Hell. He sees those five men blindfolded, walking straight toward a precipice. They are nearly there. A few more steps and they are over! Won't somebody stop them! Won't somebody rise from the dead and warn mankind of their peril!

He looks forward and sees that in a few years there will be an addition to his torment; for unless something is done to warn his family, there will come tumbling in upon him, in awful succession—one, two, three, four, five of his brothers, to add, if possible, to his misery. He cannot save his own soul, but he will do all a man in Hell can do to save his brothers.

Will you mark some of the tremendous lessons this man learned in the first five minutes in Hell.

1. He saw the reality and finality of the place called Hell.

2. He saw that all the arguments he had ever heard against Hell were utterly false and empty.

3. He saw that, if a man shuts God out of his heart in this life, God will shut that man out of his heavenly Home in the next life.

4. He saw that the cardinal folly of a man's existence is for him to care for his body and do nothing for his never-dying soul.

5. He saw the urgent necessity of something desperate being done by believers on earth to save his unsaved brothers. He saw that the ordinary church or synagogue services would not do it. They had not and they would not reach them. Something unusual, something desperate will have to be done to awake them.

6. He saw that the one only business of believing men was to spend and be spent in warning the lost of their peril. Soul winning, soul winning, soul winning—that was the burning message on the lips of this man in Hell.

Now, if a man could learn these tremendous lessons in Hell, then some preachers, yes, every preacher, ought to go there. They ought, if it were possible, to visit the lost world for five minutes to have their eyes opened to its terrible and eternal reality.

The preachers of this city have the ears of the people. They could, if they saw what this man saw, so preach that men would be alarmed to repentance and thousands would turn to God. Put in every pulpit in this city next Sunday a preacher who has spent five minutes in the lost world, let him preach the kind of sermon this man would have preached if he could have come back to earth, and a revival like unto the repentance of Nineveh would be witnessed inside a week.

You will say that a visit to the lost world is impossible. Do not forget that Paul and John were caught up into Heaven and saw the reality of the city of God. If God could allow a preacher to visit Heaven, He could allow some to visit Hell.

But we must leave that question unanswered. We are living today by faith. God wants His servants to take Him at His Word, without seeing. Fifty-three times in the Bible He has declared the reality of Hell. His Son, Jesus Christ, in language clear and unmistakable, pictured the lost world as a place of bitterest woe, and God wants us to believe in its existence just because He has said so.

It will be too late when we preachers die and are transported to Heaven and there see the reality of the unseen world, for our testimony to do any good to our generation. Our chance of saving lost men shall have passed. We may ask God then to allow us to return to earth to tell our fellowmen in a new way of the reality of Heaven and Hell, but God will not answer our request. It is now or never.

But while every preacher would profit by a visit to Hell, some would profit more than others. I will describe some of those preachers in this message.

I. THOSE WHO DO NOT BELIEVE THERE IS A HELL

There are some preachers who say that, because of the intellectual difficulties involved, they cannot believe in the Hell of the Bible. Some of these may be quite sincere in their unbelief.

Other preachers do not believe in Hell simply because they do not want to believe it. They have compromised with sin in their own lives; they value the applause of worldly church members more than the praise of God; so they believe and preach that there is no Hell.

But whether sincere or insincere, five minutes in the lost world which Christ described would sweep away their soul-destroying unbelief. Oh, what a terrible rebuke some preachers will merit from members of their congregation who find themselves in Hell and who will cry out against the preacher who did not warn them of it!

Alas for the world, and alas for such preachers, that there are so many of them. No wonder an English periodical said:

> The unalterable fact of Hell, its all but unbelievable awfulness, ought, in mercy to the world, to be made clear. Nothing is blacker than the fact that the closer Hell approaches, the less it is believed or even known.

What a masterpiece of Satan's work, that so many able ministers today have become persuaded that a fact could be intellectually difficult and even impossible, which the Lord Jesus Christ believed! Five minutes, one minute, aye, one look at the world where the rich man dwelt, would rid them of their sinful and criminal unbelief.

II. PREACHERS SHOULD VISIT HELL WHO BELIEVE IN HELL BUT DO NOT PREACH IT BECAUSE IT IS UNPOPULAR

Hell is one subject many preachers avoid, even though they believe in it. It is a terrible subject to preach. It is unpopular. The world scoffs at Hell-fire preaching. The Devil opposes every preacher who preaches on Hell. Backsliding Christians dislike such preaching. It is easier to preach on the love of God than on the justice of God; easier to preach on Heaven than on Hell.

So many preachers avoid the subject. They find a good excuse for doing so. If they can't find one, the Devil will find one for them. Every unsaved man in their congregation who closes his eyes in death, opens them in Hell; yet they preach not on this subject. They must know that the silence of a preacher regarding Hell is understood as a denial of its existence, yet they maintain such a silence while their unsaved hearers drift on unwarned into Hell.

Five minutes in the lost world, to see what this man saw, would open the eyes and mouth of every silent preacher. Oh, how they would preach when they came back! How they would try to make up for lost time and missed opportunities!

III. PREACHERS SHOULD VISIT HELL WHO THINK AN APPEAL TO FEAR IT AN UNWORTHY APPEAL

Some preachers are silent about Hell because they are convinced that an appeal to self-interest is ignoble. They insist that men should not be driven to God by fear. Pardon my bluntness, but five minutes with this man in Hell would cure them of all that drivel. How do such preachers read their Bible? Have they not read, *"Noah moved with fear prepared an ark to the saving of his house"*? Have they not read, *"The fear of the Lord is the beginning of wisdom"*? Have they not learned that men are furthest from God when *"the fear of God is not before their eyes"*?

These preachers think it is wrong to act through fear, yet they eat because they fear they would starve to death if they did not eat. They wear overcoats in winter because they fear they will catch cold if they are not warmly clad. They lock the door at night because they fear a burglar might enter if they leave the door unlocked. And when they are crossing the street and a speeding car honks, they jump aside as briskly as the preacher who believes that fear is a legitimate appeal to use in reaching men for God.

In other words, their whole life in this world is ordered on the principle of self-preservation, yet they say it would be wrong or ignoble to tell men to repent of their sin because of the terrible retribution it will bring. Oh, if such preachers could visit the lost world which Christ pictured, they would see at once the falsity of their reasoning.

Imagine such a preacher visiting Hell and meeting a group of lost souls who once were part of his congregation! They heard him preach for years, but the word "Hell" was never on his lips. He preached only on the love of God, the goodness and mercy and benevolence of God. They concluded there could be no Hell because their pastor, an able and good man, never mentioned it. Now they find themselves with the rich man in this place of awful torment. The preacher they heard visits them! They ask him if he believed in such a place. He tells them he did. They say, "Why did you not tell us about this place?" What will he say? How would his loud, swelling words about the ignobility of fear stand up before the stark awful reality of Hell? I think these lost souls would curse him for his folly, don't you? I think he would curse himself.

IV. PREACHERS SHOULD VISIT HELL WHO STRESS SOCIAL SERVICE AND NEGLECT SOUL WINNING

Preachers who spend their time in making this world a better place for unsaved people to live in and do not major on the spiritual regeneration of these people, would be helped by a vision of Hell.

I do not belittle social service as a means to an end. To make it an end in itself is putting the cart before the horse. To minister to the body and neglect the soul is virtually to deny that man has a soul. Such Christian workers superintend gymnasiums and swimming pools; they organize debating clubs and Scout activities, but do nothing about leading men and young people to a definite personal experience of Christ in the heart.

The rich man in Hell would have something to say to such preachers. He would tell them he had everything they were working for to give others. He had a fine house, a private swimming pool, three big meals a day and clothes in abundance. He had a good library and everything else a man needed in this life; but with all these things, he was lost forever in Hell!

V. BIBLE TEACHERS WHO HAVE LOST SIGHT OF SOUL WINNING SHOULD VISIT HELL

Some preachers devote their entire ministry to some particular line of truth. It may be prophecy, the deeper life, the refutation of false religions, or science and the Bible. They can preach for two weeks and never give a call to the unconverted. Such preachers would profit by a visit to Hell.

My friends, the Devil doesn't care what I preach, as long as men are not being saved by my preaching. He doesn't care how many come to my meetings, as long as no penitents come to God. He does not mind if they are standing at the back, as long as they are not kneeling at the front. It doesn't trouble him to see the gallery filled, as long as the enquiry room is empty. He doesn't mind if I preach on the Antichrist, as long as I am not getting men to come to the true Christ. He doesn't mind my preaching on the second coming, if only I forget to tell people about the first coming.

I am saying nothing, mark you, against prophecy. God forbid. I want to know more of it, not less. But prophetic sermons without soul-winning application are stones given for bread. It is Nero fiddling while Rome burns. *"He that winneth souls is wise"* and, conversely, he that winneth them not lacks wisdom.

It is true that some men are called to be evangelists and others, teachers. But the aim and object of both ministries should be the saving of the lost. What teacher could be content to dispense truth to the saints and not apply that truth to the sinners in his audience? He needs no special gift for this, any more than a man needs to be eloquent to raise an alarm of fire. If we believe a house is on fire, we will warn the occupants.

A visit to Hell would put a sob in the throat and a note of urgency in the message of any teacher, no matter what his gifts or what line of truth he is called to declare.

Is there an unsaved man reading this message? I tell you kindly but with all conviction, that you are a brother of this man in Hell. If you are without Christ, you are heading for this place of awful torment. Do not argue over the nature of that torment. Don't, I beseech you, lose your soul over whether the torment is literal or figurative. The faithful and true witness would not lie or mislead, and he said, *"In hell he lift up his eyes, being in torments."* The rich man himself cried, *"I am tormented in this flame."* Whatever the flame was, it was real suffering, wasn't it?

This man in Hell was concerned about his brothers. He was concerned about you. So should I be. He said something should be done to reach you, to arouse you. He said if someone would go back from the dead, you would repent. Is that right? Abraham, you remember, did not agree with him on that. There was quite a debate going on about you across that gulf. Which was right?

God decided to give this man in Hell the benefit of the doubt, so He sent a man back from the dead to warn the world of judgment. *"[God] hath appointed a day, in which he will judge the world. . . . whereof he hath given assurance unto all men, in that he hath raised him [Christ] from the dead."* For nineteen centuries preachers, in the name and power of this risen Christ, have warned this man's brothers of their danger.

As a preacher of the Gospel, I am taking the advice of this man in Hell. I don't want him to shout a rebuke at me across the gulf. He cried, "Testify unto them, lest they also come into this place of torment." I have been doing that all through this sermon. I have warned you. What will you do with your brother's warning, and mine? What will you do with the warning of judgment from the man whom God sent back from the dead? Your brother said you would repent. I earnestly pray that he will be right.

(This sermon is from the book, *Walking on Water,* by Evangelist John Linton; now out of print.)

V.

Is Hell a Myth?

R. G. LEE

*"And fear not them which kill the body, but are not   .e to kill the
soul: but rather fear him which is able to destroy bot   ,oul and body
in hell."*—Matt. 10:28.

I. THE ASKING—"IS HELL A M TH?"

A myth? Like Aeolus imprisoning in a leat⸍ ⸍r bag tied with a silver
string such winds and tempests as might be h⸍ ⸍tful to the further voyage
of Ulysses?

Like the cranes of Ibycus? Like the Mir⸍ ⸍taur, the fierce animal with
a bull's body and a man's head, which⸍ ⸍lemanded a tribute of seven
young men and seven young women⸍ ⸍and the killing of this beast by
Theseus with the aid of Ariadne?

A myth? As when Proserpina cr⸍ ⸍d for help and her voice was heard
by all the mothers of earth?

As Laocoon, the priest of Neptune, and the serpents of the sea in
fierce attack?

As Nemesis, the avenging deity of mythology? As the three Furies—
Alecto, the relentless—Tisiphone, the avenger—Megaera, the grim—
three woman-like creatures, with writhing snakes for hair, holding a torch
in one hand and a whip of live scorpions in the other?

A myth? As Hercules and the poison garment of Nessus? As Hercules strangling two serpents with his hands at birth? As Hercules and
his "Twelve Labors"?

As Midas and his golden touch?

As Sisyphus who made a chair with automatic workings—so that when
a creditor called upon him to collect a debt, Sisyphus invited him to
sit down, and no sooner had the fellow taken a seat when one hundred

ligaments of steel darted out and bound the fellow fast—and Sisyphus kept him there until he cancelled the debt?

A myth? As the winged feet of Mercury?

As Ulysses who filled the ears of his crew with wax and bound himself with knotted thongs to the mast—as they neared the sorcerer's shore?

A myth? As Bacchus, the god of wine—in peace wearing a purple robe, in war wearing a panther's skin, his chariot drawn by panthers?

As Atalanta and her race with Hippomenes, who threw three golden apples—and the footrace which he won?

Asking, "Is Hell a myth?" is but an interrogatory way—on the part of some—of stating that Hell *is* a myth—as much as the wild mythologies of the Greeks.

With playful raillery do many speak of the fact of Hell. With a blighting barrikin do many speak of the fact of Hell. With many Hell is the wild nightmare of a disordered brain—the fanciful fake of an erratic mind.

A myth? Just as well say a lion has the mouth of a mouse.

A myth? Just as well say an eagle has sparrow's wings.

A myth? Just as well say you can cradle a furnace in a thimble.

All of which brings us to consider some

II. ASSEVERATIONS

Asseverate means "to affirm, to aver positively or with solemnity." Many there are who, with ridicule of those who disagree, declare that there is no Hell. Atheists tell us that we die like dogs—that our souls perish with our bodies—that when the earth has swallowed us up, we become part and parcel with clay; and that is the end of the whole matter. We, believing not what atheists say, doubt if the atheists believe themselves.

But note what some say:

1. "The Dantesque picture as a place of penal flames, smoke and physical torture is an absurd picture."

2. "Hell-fire is a riot of imaginative genius."

3. "It is the feeblest form of sentimentality to believe in a Heaven, just as it is a terrible folly to believe in Hell."

4. "The pulpit teaching about Hell is an unauthorized accretion to the true doctrine—and repugnant to reason."

5. "The Hell of fire and brimstone was doomed under the revolt assisted by George MacDonald—and the doctrine of a material Hell has

gradually disappeared from the sermons of most preachers."

6. "Milton's conception of Hell was inconsistent with the character of God as revealed in Jesus Christ."

"Indeed, it is to be doubted whether men ever believed fully in the existence of such a Hell; for if preachers believed in the Hell they taught thirty years ago and had any humanity in them, they would have been unable to sleep in their beds. To talk of a Hell so horrible that no man with a heart in him would throw a dog into it and yet to preach that the Almighty Father casts the bulk of the human family into it to burn forever and ever, was to insult the very name of the Being whom we are taught to love."

7. "Hell is a state—and not a place."

"To live in harmony with what we understand to be God's law is the truest Heaven. To live out of harmony with that law is Hell."

8. "Heaven and Hell may be the same place—and Heaven will be Hell to the man who loves evil things."

9. "Many of the terms describing Hell are allegorical or metaphorical or poetical—and imply the spiritual state which is the antithesis of salvation. All such delineations as 'the blackness of darkness forever,' 'perdition,' 'the lake that burneth with fire and brimstone,' 'eternal destruction from the face of the Lord' are purely fantastical—and deserve no attention."

10. "When it comes to Hell being a place of fire, Origen taught that it was not a material fire, but self-kindled, like an internal fever—a figurative representation of the moral process by which restoration shall be effected." And Clement of Alexandria taught that "Hell-fire is a sort of spiritual fire which purifies the soul."

"It is a misconception of His words to impart the idea of literal flames." "Fire cannot burn the physical body or vehicle with which the soul will array itself when it goes forth from this mortal to immortality and from this corruptible to incorruption. Flesh and blood cannot enter the realm of the hereafter. Fire cannot feed upon the cosmic integument of the world of spirits; but what fire does for the body will be supplied by remorse, by the torturing consciousness of an absolutely wasted opportunity, by the perpetual facing of the ruined lives which have been irreparably blasted and corrupted during the earthly sojourn."

"If the Bible teaches 'everlasting punishment,' so much the worse for the Bible, because we cannot believe it; you may quote texts and have

behind the texts the very finest scholarship to justify certain interpreta-
tions, but it is no good. We are no longer the slaves of a book nor the
blind devotees of a creed; we believe in love and in evolution."

11. "If punishment is to win the verdict of our best consciousness,
it must be remedial."

"But I doubt very much whether any intelligent man or woman
believes in a materialistic Hell—that is, in a real raging fire in which people
are eternally burned."

"It is surely not illegitimate to draw the conclusion that Christ intended to teach that even the fire of remorse in the future life may purify
the spirit and so prepare it for some higher and better state."

"There never was, is, or will be, any right in the name of the Gospel
of Christ to speak of 'eternal torments.'"

12. "Endless torments are in flagrant contradiction to the goodness
of God, as expressed in His holy Word."

But, let us ask, if there is no Hell, is not the Bible a bundle of blunders,
a myth, a book of fairy tales? Are not the prophets, who spoke of God's
mercy, liars? Did not the apostles cease to perambulate around the pole
of veracity?

If there is no Hell, does not Jesus deserve to wear the label of
the imposter?

Into the valley of Hinnom, outside the city of Jerusalem, the Jews
threw the refuse of the city and the dead carcasses of animals—where
the worms would eat them and a fire was kept continually burning. Jesus
used this great valley of offal to describe the awful reality of Hell.

*"And if thy hand offend thee, cut it off: it is better for thee to enter
into life maimed, than having two hands to go into Hell, into the fire
that never shall be quenched: Where their worm dieth not, and the fire
is not quenched."*—Mark 9:43,44.

If there is no Hell, is not Calvary, with all its suffering and sacrifice
and finished atoning work, a blunder and all the voices thereof a babel
of incoherency?

By every contemptuous mouthful of spit that befouled His face, by
every hair of His beard which cruel fingers tore from His cheeks, by
every bruise of His face, by every mark of the scourge upon His back,
by every thorn that punctured His brow, by every nail that held Him
to the tree, by every breath He drew which was a pang of pain, by every
beat of His heart which was a throb of agony—by all the shadows that

covered the earth when black midnight came at noonday, we say that if Calvary be not the way of escape from an *eternal* Hell—then Calvary is a mistake.

It is not credible that the Son of God should have become man and died on the cross merely to save men from the short and temporal consequences of sin. The infinity of the sacrifice implies an infinity of punishment as that from which the sacrifice was intended to deliver those who would accept the sacrifice. If a man accepts the atonement of Christ—how can he doubt the dogma of Hell?

Now, let us ask, can there be a Heaven if there be no Hell? The Bible, Book above and beyond all books as a river is beyond a rill in reach, speaks of Heaven. But the same Bible also speaks of Hell. The same Bible that speaks of the glories and bliss of Heaven speaks of the woes and pains and miseries of Hell—as the portion of those who reject Christ.

So let us consider the

III. ACTUALITY

Though some today in the theological and educational world are "fond of a mist that rises from the ground" and rebel against the concrete, the definite, the actual—still there is a Hell. Though many vaporize every great fact and doctrine of the Christian faith and talk as though they believed that only when these great facts and weighty doctrines have been "sublimated into the mythical and poetic" are they worthy of the intellectual—still there is a Hell.

We need realities to meet realities—and we find them in the New Testament, which is not "a collection of photographed mirages" and does not "tantalize with vapors a world perishing of thirst."

Watkinson says:

> Although the New Testament is renounced, sin, devils, judgments, Hell remain potential in the human conscience. To take away Hell is to reject the physician and leave the plague, to overthrow the lighthouse and leave the hidden rock, to wipe out the rainbow and leave the storm, to take away the firelight and leave the fire to rage, to take away the vaccine and leave the smallpox. To take away Hell is to meet the tragic blackness of sin with a candle gospel, to make a mild twilight out of eternal retribution, to take away the trumpet and open the gate to enemies, to take away roses and leave the thorns, to throw away gold and press bankruptcy upon human life.

In the light of Bible truth, consider the *actuality* of Hell. If there is NOT a Hell, I do not want to believe there is. But I would rather believe and preach unpleasant truth than to believe and preach error. And as awful as the thought is, I can have no other conclusion than that there is a Hell—because I believe the Bible is the very Word of God. Inexhaustive in its adequacy, harmonious in infinite complexity, it is supernatural in origin, divine in authorship, human in penmanship, infallible in authority, infinite in scope, universal in interest, eternal in duration, personal in application, inspired in totality, immortal in its hopes, immeasurable in power.

There is not a sin in all the centuries it does not condemn, not a virtue it fails to mention. An oasis in a desert of despair, it is the only Book that makes the death room bright. In the original purpose of God, there was no manifest provision for Hell. Every being, bearing the image of the Creator, was with Him about the throne of Heaven. There was no necessity for a Hell. Necessity arose when His hosts rebelled in Heaven and were cast out. Then was the "everlasting fire prepared for the devil and his angels."

I know some people call the preacher who stands squarely upon the teaching of Christ and His apostles "narrow," "harsh," "cruel."

As to being narrow, I have no desire to be any broader than was Jesus. As to being cruel, is it cruel to tell men the truth?

Is a man to be called cruel who declares the whole counsel of God and points out to men their danger?

Is it cruel to warn people on an excursion ship that the ship has sprung a leak and they must get to the lifeboats?

Is it cruel to tell Miami that a hurricane is headed for the city?

Is it cruel to arouse sleeping people to the fact that the house is on fire?

Is it cruel to jerk a blind man away from the rattlesnake in the coil?

Is it cruel to declare to people the deadliness of disease and tell them which medicine to take?

Is it cruel to label poison with the crossbones and skull?

I would rather be called cruel for being kind than called kind for being cruel.

"Then shall he say also unto them on the left hand, Depart from me, ye cursed, into everlasting fire, prepared for the devil and his angels."—Matt. 25:41.

"And to you who are troubled rest with us, when the Lord Jesus shall

be revealed from heaven with his mighty angels, In flaming fire taking vengeance on them that know not God, and that obey not the gospel of our Lord Jesus Christ: Who shall be punished with everlasting destruction from the presence of the Lord, and from the glory of his power."—II Thess. 1:7-9.

Hell is a terrible *actuality*.

Yet some say: "Scholarly preachers have given up belief in an orthodox Hell." If so, they did not give up that belief for reasons of Greek or New Testament scholarship. If so, they gave it up for sentimental and speculative reasons. No man can go to the New Testament and not find Hell in the New Testament.

But suppose "scholarly preachers" have given up their belief in an orthodox Hell. That would not prove anything. Many times scholars have given up belief in doctrines that after all, *in the final outcome,* proved to be true.

No scholars, except Noah, believed a flood would come. But it did.

No scholars, except Lot and Abraham, believed fire would fall on Sodom and Gomorrah. But it did.

No scholars, except Jeremiah and one friend, Baruch, believed Jerusalem would be destroyed by Nebuchadnezzar. But it was!

Four leading schools of theological thought in Jesus' day scoffed at Jesus' prediction concerning the coming judgment of God on Jerusalem. But secular history tells us that, in spite of the dissent of all the scholars, it came true just as Jesus predicted.

No university in the world in the days of Luther and Huss believed in the doctrine of justification by faith. But it was so—and Luther was right—and every university of Germany, France, England, Scotland was wrong.

So if all the scholars, preachers, scientists, artists, statesmen, politicians, musicians and teachers on earth gave up belief in the doctrine of an orthodox Hell, it would not prove anything.

Some say: "I hate Hell." So do I. But if a man is going to be a preacher of Christianity, he should preach the doctrines of Christianity.

I hate to think of anybody going there. But nobody can hate Hell out of existence.

I hate snakes, but my hatred does not exterminate them.

I hate rats, but rats still live.

If we are Christians, we hate sham, but sham is here.

If we walk as wise people and not as fools, we hate the works of the flesh. But adultery, fornication, lasciviousness, idolatry, witchcraft, hatred, variance, emulations, wrath, strife, seditions, heresies, envyings, murders, drunkenness, revelings and such like are with us.

We all should hate lying, but lying is here.

We hate dishonesty, but dishonesty is abroad.

I hate infidelity, but infidelity is here.

I hate liquor, but liquor is here.

If hate were an exterminator, I could get rid of sin by midnight.

Disbelief in Hell does not put out its fires. Disbelief in poison does not do away with the deadliness of poison. You might believe you could play with nitroglycerine without danger, but that belief won't keep men from picking up your fragments in a basket. Disbelief and unbelief do not alter facts. THERE IS A HELL!

Nobody can believe in the Bible and not believe in Hell as an actuality too terrible for words to describe. And if all the terrible language descriptive of Hell is figurative, how terrible must be the actuality to which the fingers of all figures point!

Now consider some

IV. ATTESTATIONS

1. THE BIBLE.

Of course, there is only one book in this world to which to go to learn about Hell, and that is the Bible—the Book which travels more highways, knocks at more doors and speaks to more people in their mother tongue than any other. The doctrine of Hell is essentially and fundamentally a Bible doctrine. I believe what the Bible says. I have never read the Bible and said, "As I *partly* believe."

"And cast ye the unprofitable servant into outer darkness: there shall be weeping and gnashing of teeth."—Matt. 25:30.

"As therefore the tares are gathered and burned in the fire; so shall it be in the end of this world. The Son of man shall send forth his angels, and they shall gather out of his kingdom all things that offend, and them which do iniquity; And shall cast them into a furnace of fire: there shall be wailing and gnashing of teeth."—Matt. 13:40-42.

"Then shall he say also unto them on the left hand, Depart from me, ye cursed, into everlasting fire, prepared for the devil and his angels."—Matt. 25:41.

"And fear not them which kill the body, but are not able to kill the soul: but rather fear him which is able to destroy both soul and body in hell."—Matt. 10:28.

"And whosoever was not found written in the book of life was cast into the lake of fire."—Rev. 20:15.

"The same shall drink of the wine of the wrath of God, which is poured out without mixture into the cup of his indignation; and he shall be tormented with fire and brimstone in the presence of the holy angels, and in the presence of the Lamb: And the smoke of their torment ascendeth up for ever and ever: and they have no rest day nor night, who worship the beast and his image, and whosoever receiveth the mark of his name."—Rev. 14:10,11.

And if modern-day preachers from behind their pulpits say that the old-time preachers were slavishly literal in their interpretation and preaching of the doctrine of Hell, certainly the old-time preachers could, from their graves or from Heaven, accuse modern-day preachers of ignoring the reality and awfulness of it—or of neglecting to preach it at all.

But the attestations of many great preachers are in agreement with scriptural attestation.

2. DR. R. A. TORREY:

I claim to be a scholarly preacher. I have a right to so claim. I have taken two degrees, specializing in Greek in one of the most highly esteemed universities of America. I have also studied at two German universities. I have read the Bible in three languages every day of my life for many years. I have studied a large share of what has been written on different sides of the question in English and in German. I have written between thirty and forty different books which have been translated, I am told, into more languages than the books of any other living man. I say this simply to show that I have a right to call myself a scholarly preacher. Yet I believe the old-fashioned Bible doctrine regarding Hell.

3. D. L. MOODY:

The same Christ that tells us of Heaven with all its glories, tells us of Hell with all its horrors; and no one will accuse Christ of drawing this picture to terrify people or to alarm them, if it were not true. The same Bible that tells us of Heaven, tells us of Hell. The same Saviour that came down from Heaven to tell us about Heaven, tells us about Hell. He speaks about our escaping the damnation of Hell, and there is no one that has lived since that could tell us as much about it as Himself.

If there is no Hell, let us burn our Bibles. Why spend so much time studying the Bible? Why spend so much time and so much money in building churches? Let us turn our churches into places of commerce or of amusement. Let us eat and drink and be merry, for we will soon be gone if there is no hereafter. Let us build a monument for Paine and Voltaire. Let us build a tomb over Christianity, and shout over it, "There is no Hell to receive us, there is no God to condemn us; there is no Heaven, there is no hereafter!"

4. HENRY WARD BEECHER:

The thought of future punishment for sinners which the Bible reveals is enough to make an earthquake of terror in every man's soul. I do not accept the doctrine of eternal punishment because I believe in it. I would destroy all faith in it if I could; but it would do me no good. It would not destroy the thing itself. With the word *everlasting,* I should take and put it into the rack like an inquisition, until it would shriek out some other meaning, but that would not alter the stern fact.

5. F. W. FABER:

It is a good thing, and wise, for our own sakes to think sometimes of the horrid fact and place of retribution. As truly as Europe lies across the ocean and as truly as thousands of men and women over there are living real lives and fulfilling various destinies, so truly is there a place called Hell—all alive this hour with the multitudinous life of countless agonies and immeasurable graduations of despair. None, save the blessed in Heaven, have a more keen or conscious life than those millions of ruined souls—and the fearful possibility is that many who think they will *not* go there *will* go there.

6. T. DeWITT TALMAGE:

Not having intellect enough to fashion an eternity of my own, I must take the word of the Bible. I believe there is a Hell. If I had not been afraid of Hell, I do not think I would have started for Heaven.

7. C. H. SPURGEON:

Our joy is that if any one of us is made, in God's hands, the means of converting a man from the error of his way, we shall have saved a soul from this eternal death. That dreadful Hell the saved one will not know, that wrath he will not feel, that being banished from the presence of God will never happen to him.

8. PAUL STEWART:

The preaching that ignores the doctrine of Hell lowers the holiness of God and degrades the work of Christ.

9. B. H. LOVELACE:

There are foregleams of Hell all around us (Rom. 8:22). Read the tragedies that besmear the front pages of our daily newspapers, behold the victim of drink writhing in the tortures of delirium tremens, see the human wrecks strewn all along life's highway, and hear the sobs and sighs of a sin-cursed world. These are but a few sparks from the lake of fire, the eternal abode of the lost. . . .

Hell is a logical necessity. It is the ultimate and inevitable consequence of the law of moral gravitation, which begins in this life and ends in eternity. What was said of Judas Iscariot will be true of all men, "He went to his own place."

10. WILLIAM ELBERT MUNSEY:

There is a Hell. All principles of quality, character and state exist in correlative dualities. Good and evil are correlates. The very argument which gives merit its reward beyond the grave must, in virtue on a correlation, give demerit punishment beyond the grave. . . . Shut up in Hell to weep, unnoticed by mercy, forever.

11. A. C. DIXON:

There is something in God for sinners to fear. "Gone forever," said a New York preacher, "is Dante's Inferno and Michelangelo's Last Judgment." And yet within less than a mile of the pulpit from which these words were spoken, infernos fearful as Dante's were in full blast, and judgments upon sin and sinners were being executed—more terrible than Michelangelo's. S-i-n spells "Hell" in this world and the next.

It is no nightmare of medieval darkness. It is not the hallucination of a disordered brain. It is a fact which anyone with open eyes must see. The smoke of torment ascends here from the house of shame, the public-house, the drunkard's home, the divorce court, the prison, the gallows, the madhouse, the gambling den and lives of men and women who are burning in the furnace of their own lusts. . . .

When the wicked, in the flashlight of the judgment day, shall see themselves and their sins as they are, they will accept everlasting punishment as just retribution. Their sense of justice will approve it. It would appear to them an incongruous thing for God to take them to Heaven; as incongruous, indeed, as it would appear to a guilty impenitent criminal if the king of England, instead of sending him to prison, as he deserves, should take him into the palace as an associate for his wife and children . . . .

A cemetery is a necessity. The bodies of the dead must not be left in the homes of the living. A little child died in the family of a former parishioner; the poor mother, crazed with grief, would not consent to its burial. She stood, like Rizpah, over its little lifeless body and would not allow undertaker or husband to touch it. After a week of such heart-rending experience, the husband was compelled to remove her by force to another room, while some friends went with the little form to the cemetery. To have kept the dead with the living would have been unkindness to the living and have done the dead no good.

Thus every cemetery is an argument for Hell. The spiritually dead soul is like a dead body in that it is in a state of moral putrefaction and carries with it the deadly contagion of sin. If it refuses to receive life, it must of necessity be placed apart with its spiritually dead companions.

12. BILLY SUNDAY:

You will not be in Hell five minutes until you believe that there is one.

13. SAM JONES:

I believe in a bottomless Hell; and I believe that the wicked shall be turned into Hell. The legitimate end of a sinful life is Hell. Every sinner carries his own brimstone with him. How many men meet truth without a tremor in their muscles?

14. DINSDALE T. YOUNG:

If we had no Bible, no churches, no sermons, still Hell would be a philosophical necessity. But Hell is a matter of divine revelation. Nothing is more plainly revealed in the pages of Scripture than this awful fact. . . .

We must remember that the doctrine of Hell was taught by our Lord Himself; and though taught with a great reservation, it was also taught with most solemn emphasis. When we remember that the Saviour spoke more solemnly on Hell than anyone else ever spoke, we have, for all who accept His teaching, an incontrovertible argument for the existence of such a place of doom.

15. LEE SCARBOROUGH:

When we preach on the wrath of God, on the burning doctrines of an eternal Hell, we must do it with heart compassion.

16. B. H. CARROLL:

You say that you will not let God Almighty have His way. Then

God Almighty will never save your soul. There is no more hope of
your salvation than there is of expecting that this earth in one moment
shall be converted into a diamond. You are just as certain for Hell
as if you were there today.

These are only a few flowers from the garden of truth—only a few
voices from amidst many voices of truth—giving attestations concerning Hell.

But hear the voice above and beyond all voices, the voice of Jesus
attesting in these words:

*"Then shall he say also unto them on the left hand, Depart from me,
ye cursed, into everlasting fire, prepared for the devil and his angels. . . .
And these shall go away into everlasting punishment: but the righteous
into life eternal."*—Matt. 25:41,46.

Nobody goes to Hell who does not belong there.

There is a Hell, though some people—with the blandest of smiles—
come to tell us that all alike, saint and sinner, will turn up in Heaven
at last. The murderer, the seducer, the hater and the hated, the robber
and the robbed, to their surprise, will all find Heaven at last. Nero and
Paul, Jesus and Herod, Judas and Peter, Cain and Abel, Elijah and
Jezebel, Tom Paine and Murray McCheyne, will all come out at the
same side of the judgment throne. A strange Heaven indeed!—with
all the hypocrites and whoremongers and drunkards and backbiters and
blasphemers standing on the glassy sea. I say, in the name of reason,
the thought is blasphemous.

Sin is being burnt into your soul as with a red-hot iron. You cannot
throw it off as you do your clothes. It is part of your being. Look out,
men! Sin is no trifle. It will live when the sun is buried.

The popular theory of this age is: "I die like my dog. I die a sinner
and am nowhere ever after. The coffin holds my soul; and, of course,
punishment of any kind in eternity is an impossibility."

Now this theory denies the immortality of the soul; for when my body
dies, my soul dies. But God says, "The wicked shall be turned into
hell. . .Where their worm dieth not, and the fire is not quenched."

To your Bible, men, and let us have the truth, whatever it be. I cite
the eternal God Himself, and hear what He says! "The wicked shall
be turned into hell" (Ps. 9:17). You may scatter the everlasting mountains or split the sun in twain until, with shorn locks and dimmed eye,
it slumbers on the pathway of light; but you cannot alter God's Word.

I cite the tenderhearted Saviour; and three times in one chapter (Mark 9), He speaks of a worm that never dies and a fire that never shall be quenched. Take time, you, whoever you are, to read Mark 9. Now be mercilessly clear, for your soul is at stake.

Answer me this question: Did the Lord Jesus lie when He spake of the unquenchable fire? Did the Son of God picture a lie when He showed us the rich man lifting up his eyes in torments and begging a drop of water to cool his tongue? Did He mean to harrow up our souls with lying pictures of that which never existed? "It is impossible for God to lie." Well, then, it is impossible that there is no Hell; and let that settle the question forever.

Now, along with these attestations, would I have you think of some

V. ADJECTIVES

Here are some adjectives that describe the severe nature of Hell.

1. "EVERLASTING FIRE."

I am not going to split hairs to prove the fire of Hell is literal fire any more than I would split hairs to prove the gold of Heaven is literal gold. I believe when God says "fire," He means *fire*. I believe when God says "gold," He means *gold*. If the gold in the streets of Heaven is figurative, Heaven will be no less *beautiful*. If the fire of Hell can be proven to be figurative, Hell will be no less *unendurable*. All who believe they prove the fire of Hell is not literal fire have only removed physical pain, which is the least significant feature of its character. Hell is the madhouse of the universe where remorse and an accusing memory cause unspeakable torture.

All words are incapable of describing that awful place. The very thought of Hell ought to make one uncomfortable.

An Oriental legend tells of a king who acceded to his throne late in life. "Too great glory crusheth too small strength," he murmured to his vizier as he sat in state for the first time. "Verily, though my crown shineth as all the stars of Heaven reflected in one small pool, yet its weight is like to that of the water jars that all the women of my kingdom carry upon their heads!"

He bent beneath the burden and died within the year. A thousand times more should the thought of spending eternity in Hell make one uncomfortable—yea, fill one with terror.

No music—but weeping, wailing, gnashing of teeth. No rest—but the wicked wanting rest, yet forever tired. No fragrance—"smoke of their torment ascendeth up for ever." No light—"blackness of outer darkness for ever." No comfort—"tormented in flame for ever."

Though infidelity still hurls its anathemas against Christianity; though modernism still mutilates the Bible; though Faith's wings are clipped by Reason's scissors; though there is an intellectual recoil against anything emotional; right is still right, wrong is still wrong, God is still God, man is still man, Heaven is still Heaven, Hell is still Hell—no hope, no reunion, no love, no light, no peace.

2. "Everlasting fire is a real PLACE."

The rich man of Luke 16 is in Hell bodily. He wanted his brothers to know that where he was after death was a PLACE. Jesus taught that the body would be in Hell along with the soul.

"And fear not them which kill the body, but are not able to kill the soul: but rather fear him which is able to destroy both soul and body in hell."—Matt. 10:28.

3. A place of TORMENT.

"The same shall drink of the wine of the wrath of God, which is poured out without mixture into the cup of his indignation; and he shall be tormented with fire and brimstone in the presence of the holy angels, and in the presence of the Lamb: And the smoke of their torment ascendeth up for ever and ever: and they have no rest day nor night, who worship the beast and his image, and whosoever receiveth the mark of his name."—Rev. 14:10,11.

4. A place of VILE COMPANIONSHIPS.

"But the fearful, and unbelieving, and the abominable, and murderers, and whoremongers, and sorcerers, and idolaters, and all liars, shall have their part in the lake which burneth with fire and brimstone: which is the second death."—Rev. 21:8.

The Devil will be there with all demons. Read the list of the wicked persons in Romans 1:29-31:

"Being filled with all unrighteousness, fornication, wickedness, covetousness, maliciousness; full of envy, murder, debate, deceit, malignity; whisperers, Backbiters, haters of God, despiteful, proud, boasters, inventors of evil things, disobedient to parents, Without

understanding, covenantbreakers, without natural affection, implacable, unmerciful."

All of these will be in Hell for eternity if they die in their sins unrepentant and unforgiven.

All of which is to say that Hell is a hard word and a harder fact. Take all the words in the dictionary that mean something bad and ugly and terrible, and write opposite them in great black letters this one word—HELL. It means the terrible results of sin—its guilt, its pollution, its penalty, its power—sin working in an immortal soul and burning like a fire, hotter and more terrible than the fires that consume the body. Such will be the substance for those who spend the shadows to the end, forgetful of God.

5. A place from which there is NO EXIT.

In public halls we find in bold letters, EXIT. But EXIT is a word not in the vocabulary of Hell. In other places there are signs, THIS WAY OUT. But there is no sign like that in Hell. Once there, you are always there. Once in, never out.

I read in the paper the other day of some prisoners who worked a year to make their escape from prison. You could work one hundred thousand years in Hell to get out and never do so.

Jesus says: "There is a great gulf *fixed.*" It is impassable to those who would come from there here. Open your eyes and look before you enter a place from which no man has ever returned—a place where those who enter come not out forever, but lift up wailing voices to warn those who are wise enough to hear and heed.

6. A place ETERNAL.

"And these shall go away into everlasting punishment: but the righteous into life eternal."—Matt. 25:46.

No one has any trouble believing the "everlasting life" part of the verse. By every known law of exegesis, it must mean the same thing in the other part of the verse. The expression *"Eis tous aionas tou aionon"* occurs twelve times in Revelation and correctly translated means "unto the ages of the ages." Eight times it is used expressing the existence of God and the duration of His reign. One time it is used expressing the duration of the blessedness of the righteous. In every remaining instance it is used to express the duration of the punishment of the wicked. It is the strongest known expression for endlessness.

Eternal! There are ten thousand grains of wheat in one bushel, say. Multiply that by all the grains in the millions of bushels of wheat grown every year. Multiply that by the number of leaves on all the trees of the world. Multiply that product by the number of all the grains of sand on all seashores. Multiply that product by the number of all the stars in the heavens. Multiply that product by the number of inches from earth to sun.

Now, if after that many years the joys of Heaven would cease, they would not be eternal. Now, if after that many years the fires of Hell would cease, they would not be eternal.

Where will you spend ETERNITY? If Hell were nothing but a ten-year palace with no music; a fifty-year palace with no children; a one-year association with a man who killed his mother, it is too much Hell for me.

The Greek word *Gehenna* means a place of everlasting punishment. Southeast of Jerusalem was a valley where, for a long time, the idol Molech was worshiped. Little children were thrown into his fiery arms and consumed in the flames. Because of their cries it came to be known as the Valley of Lamentation or the Valley of Hinnom.

Those horrible sacrifices were abolished by Josiah (II Kings 23:10). The Jews so abhorred the place that they cast into it all manner of refuse, dead bodies of animals and of criminals who had been executed. Fires were constantly needed to consume the dead bodies, and so the place was called "Gehenna of fire." It is this word *Gehenna* that the New Testament used to describe the place of punishment appointed for the unsaved after death.

> What will you do in a world where the Holy Spirit never strives; where every soul is fully left to its own depravity; and where there is no leisure for repentance, if there were even the desire, but where there is too much present pain to admit repentance; where they gnaw their tongues with pain and blaspheme the God of Heaven?—James Hamilton.

> An immortality of pain and tears; an infinity of wretchedness and despair; the blackness of darkness across which conscience will forever shoot her clear and ghastly flashes—like lightning streaming over a desert when midnight and tempest are there; weeping and wailing and gnashing of teeth; long, long eternity and things that will make eternity seem longer—making each moment seem eternity—oh, miserable condition of the damned!—Richard Fuller.

The Lamb is, indeed, the emblem of love; but what is so terrible as the wrath of the Lamb? The depth of the mercy despised is the measure of the punishment of him that despiseth. There are no more fearful words than those of the Saviour! The threatenings of the law were *temporal*; those of the Gospel are *eternal*. It is Christ who reveals the *never-dying* worm, the *unquenchable* fire, and He who contrasts with the *eternal joys of the redeemed* the *everlasting woes of the lost*. His loving arms would enfold the whole human race, but not while impenitent or unbelieving; the benefits of His redemption are conditional. —Edward Thomson.

A SUMMARY:

Hell is a lake of fire (Rev. 20:15).

A devouring fire (Isa. 33:14).

A bottomless pit (Rev. 20:1).

Everlasting burnings (Isa. 33:14).

A furnace of fire (Matt. 13:41,42).

A place of torments (Luke 16:23).

Where they curse God (Rev. 16:11).

A place of filthiness (Rev. 22:10,11).

Where they can never repent (Matt. 12:32).

A place where they have no rest (Rev. 14:11).

A place of everlasting punishment (Matt. 25:46).

A place of blackness of darkness forever (Jude 13).

A place where they gnaw their tongues (Rev. 16:10).

A place where their breath will be a living flame (Isa. 33:11).

A place prepared for the Devil and his angels (Matt. 25:41).

A lake of fire into which people are cast alive (Rev. 19:20).

A place from which the smoke of their torment ascendeth up forever and forever (Rev. 14:11).

A place where they drink the wine of the wrath of God (Rev. 14:10).

A place where they do not want their loved ones to come (Luke 16:28).

A place where there are murderers, liars, fearful and abominable (Rev. 21:8).

Dante's Hell is a perdition which a poet had dreamed; Christ's Hell a pit He has seen—a black night of infinite darkness without one star to break its gloom. Hell—a place of utter separation from God. Hell—a place of sorrow upon sorrow. Hell—a place divested of every good. Hell—a place of hate upon hate. Hell—a place of grief upon grief.

Hell—a place of despair upon despair, where people are eternally crying out for help that never comes, with no one to hear their cries but other damned souls.

The suffering in Hell is described by the rich man desiring one drop of water. "One poor drop desired—though they were glittering on the flowers and plants of a thousand worlds, dancing over the rocks of a thousand rills, and sparkling in amber, ruby, blue, green, gold listed in the arches of a thousand rainbows, and descending in myriads upon the beggars' homes and the fields of the poor."

I would have you now think of the

VI. ASSISTANCE

Now I speak of the assistance the doctrine of Hell is in preaching to win the lost. The preaching of this doctrine is ever an asset—never a hindrance—to the success of gospel preaching. The minister of the Gospel is under obligation to preach the whole truth of God's Word. If he does, God will take care of the results.

Concerning the doctrine of Hell, we should be able to say what Richard Baxter wrote: "I preached as never sure to preach again—and as a dying man to dying men"—holding the literal interpretation of Hell and eternal damnation. If we preachers are to be messengers of God, we must tell the whole message. We must not keep back any part of the Word of God.

In a bad sense is the preacher of the Gospel to be regarded who, for fear of offending polite ears or fastidious tastes, or for the sake of conforming to fashionable whims, should gloss over the danger of Hell-fire for all unsaved ones.

It was through faithful warnings that Mary Slessor, the white queen missionary of West Africa, was converted at Dundee. And through her, thousands of others in darkest Africa got blessing. The person who set the unpalatable truth forth to Mary Slessor's mind performed a most merciful service.

If this doctrine, which has been banished from so many pulpits, is not to be preached—why is it in the Bible at all—and why so often? Is not the whole Bible studded over with the idea of "FEAR" as a motive to bring men to Christ?

"Let us therefore FEAR, lest, a promise being left us of entering into his rest, any of you should seem to come short of it."—Heb. 4:1.

"By faith Noah, being warned of God of things not seen as yet, moved with FEAR, prepared an ark. . . ."—Heb. 11:7.

If we would get people waked up and concerned about their salvation, they must be told the *whole truth*. Salvation implies danger. The appeal to fear had considerable place in Jesus' preaching. It cannot be safe or right for ministers to suppress it in theirs. The Lord Jesus was the most perfect Gentleman who has ever appeared—and He was not afraid nor ashamed to speak of HELL.

Dr. A. C. Dixon said: "If we had more preaching of Hell in the pulpit, we might have less hell in the community."

General Booth said: "If I had my way, I would not give any of my workers a three-years' training in a college, but I would put each of you twenty-four hours in Hell—the best training for earnest preaching you could have."

We need to preach this doctrine along with the truth of the cross.

Preach it—not as dainty tasters of intellectual subtleties.

Preach it—not as dealers in finespun metaphysical disquisitions.

Preach it—not as administrators of laughing gas for the painless extraction of sin.

Preach it—not with stammering tongue but as a trumpet that gives no uncertain sound.

Preach it—with broken heart and yearning soul.

Believing in the sacrifice of our Lord Jesus Christ for the sins of the whole world, we must accept the doctrine of Hell—for no lesser fate can they expect who, having heard the offer of the Gospel, deliberately reject it. How great the folly of suppressing the revealed fact of Hell!

Dr. Young said: "There is a great danger of the average Christian pulpit yielding to unfaithfulness. It is a great part of the commission of the Christian minister to warn men, and unless men are warned it seems to me that the Christian ministry cannot escape grave responsibility for the eternal fate of those who listen to it."

And we must not preach this terrible fact as though it were light fiction.

But think now of the

VII. AGONIZING

Not only of those who agonize in Hell, but the *agony* of soul we should have in prayer and in preaching with concern to save the lost. If this city had a pestilence descending on it—what would we not do to stay its onslaught? If your children were in danger of smallpox—how concerned you would be! If a mad dog were loose in a school—how you would risk life to save children from the virus of hydrophobia from the dog's fangs! How much more when there are souls in danger of Hell—eternal Hell!

Who can arrange or describe fitting funeral obsequies of a lost soul? All the tears ever shed by all the graves and tombs of earth cannot. All the moans and sobs and sighs ever uttered cannot. If the inanimate world could break her silence—would that do it? If all seas should utter their deep and dreadful wails—would that do it? If all the mountains should lift up rumbling voices—would that do it? If the sun should drape in darkness—would that do it? If the moon should refuse to give her light—would that do it? If all the stars turned to clay—would all these fitly show the dire catastrophe of a lost soul? No songs on earth, no prayers, no words can fitly show what it means to be lost!

Yet, I fear we agonize not as did Abraham over the wickedness of Sodom and Gomorrah, nor as Moses who pleaded for God to blot him out rather than the people, nor as Jacob over the disappearance of Joseph, nor as Samuel who wept all night over Saul, nor as David who cried in agony over Absalom, nor as Jeremiah who wept like a brokenhearted archangel, nor as Ezekiel who ate filth to show the horrors of slavery, nor as Job who asked God questions through lips that festered with disease, nor as Jesus who wept over Jerusalem, nor as Paul who counted all things but loss.

I am no photographer of sordid spots, but I fear that we treat our main business as an incidental. We should have and manifest the passion for souls which Whitefield had who said, "I am willing to go to prison and to death for you, but I am not willing to go to Heaven without you."

When fishermen are sent to the river to fish, they fish. When nurses are sent to a hospital to nurse, they nurse. When painters are sent to a house to paint, they paint. When soldiers are sent to battle to fight, they fight. But too often when we are sent into the world to win men, we sing, "Throw Out the Lifeline," but do not throw. We sing, "I Love to Tell the Story," and do not tell it. Our singing and our practice are so strangely at variance. We sing in cojubilant chorus, "Rescue the Perishing," and our rescue work is woefully lacking in concern, and our lack of rescue makes our lives perjure the words of our mouths.

"Rescue the perishing, care for the dying"—is short meter poetry that needs to be transposed into long meter activity. We need the passion that girded Francis Asbury as he traveled a distance equal to five circuits around the world every five years, on the average, for forty-five years—and that mainly on horseback. We need the passion that fired Livingstone and kept him aflame amid jungle dangers and twenty-seven attacks of African fever—the passion that was the power working in the heart of David Brainerd who said, "I care not what hardships I endure, if only I can see souls saved"—the passion that drove General Booth, who, with a vision of the poor of London and what Christ could mean to their lives, said, "God shall have all there is in William Booth." And deacons must not be found guilty under the indictment set forth by Bishop Theodore S. Henderson's alarming assertion: "The average church officer has not the slightest spiritual concern for the salvation of other people." God says, "He that winneth souls is wise." Let us be wise—daily wise.

A lawmaker, Zulculous, in ancient times, had a law passed when he was judge that anybody caught in the act of adultery would have both eyes punched out. The first offender brought before him was his own son. Zulculous—in much perplexity and in manifestation of mercy to his son—had one of his own eyes punched out and one of his son's eyes.

Such concern about this great truth will cause us to think agonizingly rather than lightly upon the fact of Hell.

Lastly think with me of the

VIII. ANTITHESIS

HELL! the prison house of despair,
Here are some things that won't be there:
No flowers will bloom on the banks of Hell,
No beauties of nature we love so well;
No comforts of home, music and song,
No friendship of joy will be found in the throng;
No children to brighten the long, weary night;
No love nor peace, nor one ray of light;
No blood-washed soul with face beaming bright,
No loving smile in that region of night;
No mercy, no pity, pardon nor grace,
No water; O God, what a terrible place!
The pangs of the lost no human can tell,
Not one moment's ease—there is no rest in HELL!

HELL! the prison house of despair,
Here are some things that will be there:
Fire and brimstone are there, we know,
For God in His Word hath told us so;
Memory, remorse, suffering and pain,
Weeping and wailing, but all in vain;
Blasphemers, swearers, haters of God,
Christ-rejectors while here on earth trod;
Murderers, gamblers, drunkards and liars
Will have their part in the lake of fire;
The filthy, the vile, the cruel and mean,
What a horrible mob in Hell will be seen!
Yes, more than humans on earth can tell,
Are torments and woes of eternal HELL!

(Copyrighted by Catherine Dangell in *Sweet Meditations*. Used by permission.)

But as we believe that and preach that, let us not forget to believe and preach the antithesis of that—HEAVEN!

Heaven—where no toil shall fatigue God's redeemed ones.

Heaven—where no hostility can overcome them.

Heaven—where no temptations can assail them.

Heaven—where no pain can pierce them.

Heaven—where no night can shadow them.

Heaven—the most beautiful place the wisdom of God could conceive and the power of God could prepare.

In Heaven beauty has reached perfection.

Dr. Biederwolf tells us of a little girl who was blind from birth and only knew the beauties of earth from her mother's lips. A noted surgeon worked on her eyes, and at last his operations were successful; and as the last bandage dropped away, she flew into her mother's arms and then to the window and the open door; and as the glories of earth rolled into her vision, she ran screaming back to her mother and said, "O Mama, why didn't you tell me it was so beautiful!"

And the mother wiped her tears of joy away and said, "My precious child, I tried to tell you but I couldn't do it."

And one day when we go sweeping through those gates of pearl and catch our first vision of the enrapturing beauty all around us, I think we will hunt up John and say, "John, why didn't you tell us it was so beautiful?" And John will say, "I tried to tell you when I wrote the twenty-first and twenty-second chapters of the last book in the Bible after I got my vision, but I couldn't do it."

Heaven—the land where they never have any heartaches, where no graves are ever dug.

Heaven—where there is no hand-to-hand fight for bread.

Heaven—where no hearse rolls its dark way to the tomb.

Heaven—where David is triumphant, though once he bemoaned Absalom.

Heaven—where Abraham is enthroned who once wept for Sarah.

Heaven—where Paul is exultant, though once he sat with his feet in the stocks.

Heaven—where John the Baptist is radiant with joy though his head was chopped off in the dungeon.

Heaven—where Savonarola wears a crown, though once he burned at the stake.

Heaven—where Latimer sings praises though once he simmered in the fire.

Heaven—where many martyrs sit in the presence of Jesus though their blood once reddened the mouths of lions.

Heaven—where many saints rest in peace who once were torn on torture racks.

Let Heaven come into your mind—where there are no tears, no partings, no strife, no agonizing misunderstanding, no wounds of heart, no storm to ruffle the crystal sea, no alarm to strike from the cathedral towers, no dirge throbbing from seraphic harps, no tremor in the everlasting song.

Let us have and hold and preach the Bible conception of Hell. Let us have and hold and preach the antithetical conception of that perfect vision of God which we, for lack of words to describe, call "the home of the soul"—Heaven.

Samuel Rutherford said that to see Christ through the keyhole once in a thousand years would be Heaven enough for him. Thus he did express his love for his Saviour and the joy that one glimpse of His face would yield to him. But that would not be enough for the Saviour whom he loved and adored. No, His love has something to say in this matter. It has already said it, and it is this: "I will come again, and receive you unto myself; that where I am, there ye may be also." And, "Father, I will that they also, whom thou hast given me, be with me where I am; that they may behold my glory."

There shall be no closed door in that glory to hide the Saviour from His blood-bought saints.

There with unwearied gaze
  Our eyes on Him we'll rest,
And satisfy with endless praise
  Our hearts supremely blest.
Close to His trusted side
  In fellowship divine.
No cloud, no distance then shall hide
  Glories that there shall shine.

And, most wonderful prospect, "We shall be like him; for we shall see him as he is."

(From the book, *Bread From Bellevue Oven,* published by Sword of the Lord Publishers.)

FRED M. BARLOW
1921-1983

ABOUT THE MAN:

In 1959 Dr. Fred M. Barlow was elected National Sunday School Consultant for Regular Baptist Press and the General Association of Regular Baptist Churches. He held pastorates in New York, Ohio and Michigan. Then he began a ministry to local churches and multi-church Sunday school conferences; held evangelistic campaigns; gave addresses to Bible colleges and seminaries; and was active in summer Bible camp evangelism and youth rallies.

His sermons have been prize winners in sermon contests held by the Sword of the Lord. He was the author of several books, including: *Vitalizing Your Sunday School Visitation. . . Special Days in the Sunday School. . . Timeless Truths. . . Profiles in Evangelism. . . Revival for Survival. . .* and several smaller booklets, including a biography of Dr. John R. Rice.

Dr. Barlow was a native of southeastern West Virginia.

He graduated from Baptist Bible Seminary (now Baptist Bible College of Pennsylvania, Clarks Summit, Pennsylvania) and received an honorary Doctor of Divinity degree from Western Baptist Bible College, Salem, Oregon.

Dr. and Mrs. Barlow were parents of four children.

Dr. Barlow died in 1983.

VI.

Highways to Hell

FRED BARLOW

Highway tragedies! We read of them daily in our newspapers. Some are gruesome; some are eerie and strange: blood-spattered pavement, mangled bodies, snuffed-out lives, shattered plans and bereaved loved ones.

But I suggest that Jesus, in Matthew 7, preached on the greatest highway tragedy of all time—Highways to Hell.

From our text we will see there are just two highways to travel in this life, and both lead to eternity!

Jesus, when He preached, always drew a line and divided His hearers on one side or the other. This text is typical of Christ's preaching. In this sermon Jesus divided His audience.

First, He likened them to travelers on two different roads:

"Enter ye in at the strait gate: for wide is the gate and broad is the way, that leadeth to destruction, and many there be which go in thereat: Because strait is the gate, and narrow is the way, which leadeth unto life, and few there be that find it."—Matt. 7:13,14.

For His second point, He preached that people were like trees— some good and some bad:

"Even so every good tree bringeth forth good fruit; but a corrupt tree bringeth forth evil fruit. . . . Every tree that bringeth not forth good fruit is hewn down, and cast into the fire."—Vss. 17,19.

For His third point, Jesus warned that every human was like one of two builders: either like the foolish man who built upon the sand and lost his house in the storms; or like the wise man who built his house upon the rock, and it fell not in the storm—vss. 24-27.

Yes, every time and everywhere Jesus preached, He put everybody in one crowd or the other: either saints or sinners, either saved or lost, either for Christ or against Him. They either loved Him or hated Him; they either received Him or rejected Him; they either crowned Him Lord or crucified Him as a criminal; they either confessed Him or denied Him; they were either on the road to Heaven or the road to Hell.

My friend, the issues are still the same! Everyone who reads this is on one of two roads—either on the road to Heaven or on the Highway to Hell! The most important question you must ever answer, and that now, is, "Are you walking in God's way to Glory, or in your own way to Hell?"

Will you see with me from our text there is a broad, streamlined, easily accessible and much-traveled Highway to Hell.

People in our day are highway-conscious. Cities are pouring millions of dollars into city expressways and freeways. Why all this? To move more traffic, more quickly, more easily! That is just like the Devil and sin! There are Highways to Hell to move more people, more quickly, more easily to that land of perdition and destruction.

ROUTE 1—PROFESSION OF RELIGION

When I use the term "religion," I mean it to be understood as it is defined and not as it is many times intended to mean! Religion—a word used only five times in the Bible—means "the outward act or form by which men indicate their recognition of a god or gods, etc."

The Athenians were religious, said Paul. They showed their religion by erecting idols to every god they had heard of, and one to "THE UNKNOWN GOD," if any! In some parts of America religion means "salvation" or "born again," but I use it here in its defined sense.

Religion is a broad, much-traveled, easy-accessible highway; but it is a Highway to Hell! It is popular today to have broad and liberal views on religion. But I note that everyone is quite narrow and fanatic about doctors, lawyers, etc.

The religionist cries, "Any religion is all right. I'm not against any church or denomination. They are all going to the same place." (I agree they are all going to the same place—Hell!) But when he is stricken with cancer, he does not go to the doctor who says, "Oh, well, take anything you want—pills, surgery, fluids, therapy. One is just as good as another. All get you to the same place!" He doesn't want to wind up in the grave, so he seeks out a fundamental doctor with fundamental narrow beliefs that will cut out the diseased killer!

And when you take your vacation in Michigan, you don't get a Utah map! Why not if "one road is as good as another"? When you are lost on the highway, you ask for information and try to follow it to the letter, because you want to get on the right road!

Why not be as consistent and honest about your never-dying soul and get off this highway of religion—Gentile or Jew, Trinitarian or Unitarian, modernist or fundamentalist, Christian or pagan—any one religion is as good as another, just a different highway to the same place!

How often Jesus warned us of the fatality and hellish destiny of religion! In Matthew 7:21-23 He warned:

"Not every one that saith unto me, Lord, Lord, shall enter into the kingdom of heaven; but he that doeth the will of my Father which is in heaven. Many will say to me in that day, Lord, Lord, have we not prophesied in thy name? and in thy name cast out devils? and in thy name done many wonderful works? And then will I profess unto them, I never knew you: depart from me, ye that work iniquity."

Yes, Jesus warned us that many who intended, planned and expected to go to Heaven and even preached, taught and did miracles, go to Hell. Here Jesus warned preachers, teachers of Sunday school classes, personal workers, yes, even miracle workers, that they may be trusting their religion instead of Christ and be on the Highway to Hell.

In Matthew 13 He warned by parables that many were religious but lost! The parable of the seed should warn us that, even if we have heard hundreds of sermons and make mental agreement and physical action as a result, we may be rootless, shrivel up and go to Hell! Yes, people look like Christians, act like Christians and talk like Christians; and you may be one of such, yet be only a "tare"—a fake, imitation wheat!

Certainly Jesus meant to warn us of mere outward profession but not possession of salvation in His teaching of the five foolish virgins in Matthew 25. No oil—too late—shut out. Oh, I am so afraid that will be the sad story of many of my hearers!

Again in Luke 18:9-14 Jesus told us the story of the religious Pharisee who went home lost. Yes, he was moral, but he was lost. Yes, he tithed his money to God, but he was a lost sinner. Yes, he fasted (prayed and missed meals to commune with God), but he was lost.

Oh, Jesus' sermons were full of warnings, and the Bible is full of warnings to be sure you are saved and not just religious.

Peter, in II Peter 1:10, warns us ". . .give diligence to make your calling and election sure." And well he might. He had seen Judas preach and do miracles in the name of the Lord, along with the other eleven disciples. He had watched him for over three years act like a Christian, but Judas was a son of perdition and on the Highway to Hell!

Friend, it would be terrible enough to go to Hell because of a willful rebellion in sin or with a clenched fist of atheism or infidelity. But it must be one of the saddest, most remorseful, most tormenting remembrances in Hell to look back and remember you had figured you were going to Heaven but you were deluded, deceived and damned because you trusted in a church or a creed or a ritual like baptism or any or many religious rites, instead of God's way—Jesus Christ (John 14:6).

Get on the narrow road, enter the strait gate and be saved today.

ROUTE 2—THE PLEASURE OF SIN

It has taken no stretch of the imagination for me to visualize this broad, smooth-ribboned road to perdition teeming with the pleasure-hungry, sin-seeking, Christ-rejecting crowd. On Sunday nights in villages, in towns and in our largest cities I have watched these two classes Jesus spoke of on the two roads.

I have seen the masses on their way to a night of sin, revelry and on to Hell, and the "handful" on their way to God's house because they have found the narrow road to Heaven and its gate of life.

I have heard enthusiastic and good-intentioned but mistaken and misinformed preachers cry out to audiences, "There is no pleasure in sin." Moses knew better than that. He had to make a choice between sin and the Saviour. He had to make the same decision you must make—sin or Saviour. The Holy Spirit tells us of Moses "choosing rather to suffer affliction with the people of God, than to enjoy the pleasures of sin for a season" (Heb. 11:25).

Yes, there are many places of pleasures on the Highway to Hell. *There is the house of impurity and adultery.* Many enter in at it.

You know the staggering number of illegitimate children born in America to high school girls. You know of the millions of homosexuals in America—the sin that wiped out Sodom and Gomorrah. You know of the pornography, the millions of sex magazines printed monthly and read by the American people. You know of the millions who have venereal disease or the deadly AIDS. You know that multitudes of girls disappear every year into white slavery. You know of the millions of illegal abortions performed annually. You know of the parade of nudity and filth on the movie screen, on TV, in the magazines, papers and calendars.

But hear the Word of the Lord in I Corinthians 6:9,10,

"Know ye not that the unrighteous shall not inherit the kingdom of God? Be not deceived: neither fornicators, nor idolators, nor adulterers, nor effeminate, nor abusers of themselves with mankind. . . shall inherit the kingdom of God."

James 1:14,15 promises the same,

"But every man is tempted, when he is drawn away of his own lust, and enticed. Then when lust hath conceived, it bringeth forth sin: and sin, when it is finished, bringeth forth death."

The Highway to Hell.

Certainly on the Highway to Hell is the dance hall. Harry Vom Bruch said, "The seventh commandment has no more show in a dance hall than a glass fort in front of a howitzer."

There is pleasure in the sin of dancing. But there is the payoff. You pay the piper when you dance.

Dr. Frank Richardson, speaking before the Homeopathic Medical Association of New Jersey, summed it up: "Dance halls are the modern nurseries of the divorce courts, training ships of prostitution and graduating schools of infamy and vice." He could have added—Highway to Hell—for Galatians 5:21 warns, "Envyings, murders, drunkenness, revellings, and such like: of the which I tell you before, as I have also told you in time past, that they which do such things shall not inherit the kingdom of God."

The pleasure-mad *Highway to Hell is walked upon by multitudes who drink booze.* When we remember the billions of dollars spent yearly for booze, then we must admit there is pleasure in the sin of drinking alcoholic beverages.

Oh, but the drink is only a seasonal pleasure.

"Who hath woe? who hath sorrow? who hath contentions? who hath babbling? who hath wounds without cause? who hath redness of eyes? They that tarry long at the wine; they that go to seek mixed wine."—Prov. 23:29,30.

Yes, those who drink Four Roses end up with "red noses." And the drink that gives you a "lift" also gives you a chain! Proverbs 23:25 says, "I will seek it yet again." Booze shackles and chains its victims.

There are 16 million problem drinkers in the U.S.A., four million alcoholics and one million skid-row victims (1959 figures).

Go with me to the missions I preach in, and I will show you the forlorn, emaciated derelicts. Hear their tale of woe. See these 'who seek it again.' If they can't get Seagram's, they will take beer. If they can't panhandle the money for beer, they will take rubbing alcohol or shoe polish or antifreeze—anything with the soul-slaying, thirst-maddening, eternity-damning alcohol in it. "For the men of distinction become men of ex-tinction" on their shuffling march down the Highway to Hell!

On the Highway to Hell is the pleasure-mad throng. Jeremiah preached when he told of those who "came to the pits, and found no water; they returned with their vessels empty" (Jer. 14:3). Today multitudes are lowering empty buckets into the empty cisterns and wells of this world and returning with empty vessels.

Not at the race track, not at the tavern, not at the movie house, not at the burlesque show, not at the casino do you find peace of heart and rest of soul. These are dead end streets on the Highway to Hell.

Dr. Robert Lee preached it vividly when he penned,

> The world promises substance—and gives shadow; the world prom-ises velvet—and gives a shroud; the world promises liberty—and gives slavery; the world promises nectar—and gives gall; the world promises fruit—and gives rinds and hulls; the world promises perfumed garments—and gives rags; the world promises revelry—and provides burlesque; the world promises sleep—and sends nightmares; the world promises rest—and gives weariness!

He could have added one more phrase: "The world promises Heaven—and gives Hell," for God's Word warns, "Stolen waters are sweet, and bread eaten in secret is pleasant" (Prov. 9:17). The payoff is found in verse 18, "But he knoweth not that the dead are there; and that her guests are in the depths of hell."

ROUTE 3—LOVE OF MONEY

God's Word says, "But they that will be rich fall into temptation and a snare, and into many foolish and hurtful lusts, which drown men in destruction and perdition" (I Tim. 6:9).

This verse does not say all rich people go to Hell. But it does warn that all who covet, desire and are greedy to be rich go to Hell!

Oh, what a grip and hold money and wealth hold over the souls of men! Judas sold his soul to Hell because of the love of money. He denied Christ and betrayed Him for thirty pieces of silver. Jesus said, "It is easier for a camel to go through the eye of a needle, than for a rich man to enter into the kingdom of God" (Matt. 19:24). Surely that was the case of the rich young ruler who wanted to have eternal life but went away empty, disappointed and grieved, "for he had great possessions" which he would not give up (Mark 10:22).

But you don't have to be rich. Desirous, covetous, grasping, greedy-souled appetites send men to Hell! Jesus in His sermon preached, "For what shall it profit a man, if he shall gain the whole world, and lose his own soul?" (Mark 8:36).

What are you selling your souls for, friends—gold, stocks, bonds, houses, lands, cars? It is a bad bargain! Get off the Highway to Hell. The rich man of Luke 16 has been there crying in torments, writhing in pain, remembering with remorse his futile life that was laid up in treasure for himself, and not rich to God!

ROUTE 4—UNBELIEF

How wicked is this Devil who would blind our eyes and close our hearts to the truth of the Word of God! For God has warned us all through the Word that the sin of unbelief is a damning, Hell-insuring sin. Christ's commission to His disciples insured salvation to the believer and destruction to the unbeliever: "Go ye into all the world, and preach the gospel to every creature. He that believeth and is baptized shall be saved; but he that believeth not shall be damned" (Mark 16:15,16).

Again Jesus warned in His promise of eternal life to all who believe on the Son and perdition to the unbeliever: "He that believeth not the Son shall not see life; but the wrath of God abideth on him" (John 3:36).

You may be an atheist so-called! But remember, "He that believeth not is condemned already" (John 3:18). You may be an infidel who argues and dissects the Bible! But remember, "He that believeth not is condemned already." You may be an agnostic and claim you cannot know or understand. But remember, "He that believeth not is condemned already." You may be charmed by sin that has blinded your eyes to the reality of eternity. But remember, "He that believeth not is condemned already."

I say this earnestly as I have looked down the long Highway to Hell, broad and beautiful: Most travelers on their way to the brink of ruin and Hell are those who plan and expect to get off the road to Hell and on to the road to Heaven.

I have only talked to two of hundreds and thousands who really didn't care whether they went to Hell or not! And I have talked to every kind of a sinner there is, I believe. All but two really wanted someday to quit their sin and be saved and go to Heaven.

Yes, the most terrible tragedy on the Highway to Hell is that most of the travelers don't mean or want to end up in Hell! But the sad, sad truth is that more will stumble into Hell than march gloriously into Heaven! Jesus said so in our text.

Norman Lewis, long a missionary in South America, told of a night ride. It is night. Along the highway skims a car. The speedometer hovers between 70 and 75 as roadside objects flit past. But as the car sweeps around a wide curve, its probing lights suddenly pick out a swinging red light. On go the brakes—hard. Three hundred yards ahead there has been a bad accident, and two wrecked cars block the highway. To crash into those cars at full speed would mean shattering ruin and horrible death. How fortunate a man is already stationed there beside the road swinging a red light to warn of the awful danger.

Lewis asks, "Is man more merciful than God?"

No, friend, for on the Highway to Hell God has His warnings to stop us on our headlong, midnight ride to Hell and ruin. "Turn ye, turn ye," He warns, "for why will ye die?" "Prepare to meet God," cries another warning. "Boast not thyself of to morrow; for thou knowest not what a day may bring forth" (Prov. 27:1). For "to day is the day of salvation," says the Lord. Again He warns us, "He, that being often reproved hardeneth his neck, shall suddenly be destroyed, and that without remedy" (Prov. 29:1).

And just before the wild ride ends in Hell, God warns us again— maybe your last warning, "How shall we escape if we neglect so great salvation?"

VII.

Tormented in Hell

BILLY SUNDAY

"And in hell he lift up his eyes, being in torments. . . . "—Luke 16:23.

If I were going to choose my subject this afternoon, I assure you I would not speak upon this topic. I always do so with a reluctance. I shrink from it. It is not a pleasant subject for me to speak upon. Neither is it pleasant for you to listen to. But a minister has no business to choose his subjects. He must go to the Bible to find out what that teaches and then preach it to the people. If he doesn't, he is not a faithful minister, no matter whether what he preaches is pleasant to his audience or not.

Hell Is Necessary if There Be Wicked Men and a Righteous God

I wish I could believe that there is no Hell. Nothing would rejoice or delight me more, when I leave here, than to know that every man, woman and child in Pittsburgh had repented and accepted Jesus Christ as their Saviour.

But if men persist in living in sin, if they persist in rejecting Jesus Christ and defying God, then it is right and proper that there should be a Hell in which they be confined. If men choose sin rather than salvation, if they choose iniquity rather than God, then it is right and just—it is for the good of the universe and for the glory of God—that there be a Hell.

It is right and just that there should be jails and penitentiaries in which to confine people who will not keep the law. And if it weren't for jails and penitentiaries, if it weren't for the fear of punishment, neither your life nor your property would be safe. It is the fear of punishment that holds many a man and woman in restraint. Remove the penalty for wrongdoing, and you lift the floodgates of iniquity. Remove the penalty for taking life, and our streets would flow with blood. Remove the penalty for breaking into a house or for cracking a safe, and burglary and theft would be rampant.

It is the fear of punishment, of jails, of penitentiaries and of the rope or the electric chair that holds many a man and woman in restraint. Remove the fact that there is punishment for wrongdoing, and you lift the floodgates of iniquity.

Hell is just as much a manifestation of the love of God as is Heaven. It is right and proper to have jails if people want to keep the law. Those who break the law are not entitled to the same liberty as the man who keeps the law, and the man who doesn't serve God is not entitled to the same privileges as the man who does. Your common sense tells you that much.

Sending them to jail, God demonstrates His justice in that He will uphold His law, and He demonstrates His love in that He has provided a way whereby you can escape. And sooner than repeal His law or suffer the people to trample it beneath their feet, God was willing to give His Son to open up a plan whereby people might be kept out of Hell. The fact that God did it takes the responsibility off God's shoulders and puts it on you. If He hadn't cared, He wouldn't have provided redemption.

I wish all people would repent and make Hell unnecessary so far as the human race is concerned. Hell wasn't prepared for man but for the Devil. The devils were once bright, shining angels. Their first estate was Heaven, but they left their first estate. When Jesus Christ came into the world and died on the cross, He didn't redeem the devils. So God is desirous of saving people and is doing all He can. When Jesus died on the cross, He didn't redeem the devils because He would have had to take the nature of each individual angel. You and I are the offspring from Adam and Eve, every one of us. We have their nature.

When Jesus came on earth, He took our nature and shed His blood and paid the penalty to redeem the people whose nature He took. He didn't take the nature of angels. He took the nature of human beings. Jesus Christ came into the world to die to save us.

One Who Preaches God's Warning
Is Your True Friend

I would rather believe and preach a truth, no matter how unpleasant it is, than to believe and preach a pleasant lie. I believe there is a Hell. If I didn't, I wouldn't have the audacity to stand up here and preach to you. If there ever comes a time when I don't believe in Hell, I will leave the platform before I will ever preach a sermon with that unbelief in my heart. I would rather believe and preach a truth, no matter how unpleasant, than to believe and preach a lie simply for the friendship and favor of some people.

You cannot reconcile the doctrine of universal salvation with the teaching of Jesus Christ and the apostles. You have to give up one or the other, and I am aware of the fact that the man who stands four-square on the Word of God and without fear or favor preaches the Bible just as it is given here, is called bigoted, narrow, cruel, puritanical and all that. And they say a fellow who doesn't believe that Jesus is the Son of God or who does not believe in eternal damnation or who preaches that everybody is going to be saved, is a liberal preacher. I say he is an old fool.

The man who preaches the truth is your friend. I have no desire to be any more broad or liberal than Jesus, not a whit. And nobody else has any right to be more liberal than Jesus and claim to be a preacher.

Is a man cruel who tells you the truth? If you summon a doctor and he says your child has diphtheria, is that cruel? I rush up and tell you your house is on fire and give the alarm. Am I cruel because I warn you? No, sir. I'm your best friend. Then am I cruel because I tell you there is a Hell? No, sir. The man who tells you there is not a Hell is the cruel one, and the man who tells you there is a Hell is your friend. So it's a kindness to point out the danger. God's ministers have no business holding back the truth.

Many preachers in these days are flippant of speech. They say, "Let's eat, drink and be merry. We are all going to be saved." You ask many a man about being a Christian, and he says, "I believe in a God of love. God is too good to damn anybody. I don't need to forsake sin. I know I'm an old sinner and a reprobate, but God is good; there is no Hell. Do you think that a good God would permit a Hell? Do you think that God would take me and damn me? I am trusting in the goodness of God. I don't need to forsake my sins."

What's the use of building churches and hiring preachers to preach to you if everybody is going to be saved? It doesn't appeal to any man's common sense or reason. Does that meet the highest demands of your conscience? When your conscience points out that you are a sinner, does it meet the highest demands of your conscience to say, "I know I'm sinning, but God is good. He gave His Son to die"? Does that meet the highest demands of your conscience? If it does, you have a mean, lowdown, rotten conscience. If it meets the highest demands of your conscience to know that you are a sinner, dragging God's law beneath your feet and making God's law the excuse for your cussedness, then you are too lowdown for me.

Suppose your mother, who had cared for and loved you all your life, should ask you not to do something. You, because you know your mother loves you, go and do just the thing she does not want you to do. Does that meet the highest demands of your conscience?

The One Sure Source of Truth About Hell: the Bible

I am not going to give you my speculations or theories or opinions. They are worth no more than any other fool's speculations, theories or opinions. And any man who preaches his speculations, theories or opinions is a fool. But I am going to preach the Word of God. God knows all about it and has told us all about it. One ounce of God's revelation is worth forty million tons of man's speculations and theories.

To perdition with your opinion. What do I care about your opinion? When God's Word says one thing and your opinion thinks another thing, you have another think coming, old fellow. Listen to me. I am going to give you the law.

I stand before you this afternoon and say, "It's the law." You have to take it. You can't get around it. It's our authority. So I'm not preaching anybody's speculations or theories. It's the law. It's the only authority we have on the question. That being true, listen! Hell is certain; it is absolutely certain. There is a Hell.

A fellow once said to me, "Mr. Sunday, don't you know that most of the scholarly ministers have given up their belief in Hell?"

Well, that's a lie. Some fools have, I'll admit that. That's always an argument with a fellow who has a weak cause and wants to bolster the thing up by a strong assertion, so he says, "Don't you know that the scholarly ministers have given up their belief in Hell?"

What do I care about those old lobsters? Some have given it up, I'll admit that. But they didn't give it up because the Bible didn't teach it or because it's not in the New Testament. They did it for speculative principles, to be sentimental, to be popular with the clique and a crowd that doesn't want God's truth.

No man on God's earth can go to the Bible to find out what it teaches about eternal damnation and not stand up and preach that man will be eternally damned if he doesn't repent of his sins. The man doesn't live that can go to the Bible to find out what it teaches in order that he may preach what it teaches, then not stand up and tell the people there is an eternal Hell for the people who won't repent.

And supposing they have given up their belief in the doctrine of eternal Hell. That wouldn't prove anything. Anybody familiar with the history of the world knows that there is not an invention, a discovery or a doctrine that is known and accepted and believed today which, when it was first propagated, wasn't ridiculed.

Galileo said, "The earth moves," and on his knees he was compelled to retract. And as he arose he said, "It moves notwithstanding." Who was right, Galileo or the people who sneered at him?

I say there isn't a discovery or an invention or a doctrine that wasn't disbelieved, but that disbelief didn't prove that Galileo was wrong. That didn't change the truth.

People ridiculed Noah when he built the ark, but the Flood came. Jesus prophesied that in forty years one stone shall not stand above another, and they laughed; but the Romans leveled the city just the same.

We are certain there is a Hell because Christ says so, the apostles say so, God says so. We are more positive there is a Hell than we are that the sun will rise tomorrow. I have not one word of authority to tell you that the sun will rise in the morning. I suppose it will. I hope it will. I should be disappointed if it should not, but I haven't one word of authority to tell you that it will. But I have authority to tell you that there is a Hell, and that is the Word of God.

I have no authority to tell you that you will live until tomorrow morning. I expect you will. I hope you may. I would be disappointed if you didn't but I haven't one word of authority to tell you that you will. But I have authority in the Word of God to tell you there is a Hell. There is a Hell because God says there is, and the only thing against it that I have ever found is simply the speculations of a lot of theologians and the dream of a lot of poets and old novel writers and old backsliders in the church.

Sin is a moral ulcer. It may be some time before it will stamp itself on your body, but it will.

Everybody knows that the farther a man goes into sin, the farther he goes. And you let a man go on and on until repentance is passed, and what has he left but Hell; and the only theory against Hell is the speculation of theologists and some old fool philosophers.

When on one hand I have the speculations of men, the theories of philosophers and the opinions of some theologians, and on the other hand I have the Word of God and the Word of Christ, it does not take me long to make up my mind which I'll choose.

I want to tell you the next time you read a book—and I don't care who wrote the book; the next time you listen to a lecture—and I don't care a continental who delivers it; the next time you listen to a sermon—and I don't give a rap who preaches it—if that book or that lecture or that sermon says there is no Hell, then that lecturer or that book or that preacher is a liar. We have the authority. That is the law, and you can't get around that to save your life.

Hell Is a Place of Bodily Suffering

"In hell he lift up his eyes, being in torments." That Hell is a place of bodily suffering is plain from the New Testament.

The rich man left five brothers back on earth, and they all knew they must endure the same torment if they did not repent.

The words that God uses to express the doom of the unsaved are death and destruction. Now, listen! I will quote to you from the Word of God to clear your mind.

"The beast that thou sawest was, and is not; and shall ascend out of the bottomless pit, and go into perdition: and they that dwell on the earth shall wonder, whose names were not written in the book of life from the foundation of the world, when they behold the beast that was, and is not, and yet is."—Rev. 17:8.

"And the beast was taken, and with him the false prophet that wrought miracles before him, with which he deceived them that had received the mark of the beast, and them that worshipped his image. These both were cast alive into a lake of fire burning with brimstone."—Rev. 19:20.

"And the devil that deceived them was cast into the lake of fire and brimstone, where the beast and the false prophet are, and shall be

tormented day and night for ever and ever."—Rev. 20:10.

"And cast him into the bottomless pit, and shut him up, and set a seal upon him, that he should deceive the nations no more, till the thousand years should be fulfilled: and after that he must be loosed a little season."—Rev. 20:3.

If we can find where the beast goes, we can find God's definition of perdition or destruction. And I read these words, "And the beast was taken, and with him the false prophet that wrought miracles before him, with which he deceived them that had received the mark of the beast, and them that worshipped his image. These both were cast alive into a lake of fire burning with brimstone."

By the Word of God, his definition of perdition or destruction is "a place in the lake of fire."

Now, let's see if we can find God's definition of death. A lot of people seem to think that means total annihilation.

Then, my friends, perdition is a place of torment in the lake of fire and brimstone. The second death, by the Word of God, is a place of eternal torment for the unsaved. Those are the words God uses to describe the doom of the unsaved—perdition and death. Perdition is a place in the lake of fire and brimstone forever and forever. Death is a place in the lake of fire and brimstone. So death doesn't mean annihilation at all. It means eternal damnation, according to the Word of God.

A preacher said to me, "I built that church." He didn't lay a brick or stone in it. He simply raised the money to build it. Hell is certain. My friends, the fact is, there is a Hell. Back of that is the fact that people are going to go to Hell if they reject Jesus Christ.

Hell Is a Place of Remorse

The rich man didn't take his money, but he took his memory. You will not take much with you if you go. I hope you won't go. You will take your memory. You won't take your money or your stocks. You will remember the poor you didn't help. You will remember that you lived for the almighty dollar. The gambler will remember that he lived to fleece people out of their money. And the seducer will remember that he lived to assassinate virtue and rob womanhood.

And the drunkard will see again and remember his home of want and squalor and how he treated his wife and children.

And say, if the Lord would let me go down to Hell and give the invitation, I'd depopulate it in fifteen minutes. I wouldn't need to preach for eight weeks.

And the murderer, he will again see the blood ooze as it falls from the wound of the one whose life he has taken.

Ah, yes, you Christ-rejecters, it will all come before you in Hell. You will remember that you heard the preacher's voice.

Hell will be a place of remorse. Ah! There is no torment like the Hell of an accusing memory. In jails and penitentiaries men go insane thinking over their crime and the thought that they have been deprived of their liberty. I have had men and women come into my presence and turn ashen pale, fall on their knees and gasp. Why? Over the memory of their sins. In Hell you will remember.

"Out, out, damned spot," cried Lady Macbeth as she grabbed at her lily white hand; then she cried: "Will not all great Neptune's seas wash this blood away?" There was no blood there, only the guilt of the murder on her miserably guilty soul. It was her memory.

Hell is a place of remorse and of memory. In Hell you will remember the chances you had and let pass by.

In Hell we will carry with us the desires we build up. No doubt people will be in Hell who were great on earth.

Hell Is a Place Without Hope

Some people will tell you that the word *everlasting* doesn't mean everlasting. If Hell isn't everlasting, then Heaven isn't everlasting. Listen! "And these shall go away into everlasting punishment, but the righteous into life eternal." Then, if eternal life is eternal, eternal punishment is eternal, by all the laws of common sense, and I have looked through that old Bible and I am frank to tell you that I can't find one word of hope for Hell.

Some quibbler comes on the scene and says that Matthew 1:21 reads: "And she shall bring forth a son, and thou shalt call his name JESUS; for he shall save his people from their sins." Sure, but He won't save you *in* your sins, don't forget that. Paul says, "For as in Adam all die, so in Christ shall all be made alive."

Say, if God should commission an angel to come to this world to deliver to everybody a personal message of God's love, and if you should condescend—should agree—to accompany that angel on his rounds, you would have to stop in front of the door of the multimillionaire; you would have to go down into the hovels of the poor; you would have to speak to the workingman hurrying along with his dinner pail; you would have to go into the saloon and speak to the drunken bum; you would have to go to the home of squalor and want; you would have to go into the jails and penitentiaries; you would have to stop the highwayman as he is about to put a gun under your nose; you would have to walk up to the burglar as he is drilling a hole in the safe; you would have to go to India's teeming millions; to China's millions; you would have to go to the jungles of Africa and speak to the black man, bowing down to idols of wood and stone; you would have to visit the islands of the seas where the blackskinned mother rocks her babe to sleep to the lullaby of the ocean's wave; you would have to go to India's coral strand and Ceylon's perfumed shore. Then, then, then, lest there should be some poor unfortunate to whom the angel had not paid a visit, God Almighty would blaze in letters that have shone through the ages, "He so loved the world that He gave His only begotten Son," to open up a plan of redemption to keep you out of Hell, and yet you repudiate God's plan and pass it by.

Jesus Christ is anxious to save you from Hell. He is anxious to keep you out of perdition if you will yield your heart and life to Him. "In hell he lift up his eyes, being in torments."

HYMAN J. APPELMAN
1902-1983

ABOUT THE MAN:

Dr. Appelman was born in Russia and was reared and trained in the Jewish faith. He could speak many languages. The family moved to America in 1914. Dr. Appelman graduated with honors from Northwestern University and from DePaul University where he was one of the highest in the class and was awarded a scholarship. He received his license to practice law from DePaul Law School and was a trial lawyer in Chicago before his conversion—from 1921-25.

At age 28 he was converted. His Jewish family, then living in Chicago, disowned him. His father said to him, *"When your sides come together from hunger and you come crawling to my door, I will throw you a crust of bread as I would any other dog."*

Feeling a definite call to preach, he attended Southwestern Baptist Theological Seminary in Fort Worth from 1930-33.

In 1933 he was elected to be one of the State Evangelists for Texas; he faithfully ministered for eight years in this capacity for the Southern Baptist Convention. Later he launched into larger meetings, both in Texas and outside, and soon was spending some time, year after year, in a foreign country. His meetings were large meetings, with hundreds, sometimes thousands, of conversions in each.

Dr. Appelman made eight or nine trips around the world and several trips to Russia as an evangelist.

His schedule left one breathless. It was hard to find a day in his long ministry of fifty-three years that he was not preaching somewhere. He averaged two weeks at home out of a year. That was the intenseness of a Jew! Of this Jew, at least! His prayer life, hard work and biblical preaching reminded one of the Apostle Paul.

Dr. Appelman was the author of some 40 books.

VIII.

Hell — What Is It?

HYMAN J. APPELMAN

"There was a certain rich man, which was clothed in purple and fine linen, and fared sumptuously every day: And there was a certain beggar named Lazarus, which was laid at his gate, full of sores, And desiring to be fed with the crumbs which fell from the rich man's table: moreover the dogs came and licked his sores. And it came to pass, that the beggar died, and was carried by the angels into Abraham's bosom: the rich man also died, and was buried; And in hell he lift up his eyes, being in torments, and seeth Abraham afar off, and Lazarus in his bosom. And he cried and said, Father Abraham, have mercy on me, and send Lazarus, that he may dip the tip of his finger in water, and cool my tongue; for I am tormented in this flame. But Abraham said, Son, remember that thou in thy lifetime receivedst thy good things, and likewise Lazarus evil things: but now he is comforted, and thou art tormented. And beside all this, between us and you there is a great gulf fixed: so that they which would pass from hence to you cannot; neither can they pass to us, that would come from thence. Then he said, I pray thee therefore, father, that thou wouldest send him to my father's house: For I have five brethren; that he may testify unto them, lest they also come into this place of torment. Abraham saith unto him, They have Moses and the prophets; let them hear them. And he said, Nay, father Abraham: but if one went unto them from the dead, they will repent. And he said unto him, If they hear not Moses and the prophets, neither will they be persuaded, though one rose from the dead."— Luke 16:19-31.

The entire passage provides the framework for this message, but I want to stress especially the phrase, "and in hell." Let us consider: the *certainty* of Hell, the *crowd* going to Hell, the *character* of Hell, and the *cross* that saves from Hell—the cross that God has put in the paths of all of us to keep us from taking the road to Hell.

Three things are going to happen to you. First, you are going to die. You are not going to live forever. Second, you are going to face the judgment. You are not going to escape it. Third, you are going to sink into Hell if you die in your sins, without God, without Christ, without the blood, without the cross, without hope, without salvation.

The Certainty of Hell

I know there is a Hell, not because I was taught the fact in seminary. I know there is a Hell, not because my denomination believes it. I believe there is a Hell, not because my people, the orthodox Jews, have always believed it. I know there is a Hell, not because all orthodox, fundamental Christians in all the world, of every persuasion, believe it. That is not enough. Men may be mistaken. The best of them may be wrong. Men may devise a theory which spreads universally but is wrong nevertheless. **I believe that there is a Hell because God says so in His holy Book.**

A Texas evangelist, a powerful preacher and soul winner, declares frequently, "God says it. I believe it. That settles it." Most Christians know that the Bible says more about Hell than about Heaven. For every statement in the Bible about the land of bliss, there are at least ten concerning the pit of torment. The reason is simple. Anyone can understand it.

We have all had the experience of driving down a paved highway maintained by the state and the nation, or the state or the national government. As long as that highway is in proper condition there are few markers needed. You will encounter a railroad crossing, a crossroad, a curve or a "turn" sign. You will be told of an approaching town, city, village, school or church. However, when there is on the road a threat to the traveler's safety, such as a washed-out bridge on which men are working, there is sign after sign after sign warning of what is ahead. On a straight road there is no need for such a warning. A good road does not need warning signs. But a road that leads to possible disaster needs such markers.

Everyone wants to go to Heaven. Everyone who believes in Heaven desires to go there. God does not want anyone to go to Hell. Consequently, He has put markers, warning signs, detour signs, on the way to destruction, to warn of the desolation, the death, the punishment ahead.

God's Word declares, "The wicked shall be turned into hell, and all the nations that forget God." Isaiah said, "For Tophet is ordained of old; yea, for the king it is prepared; he hath made it deep, and large: the pile thereof is fire and much wood; the breath of the Lord, like a stream of brimstone, doth kindle it."

The Bible's worst description of Hell came from the lips of the sweet, tender, gentle, soft-spoken, compassionate Jesus Christ. The worst description of Hell in the entire Bible is in chapter 9 of Mark, beginning with verse 43. Jesus is speaking:

"And if thy hand offend thee, cut it off: it is better for thee to enter into life maimed, than having two hands to go into hell, into the fire that never shall be quenched: Where their worm dieth not, and the fire is not quenched. And if thy foot offend thee, cut it off: it is better for thee to enter halt into life, than having two feet to be cast into hell, into the fire that never shall be quenched: Where their worm dieth not, and the fire is not quenched. And if thine eye offend thee, pluck it out: it is better for thee to enter into the kingdom of God with one eye, than having two eyes to be cast into hell fire: Where their worm dieth not, and the fire is not quenched."

In II Thessalonians Paul declares,

"When the Lord Jesus shall be revealed from heaven with his mighty angels, In flaming fire taking vengeance on them that know not God, and that obey not the gospel of our Lord Jesus Christ: Who shall be punished with everlasting destruction from the presence of the Lord, and from the glory of his power."

The Holy Spirit, in chapter 14 of the book of Revelation, says,

"The same shall drink of the wine of the wrath of God, which is poured out without mixture into the cup of his indignation; and he shall be tormented with fire and brimstone in the presence of the holy angels, and in the presence of the Lamb: And the smoke of their torment ascendeth up for ever and ever: and they have no rest day nor night."

Let us go back to Christ's statement: "If thy hand offend thee, cut it off." Chop off your hand and suffer physical pain rather than go into the Devil's Hell. If your foot offends you, take that same knife and, without mercy, chop off the offending member. It is better to suffer that frightful pain than to be cast into the tortures of the burning pit. If your eye offends you, dig the eye out and throw it away. It is better to endure that indescribable anguish, even to inflict it upon yourself, than to go with both eyes into the torments of desolation.

Our Lord's statement needs no amplification. I have told you what the Bible says about Hell. God is not a man that He should lie. The Bible is not a book of vague imaginings, that there should be any question, any doubt, any uncertainty about the subject.

The Crowd Going to Hell

Who is going to Hell? God says:

"Except ye repent, ye shall all likewise perish."

He declares also, *"Except ye be converted, and become as little children, ye shall not enter the kingdom of heaven. . . . Except a man be born again, he cannot see the kingdom of God. . . . Except a man be born of water and of the Spirit, he cannot enter into the kingdom of God."*

It is written, *"He that believeth not is condemned already, because he hath not believed in the name of the only begotten Son of God. . . . He that believeth not the Son shall not see life, but the wrath of God abideth on him. . . . Whosoever was not found written in the book of life was cast into the lake of fire. . . . But the fearful, and unbelieving, and the abominable, and murderers, and whoremongers, and sorcerers, and idolaters, and all liars, shall have their part in the lake which burneth with fire and brimstone: which is the second death."*

Let us emphasize the opening words of this last verse, found in Revelation 21:8: "But the *fearful.*" You may say, "I am not fearful." I am glad indeed that you are not fearful, but have you accepted Jesus Christ as your personal Saviour? If you have not, then you are unbelieving.

This verse says also, "But the fearful, and *unbelieving,* and the *abominable.*" You may say, "I am not abominable." I am glad indeed that you are not. I hope you never will be. Tell me, however, have you been born again? Does your spirit bear witness with God's Spirit that you are a child of God? You may say, "I do not know." You may say you have no such feeling. Then you are unbelieving.

"But the fearful, and *unbelieving,* and the abominable, and *unbelieving,* and murderers, and *unbelieving,* and whoremongers, and *unbelieving,* and sorcerers, and *unbelieving,* and idolaters, and *unbelieving,* and all liars, and *unbelieving,* shall have their part in the lake which burneth with fire and brimstone."

Who is going to Hell? Every unbelieving man, woman and child in all the world; every Jew, every Gentile anywhere and everywhere, to the ends of the earth, is lost, is on the road to torment. But who is going to Hell?

1. First of all, *the out-and-out sinners,* the drunkards, the cheaters, the dishonest, all those who live in open, notorious sin, those who live as though there were no God, no Christ, no Ten Commandments, no death, no resurrection, no judgment, no Heaven, no Hell. You will agree that these out-and-out sinners are going to Hell.

2. Then Hell will be occupied by the *moral, worldly crowd,* the leaders in civic activities, in fraternal organizations, in lodges, in societies, in P.T.A.'s, who have not Christ as their Saviour. Good, moral, clean, fine though these people may be, they are all going to Hell. There are good people, clean people, moral folk with excellent reputations, people who are above reproach, but who are not right with God. They have not accepted the shed blood of the Lord Jesus Christ. They have not repented of the sins they have committed. Moral worldlings are going to Hell—but they are not the only travelers to perdition.

3. There is another crowd on the road to Tophet. That crowd consists of the *procrastinators.* They are not notorious sinners. They do not hold themselves up to be moral worldlings. They know they are sinners. They know they have done wrong. They know they need Christ. They believe the Bible as definitely as I do. They believe Jesus Christ died for their sins. They know He can save them. They want Him to save them. They intend to have Him save them. They are not infidels. They are not atheists. They are not "smart alecks." They want to be saved. They mean to be saved. They don't intend to go to Hell.

Nevertheless, they are listening to the Devil whisper, "Not now. Not now." The Devil doesn't have to get anyone to commit some big sin in order to take him to Hell. He doesn't have to get anyone to be unusually vile or extraordinarily wicked. The Devil has only to get a boy, a girl, a man or a woman to put off salvation long enough, and he has accomplished his purpose. To put off accepting Christ long enough is to reject Christ, is to die in sin, is to be tormented forever.

4. There is yet another group that is going to Hell. Not only are the out-and-out sinners, the moral worldlings, the procrastinators going to Hell: *the professing but not possessing church members are also doomed and damned.* Those who are Baptists but not Christians, those who are Methodists but not Christians, those who are Presbyterians but not Christians, those who are of any other church or persuasion but are not Christians will, I believe, have to suffer deeper, hotter Hell than others. They have made their choices. They have had their opportunities. They have been to church services. They have heard the Gospel. They have seen people saved. They have pretended to have salvation.

Do not misunderstand. I'm not criticizing the church. Every Christian ought to belong to some church. The church, however, is not for salvation. The church is not for sinners. The church is for the saved. The church is for the saints. We have the church because people are saved.

I have mentioned, by the authority of God's Word, the crowds who are going to Hell. They are the out-and-out sinners. They are the moral worldlings. They are the procrastinators. They are the bitter host of professing but not possessing church members.

The Character of Hell

What about the character of Hell? What kind of place is it? Many people ask the question, "Is Hell a place of literal fire?" Yes, it is a place of literal fire. Suppose I said, "No, it is not literal fire"? Would that put out the fire?

I have never been there. I know that I'm never going to be there. Glory to God, I shall never by personal experience know what kind of place Hell is! I do not want you to discover its character by personal experience because then it will be too late to escape its awful pain.

Even though I have never been in or seen Hell, I know someone who has seen it. I know someone who ordained Hell. He established it originally for the Devil and his angels. If you insist upon forcing your way into it, you are an interloper. God does not want you to go there. He did not prepare Hell for you. He prepared it for the Devil. The Lord Jesus Christ knows about Hell. It is He who gives us a description of it in the terrible words of my text from Luke. Let Jesus tell what kind of place it is.

Jesus says that Hell is a place of pain.

"And in hell he lift up his eyes, being in torments, and seeth Abraham afar off, and Lazarus in his bosom. And he cried and said, Father Abraham, have mercy on me, and send Lazarus, that he may dip the tip of his finger in water, and cool my tongue; for I am tormented in this flame."

Consider the agony, imagine the pain, picture the anguish, witness the suffering of that poor lost soul to whom a drop of water (how much water can a man hold on the end of his finger?) on the end of Lazarus' finger and put on the sufferer's tongue would have been a taste of Heaven.

Oh, the pain, the punishment, the unsatisfied appetites, the unassuaged desires, the unsatisfied longings! On earth the sinner can find at least some satisfaction in pursuing sin, but in the Devil's Hell no sinner will be given an opportunity to satisfy any sinful passion, any sinful emotion, any sinful appetite, any sinful desire. Increasingly, with every endless eon, the awful sins of the sinner's life will grind, blind, bind, cripple, corrode, corrupt, condemn, curse, throughout the passing of the endless procession of the centuries.

There is no liquor in Hell. Hell is a place where prohibition is strictly practiced. There are no shows in Hell. There are no dances in Hell.

In Hell there is something infinitely worse than pain.

I recall an incident in my seminary days. I was sitting in the office of one of my professors who was to meet a small class of us in a seminary course. I was early. I had just come from the post office. I had received a letter from Chicago, a letter which contained news that stirred my soul to the depths and hurt me dreadfully. I sat there. I did not want to go home. My wife would see my tears, and her day would be spoiled also. There was not a thing she could do about it. The problem was a ghost out of my past.

I sat in that professor's office, bowed my head in my hands and started to pray and cry. I did not hear the professor as he came in. His rubber heels on the carpeted floor made no sound. Besides, I was crying, and I would not have heard him.

Tapping me on the shoulder, he asked what was the matter. I told him I was troubled by something personal out of my past. Out of his great, gracious heart he insisted that if the problem was not too personal, I should tell him about it and perhaps he could help me.

Looking at him, I said, "Doctor, there are so many things in my past I wish I could forget."

After walking to the window and looking out across the campus, he turned back to me, after a minute or two, and the tears trickled down his cheeks as he said, "Son, you are not the only one."

I do not doubt my salvation. I know my sins are forgiven. I know I am a child of God. I know I am going to Heaven. But, oh, I wish I could forget my sins! I wish I could forget the blame of them, the shame of them, the agony of them, the pursuit of them. Thank God, when we cross chilly Jordan, when the waters of that dark river wash across our souls, even the memories of our sins will be gone! But if you die in your sins, the memory of those transgressions will become stronger and stronger with every passing age. There will be no surcease, no losing yourself in forgetfulness.

Those who die in their sins will sink into Hell. Forever after they will remember endlessly, without cessation, without forgetfulness, the sins that sent them into the pit of perdition. They will recall their opportunities to accept the Lord Jesus Christ. They will remember the services they attended, the songs and the sermons they heard. They will remember the prayers that were prayed for them, the tears that were shed over them, the personal testimony that was delivered in their hearing. They will remember that they could as easily have been in Heaven as in Hell. But there they are, endlessly chained to the stake of torture.

Here upon this earth you may lose yourself in a movie; you may lose yourself in a book; you may lose yourself in a dance; you may lose yourself in a baseball game; you may lose yourself in some other sport or amusement; you may lose yourself in the visit of some friend. You may lose yourself in drink. If the going gets hard, the doctor may give you sleeping pills to knock you out for awhile. You may ease your tormented conscience with the balm of sleep. You can take poison; you can blow your brains out; you can hang yourself and believe you have left your difficulties behind.

But there is no poison in Hell. There are no guns in Hell. There is no death in Hell. There are no shows in Hell. There are no saloons in Hell. The Devil is strictly a teetotaler. There are no dances in Hell. The Devil is in the drinking and dancing business only here upon this earth. You will dance in Hell, but not to a jazz orchestra. There are no books in Hell. There are no opiates in Hell. There are no doctors' prescriptions in Hell. There is no rest, no death, no ceasing of burning, blazing memory there.

But there is something even worse about Hell. This may seem to be an exaggeration, but Scripture declares the fact:

"And beside all this, between us and you there is a great gulf fixed: so that they which would pass from hence to you cannot; neither can they pass to us, that would come from thence."

The worst thing about Hell is that it is a world absolutely without hope. There is no way out of Hell. There is nothing even God can do to take someone out of Hell.

One does not need an abundance of imagination to picture this awfulness. God forbid that any man, that any woman, that any child should be Hellbound. If you die in your sins, you will go to Hell. As you look up, up, up, in the dim distance, you will see the mansions of bliss, the gates of glory, the golden streets, the tree of life, the river of life. You will see God on His holy throne. You will see the angels flitting about on God's errands. You will see the blessed saints dressed in white robes of righteousness strumming their harps and singing the Saviour's eternal praises.

You will recognize features, faces, forms, figures of loved ones, of friends, of people who even now are at your side, folk who have lived in your home, business associates, schoolmates. You will remember that you had the same opportunity as they to escape Hell. But between you and Heaven will be the smoke of ten thousand times ten thousand fires, and you will remember only the frightful word, "Forever! Forever!"

You will sink back into the pit. A thousand times a thousand endless years will drag their slow feet in leaden procession over your tormented soul. Again you will lift your head above that lake which burns with fire and brimstone. Again you will look about you and you will see the gates, the bars, the bolts, the locks, the studded nails of the penitentiary of the damned.

Hell is a world without hope. Its burning torments sear the flesh, but there is no relief. As the demons of Satan dance mockingly, laughingly, gloatingly, they, too, sing in bitter, biting, blighting voices, one song, one note, one cadence, one refrain: "Forever! Forever! Forever! Forever! Forever!" Should you make your abode in Hell, you will see the burning faces, the glazed eyes, the tortured hands of fellow-prisoners of damnation. You will recognize, God forbid, husband, wife, father, mother, brother, sister, son, daughter, friend, neighbor, that you could as easily have taken to Heaven as dragged down to Hell.

Oh, that awful mass of weeping, wailing humanity that inhabits Hell! They, too, cry one Heaven-searching cry to God, but, alas, too late. All cry that endless refrain, "Forever! Forever! Forever!" Beyond God forever! Beyond Christ forever! Beyond the Spirit forever! Beyond the Bible forever! Beyond the Gospel forever! Beyond the cross forever! Beyond the blood forever! Beyond tears forever! Beyond repentance forever! Beyond faith forever! Beyond confession forever! Beyond time forever! Beyond eternity forever! Forever! Forever! Forever!

Many Christians do not believe this to be true. If they did, they would have prayer meetings morning and night. They would run up and down the streets weeping, agonizing, pleading with lost souls to be reconciled to God through the Lord Jesus Christ.

Christian, whether you believe it or not, the Bible teaches in chapter 14 of Revelation, "The smoke of their torment ascendeth up for ever and ever, and they have no rest day nor night."

The Cross That Saves From Hell

If one were to multiply a thousand times, a million times, the horrors I have described, he would still not approximate the frightfulness of Hell. But, thank God, there is a way out of Hell; there is a way for every man, for every woman, for every child in all this world to keep out of Hell. That way is the way of the cross—the way of the cross that leads home. It is written:

"And as Moses lifted up the serpent in the wilderness, even so must the Son of man be lifted up: That whosoever believeth in him should not perish, but have eternal life. For God so loved the world, that he gave his only begotten Son, that whosoever believeth in him should not perish, but have everlasting life. For God sent not his Son into the world to condemn the world; but that the world through him might be saved. He that believeth on him is not condemned: but he that believeth not is condemned already, because he hath not believed in the name of the only begotten Son of God."—John 3:14-18.

You may take the cross or the curse. You may take the blood or the blame. You may accept salvation or be banished forever from God's presence.

This was true of all Christians. All were sinners on the way to Hell, with the curse and the doom of their sins dragging them into the pit. They saw the cross. They believed. They received. Now Hell is a closed book to them and Heaven is ever open before them.

Jesus loves you. God loves you. The Holy Spirit loves you. Other Christians love you. There is nothing in the way except your own will. God stands ready to forgive your sins for Christ's sake. You have all that is required, in the way of recommendation, to cause Jesus to blot out your transgressions in His own blood. Accept the blood-written offer of God's mercy.

A fellow preacher, the editor of a denominational paper, told the following interesting story.

Years ago when he first started to preach, he was pastoring a church in the Delta area, the richest land block in America and perhaps in the world. In those early days there lived in the town where my friend was pastor a plantation owner, a widow in her late eighties. She grew old, tired, sick, the result of old age. The doctors did all they could.

One day, in the presence of her firstborn son who was living with her and managing her great properties, the family physician told her that she was going to die. The doctor said he did not know how long she would live, but that it would not be long. He told her to prepare for death and without delay.

When the doctor left, she called her firstborn child to her and told him to summon all her children, grandchildren and great-grandchildren. The son, wiring, calling, visiting, sending messages, gathered the family together. Three or four days later they were all in the grandmother's room, all fifty-three of them.

After praying with them, she kissed them all, said goodby to each and told them she wanted all except her own nine children to leave the room.

She asked that the children form a line against the wall at the foot of the bed. "I want you," she said, "to come to me one by one. I want to bless you, to say goodby to you."

The old mother was crying, as were the children. Moments of emotional stress passed. The first son walked to the bed, dropped to his knees and bowed his head against his mother's body. Patting his bowed head, praying whisperingly over him, lifting his face, kissing him, she said, "Good night, son. Good night. See you in the morning, darling."

The second child came. The third child came. The fourth child came.

The fifth child came. The sixth child came. The seventh came, and the eighth. To each of them, bowed beside her bed, she spoke the same words.

The last of the children came, a man in his late forties, a good man but not a Christian. He was not a wicked man in the sense of being vilely immoral, but he was not a Christian. His mother knew it. He knew it. The rest of them knew it. Without looking into the face of his dear mother, he dropped beside her bed.

She tried to raise herself to a sitting position, but she could not. Clasping her hands, she wrung her fingers until her knuckles were almost white. The man still wouldn't look at her but kept his head bowed between his hands. Patting his head, whispering a prayer, she lifted his face, kissed him, and said, "Goodby, son. Goodby. Goodby, son."

Standing, the man started back to the others. Suddenly he stopped. Thinking of what his mother had said, he took one step back to the bed.

"Mama," he said, "you didn't say it right. You didn't say it right to me."

"Son, what didn't I say right?"

"Mother, you said 'good night' to the rest of them, 'see you in the morning,' but you said *goodby* to me."

Raising herself to a sitting posture by sheer force of will, extending her hands out and up to him, the mother said slowly, agonizingly, "Son, you are not a Christian. It is 'good night' to them, 'see you in the morning,' because they are saved. I shall see them in the resurrection morning. You are not a Christian. You are lost. Oh, unless you change, it is *goodby* to you!"

Red with sudden rage, the man, clenching his fists, started to say something but, thinking better of it, went to the door. His hand was on the knob when the Spirit of God touched him and broke his heart. With a great cry, he released the door handle and, taking one step across the room, fell across his mother's bed and sobbed, "Mama, I don't want it to be goodby. Mama, I want to see you in the morning, too. Mama, tell me, what must I do? What must I do?"

Putting her hands under him and raising him until their faces were opposite each other, until they were looking into each other's tear-filled eyes, the mother sobbed, "Son, it does not have to be *goodby*. It can be *good night* if you will believe in Jesus Christ."

"Mama, I do believe in Jesus Christ. I have always believed in Him."

"Son, will you then, right now, accept Jesus Christ and confess Him as your personal Saviour? Right now, son, will you do it?"

"Yes, Mama, I will. I do accept Him as my Saviour. I am sorry I did not do it before now. Yes, Mama, I will. I do trust Jesus Christ. I do accept Him and confess Him as my Saviour."

Putting her hands on his shoulders, the mother pushed him gently to his knees. Bending, she kissed him on the lips. Caressing him, she said, "Good night, son. Good night, baby. Good night, darling. See you in the morning."

What is it going to be with you? How is it going to be with you? All you have to do is say, "Lord, have mercy on me, a sinner." God, who has never broken a promise that He has given, will not break His promise to you. He will save you from your sins.

WILLIAM ELBERT MUNSEY
1833-1877

ABOUT THE MAN:

Methodism in early America was a great force for revival and righteousness. A roll call of some of its men is a roll call of giants for God—Asbury, Cartwright, Sam Jones being among them.

Add to that list of Methodist worthies William Elbert Munsey.

Born in Bland County, Virginia, in 1833, young Munsey learned early to help his father eke out a living on the old farm. When he was only twelve his father died, and the youth assumed the responsibility of providing for his mother and five younger brothers.

Denied formal school except for one year, Munsey mastered books. Dr. John Rice wrote of this intellectual giant, that at age ten "he had read the whole works of the Jewish historian Josephus several times" and that "he studied everywhere and always. . . . While plowing he would prop a book up at the end of the furrow, read a section, then leave the book and fix in his mind what he had read while he plowed the next furrow."

Munsey was converted at an old-fashioned Methodist camp meeting at age seventeen, and soon after became a Methodist preacher. Throughout Tennessee and Virginia he was well known.

Though intellectual, his sermons were not dry-as-dust. He was a preacher of such power and such performance that the Knoxville *Tribune* tabbed him "the most eloquent public orator of the South."

Those sermons must have been something to hear. Often an entire congregation would stand up under the spell of his preaching—sermons that were often two hours long. People thronged his churches, especially at Alexandria and Richmond, Virginia, where the churchhouse would be filled two hours before meeting time.

He was a genuis in painting word pictures. His sermons on future and eternal punishment are not only classic; they are probably the finest of their kind.

In these dark, desperate days we need preaching on: death is sure, Hell is hot, eternity is forever, sin is the reason, Christ is the cure.

We need more men like Munsey!

He died in 1877 in Jonesboro, Tennessee, burning himself out at age forty-four.

IX.

The Awfulness of Eternal Punishment

ELBERT MUNSEY

"If thy hand offend thee, cut it off: it is better for thee to enter into life maimed, than having two hands to go into hell, into the fire that never shall be quenched: Where their worm dieth not, and the fire is not quenched. And if thy foot offend thee, cut it off: it is better for thee to enter halt into life, than having two feet to be cast into hell, into the fire that never shall be quenched: Where their worm dieth not, and the fire is not quenched. And if thine eye offend thee, pluck it out: it is better for thee to enter into the kingdom of God with one eye, than having two eyes to be cast into hell fire: Where their worm dieth not, and the fire is not quenched."—Mark 9:43-48.

The word in these verses translated Hell is *gehenna,* not *hades.* The Hebrew word *sheol* and its equivalent, *hades,* often translated Hell in our version, mean the invisible world—the unseen world of spirits—of spirits both bad and good. They are sometimes used to represent the grave—the invisible abode of dead bodies—but this use is figurative. *Sheol* among the Hebrews (as well as *hades* among the Greeks) means the invisible world of spirits.

It was in *sheol* where the patriarchs are represented in dying as being "gathered to their people." "Gathered to their people" is recorded as something distinct from burial, and as preceding burial, and this shows us the meaning of *sheol* and *hades,* and that the doctrine of the immortality of the soul is taught by being recognized in the Old Testament.

Abraham "gave up the ghost. . .and was gathered to his people," before his burial in the cave of Machpelah. It certainly could not mean Machpelah, for Abraham had no people there—Sarah was the only one buried there. Moses was "gathered unto his people," and so was Aaron, and their graves were solitary. It was in *sheol* where Jacob expected to meet his son.

The common name of grave in the Hebrew is *keber.* In the Greek it is *taphos,* or some equivalent word.

Sheol, translated "Hell," sometimes means that part of the invisible world in which the wicked are punished till the judgment, as in the verse, "The wicked shall be turned into hell [*sheol*], and all the nations that forget God." It certainly here cannot mean the grave, for those who are not wicked and who do not forget God, go to the grave, as well as the wicked and all the nations that do forget Him. It cannot simply mean the place of spirits good and bad, for then there is no sense in saying that the wicked and the nations that forget God go there, for certainly if all people go there after death, they will go.

Speaking of the people in two classes, and saying that one class— the wicked—go to *sheol* when they die, implying that the good class do not go there, shows that the word here means the place of future punishment. It is so used by Solomon in the verse, "Thou shalt beat him [i.e., thy child] with the rod, and shalt deliver his soul from hell" (*sheol*). Whether he correct his child or not, he will go to the grave and invisible world. The Greek equivalent of *sheol* is *hades.*

It also sometimes means the place of future punishment for the wicked, as in the verse, "The rich man died, and in hell [*hades*] he lift up his eyes, being in torments"—"torment" as a state of misery. John says, "Death and hell [*hades*] were cast into the lake of fire: this is the second death." This certainly means the wicked only.

Now the word *tartaros* is never used but as the prison of the wicked, and is used in II Peter, "God spared not the angels that sinned, but cast them down to hell, and delivered them into chains of darkness, to be reserved unto judgment." This is in harmony with the other verses and corroborates what I have said about them.

Gehenna is the word used in the text. It is compounded of two Hebrew words *Ge* and *Hinnom*—Valley of Hinnom. This valley was southeast of Jerusalem and near the city. In this valley was an image of Moloch, Baal or the Sun, and in the valley the idolatrous Jews, in the worship of this god, burned their children alive. This valley is also called Tophet, from *toph,* meaning a drum, because the cries of the burning children were drowned by the beating of drums.

Josiah, who abolished the worship of Moloch, to render this valley odious, turned all the filth of Jerusalem into it. The dead of animals and the dead bodies of malefactors were thrown into it. The sewers of Jerusalem also emptied their filthy contents into it. To consume this filth a fire was kept there perpetually burning. The valley, by natural law of all ideas, became the symbol of cruelty, misery, pollution and of perpetual burning. Thus, by a law of language, its name was transferred to the place of punishment for the wicked and is so used in the text and other places.

The Universalists say that when the word is used in the Bible it always means the Valley of Hinnom near Jerusalem. They have written books to prove that it has no reference to such a place of future punishment for the wicked as we claim. It is a pet argument of theirs. Let us read some of the Scriptures in which *gehenna* is used according to their argument and mark well the consistency, beauty and sense, and if the inspired writers are not crazy, craziness cannot be proven by the productions of a man's pen.

"Fear not them which kill the body, but are not able to kill the soul: but rather fear him which is able to destroy both body and soul" in the Valley of Hinnom, which is near Jerusalem—"in hell."

"Woe unto you, scribes and Pharisees, hypocrites! for ye compass sea and land to make one proselyte, and when he is made, ye make him twofold more the child [of hell]"—of the Valley of Hinnom, near the city of Jerusalem—"than yourselves."

"Ye serpents, ye generation of vipers, how can ye escape the damnation [of hell]"—of the Valley of Hinnom near Jerusalem?

"The tongue is a fire, a world of iniquity: so is the tongue among our members, that it defileth the whole body, and setteth on fire the course of nature; and it is set on fire (of hell)"—of the Valley of Hinnom near Jerusalem.

The word *Gehenna* is used twelve times in the New Testament. It never literally means the Valley of Hinnom. It may in a few instances mean the misery of the Jewish nation, but its general meaning is a place of great suffering in the future for sinners. Take one verse already quoted: "Fear not them which kill the body, but are not able to kill the soul: but rather fear him which is able to destroy both body and soul in hell"— *geenne*, another form of the same word. The soul is here distinguished from the body and is said to be indestructible by man and is said to live after the body is killed. It says that God only can destroy it, and that God will cast it with the body in *Gehenna*. The fact that this will occur after the body has been dead shows that it will be after the resurrection; hence *Gehenna* is the abode of the damned after the judgment, as *hades* is their abode after the death of the body and before the judgment.

The conclusions from this verse, and that the punishment is in the future, are more clearly taught in Luke: "Be not afraid of them that kill the body, and after that have no more that they can do; but fear him which, after he hath killed, hath power to cast into hell." The preposition *meta,* in the phrase "after that," is properly translated—it always means "after" when it governs the accusative as in the text. It means "with," "together with," when it governs the genitive.

Because the word *Gehenna* is compounded of *Ge* and *Hinnom*—Valley of Hinnom—to make the word when it is used with reference to the wicked apply to the Valley of Hinnom near Jerusalem is philological stupidity. The invisible is always represented by a word made from the visible.

The word *paradise* meant originally in Persia, "a park or pleasure ground, well watered and planted and stocked with animals for the chase." When Christ said to the dying thief, "To day shalt thou be with me in paradise," do you suppose He meant one of those Persian gardens? Do you suppose Paul, when he said—and I quote—that he "was caught up into paradise, and heard unspeakable words, which it is not lawful for a man to utter"—that is, "not possible for a man to utter," as the marginal reading is—that he meant a Persian garden? If so, Persia is in the third heaven and is "up"—"caught up"—for Paul says in two verses before, "caught up to the third heaven." Our word meaning heaven just means the region of air around us.

Are the damned to be sent to the Valley of Hinnom near Jerusalem and the saved into a garden in Persia? If one is to be taken this way, the other must. If Gehenna is not the place of future punishment for the wicked, we have no Heaven or Paradise either. The same arguments can be used against both; and the reason they are used in favor of Hell and not Heaven is that those who use them, as a general rule, would love to go to Heaven but feel they are not prepared for it, and they want to get a future Hell out of the way.

I do not want to offend anyone, but with my convictions I can say nothing else, and God helping me I will not go to the judgment with your blood on my skirts. I feel it my duty, and I know no policy in the pulpit.

The existence of the atonement is evidence of a state of future punishment. I lay down three propositions: 1. Man's body is mortal. 2. Man's soul is immortal. 3. Sin has produced the mortality of the body; corrupted the moral character of the soul, but cannot destroy the immortality of the soul.

Take these three facts laid down as premises, and think over them but for a moment. Man's body is mortal—who would ask proof of it? Man's soul is immortal—all of you believe it; if there is a person here who does not, then he is prepared to hear no argument whatever upon either Heaven or Hell. Sin produced the mortality of the body but cannot destroy the immortality of the soul. The basis of the soul's immortality is found in the capabilities of its constitutional essence—the reason is found in God's will thereto agreeing. Sin from its nature affects the moral character of the soul, not its constitution and essence. What the soul is capable of having in virtue of its constitution and essence independent of its moral character sin cannot touch or destroy.

Now hear the conclusion: If man's body is mortal, if man's soul is immortal and sin produced the mortality of the body but cannot destroy the immortality of the soul, and there is only a state of eternal blessedness in the future for departed spirits—which is the theory of one class of Universalists—all spirits must necessarily go there after the death of the body, and we have universal salvation irrespective of character.

Where, then, is the necessity for a Saviour and the scheme of redemption of which He is the subject? There is none. The existence of the atonement is evidence there is a state of future punishment. If there is no state of future punishment, the atonement is at once perceived to be a supererogation—a something superinduced upon the grand system of God's moral government, for the existence of which there can be no sensible reason assigned.

If it be said by another class of Universalists that there is a place of future punishment but that the punishment of the wicked is limited and that after a time they will all go to Heaven, the following conclusions inevitably follow: 1. that suffering can compensate for sin; 2. that suffering involuntarily endured can compensate for sin voluntarily committed; 3. that suffering can purify man's nature.

These conclusions are unphilosophic and unscriptural; and the result is as before—there is no necessity for Christ or the atonement. The very existence of the atonement is evidence of a state of eternal future punishment for the wicked.

This punishment is eternal as a matter of fact, as I have shown; and it is eternal as a matter of right. I can present my arguments because of what has preceded them in this series, as briefly and compactly as I choose. As a matter of course, I go upon the doctrine that the true sense of future punishment is that of retribution, not that it is disciplinary. This has been shown inferentially from every argument all the while. I may in a future discourse touch upon it more explicitly.

The penalty must be in proportion to the amount of guilt. This arises out of the very relation between penalty and guilt. The guilt of any offense of man against God is in proportion to the superior dignity of God's nature. This will not do as a general rule. It is not true when both parties are finite and never true with reference to the accidental dignity of mere office and circumstances but only with reference to dignity of nature. It is only true with reference to a finite creature and an infinite God, where such relations exist as do exist between the infinite God and all finite creatures.

Man's nature is finite. God's nature is infinite. There can be, therefore, no proportion in point of dignity of nature between the two. There can be no proportion between two things unless the one subtracted from the other creates a visible diminution. Subtract the finite from the infinite, and there is no diminution—the infinite remains. Let the infinite be your minuend; the finite, your subtrahend; and the infinite is your remainder.

Now, if the penalty is in proportion to the amount of guilt and the guilt of man's offences against God is in proportion to the superior dignity of God's nature, and between God and man there is no proportion in point of dignity of nature because God is infinite; then the penalty of sin as a matter of right is infinite in the only direction in which it can be—that of duration.

Again, the penalty of sin must be in proportion to the amount of guilt. The guilt of sin consists in its being the violation of an obligation; therefore, it must be in proportion to the amount of obligation violated. This is also clear.

The whole question turns upon the character of man's obligations to God. These are infinite. God is the Creator, Preserver, Benefactor, Governor and Redeemer of men, infinitely and absolutely. If man really owns, originates or preserves by any right or power within himself anything subjectively or objectively, just so far as that thing was worth, he would lack of being under infinite obligations to God.

But where is there such a thing? From the nature of God and His relations to man, the character and value of man's obligations must be estimated from the infinite nature and plans of God, the obligee! and not from man, the obligor. Man is under infinite obligations to obey God. If man's obligation to obey God is infinite, the guilt of disobeying Him is infinite. And if the guilt of disobeying Him is infinite, the penalty, *as a matter of right, is infinite.* The penalty must be in proportion to the amount of guilt; the amount of guilt must be in proportion to the amount of obligation violated. Man's obligations to God are infinite; the penalty, as a matter of right, must be infinite.

Is eternal punishment a fact, and is it right? Our God is a consuming fire. The capacity and power to love shows the capacity and the power to hate. Those who would say that anger and wrath are inconsistent with the character of God make God a cold and chilling abstraction unable to love. If you want a God capable of love and infinite love, He must be capable of wrath and infinite wrath. Indeed, love of the good and love of good men is anger of evil and evil men. Anger is but love itself, the burning reflex of divine love which warms and rejoices Heaven, kindling into a flame of unquenchable wrath for evildoers.

The existence and happiness of the righteous depend upon the integrity of God's system and government. And God loves the righteous so well that He is angry with every sinner who would destroy the integrity and rectitude of His system and government. Destroy God's government, and the righteous are ruined. Sin is treason, and the sinner is a rebel, and God must punish him.

Away, you sickly sentimentalists! While you say God cannot hate, you say He cannot love; and every argument you use against Hell is an argument against Heaven.

Is eternal punishment a fact, and is it right? God's justice answers in the affirmative, and the divine mercy says, "Yes." After all that mercy has done to save a sinner, to follow him with its offers after this probation would be to give a premium for sin. And in the magnificent family of God's attributes, mercy is the sweetest, loveliest and most beautiful. Her form is perfect symmetry, her eyes a celestial blue, her locks are golden, her face the fairest in Heaven; and a glittering circlet of gold set with sparkling diamonds and intertwined with leaves and flowers of fadeless amaranth rests upon her white and pure brow. She is the friend of man; and though she leans upon the brawny arm of justice—with his dark brow, flashing eye and stalwart form—she is as strong as he. A glance of her eye has often stayed his hand, and her fingers have unstrung his bow; and if an arrow has flown, with leaves plucked from the tree of life she stanches and heals the wound in man the arrow made, if the man will permit her.

But, oh! she is oftener cursed by the man than blessed in her mission. And in the moment the sinner passes over the river, holding in one hand a list of her slighted offers and unappreciated blessings, with the other she wields the fiercest whip on the backs of the damned, and her voice is loudest and clearest in asserting the rightfulness of eternal punishment—

> **Bow ere the awful trumpet sound,**
> **And call you to His bar!**
> **For Mercy knows the appointed bound,**
> **And turns to Vengeance there.**

Is eternal punishment a fact, and is it right?

The Bible, born in the wilderness and rocked by the hand of God—Horeb's fiery thunders beating its lullabies on the bare and granite crags and the red lightnings flashing around its cradle—and who was baptized by water and blood, kneeling at the foot of the cross—God's eternal truth standing sponsor—and who in mature manhood was crowned and commissioned on the cliffs of Patmos, the blue waters of the Grecian sea laving their base, and which rippled in music around the boats and oars of hero and warrior in classic story—comes forth with a casket in its right hand and a quiver in its left. The casket is filled with jewels—bright and sparkling from the mines of Heaven—jewel promises which it empties into the lap of the church and scatters on our closet floors to shine, glitter and light up these temples when we pray, and sows along the pathway of the Christian until the road to Heaven, through the gloom and night of this probation, is shining and paved with gems—the road itself leading to a city whose foundations are precious stones.

The quiver is filled with arrows—pointed, barbed and deadly—fiery threatenings which it ever hurls upon the heads of the wicked to force them to come into the marriage supper of the Lamb—or, refusing, to beat in one tempestuous storm of hissing and piercing shafts upon their naked heads as they run and scream over the fields of perdition. No grotto or overhanging rock can shelter from the pitiless storm, for the bolts of God can pierce all rocks and burn through every defense. There is a curse for every promise, and both alike are the Bible's answer to our question.

In Palestine there are two mountains rising on steep and rocky precipices about 800 feet high, on both sides of a narrow valley about 300 yards wide. They are called Ebal and Gerizim. God commanded the children of Israel by Moses when they entered the promised land, that six tribes of them should stand upon Mount Ebal and the other six tribes on Mount Gerizim and that the Levites should pronounce the curses and blessings of the law—the tribes on Mount Ebal responding "Amen" to the curses, the tribes on Mount Gerizim responding "Amen" to the blessings. This was doubtless the grandest ceremony in the history of the nations.

Mount Ebal and Mount Gerizim are on every page of the Bible and on every field of divine providence, and in the valley between them will sit the throne of judgment—and to every blessing and every curse all the people will say "Amen," and the universe shall acknowledge that eternal punishment is right.

The blessed Saviour sat down probably on the eastern horn of the Hattin, a ridge between Tabor and Tiberias, and preached His first sermon. It was a sermon of blessings: "Blessed are the poor in spirit—Blessed are they that mourn—Blessed are the meek—Blessed are they which do hunger and thirst after righteousness—Blessed are the merciful—Blessed are the pure in heart—Blessed are the peacemakers—Blessed are they which are persecuted for righteousness' sake"—a sermon of blessings. Certainly it would be inconsistent with Christ's character to curse. Would not the universalist quote these all the day? To pronounce curses would not suit that kind face and be in harmony with His mission.

This was His first sermon. Now hear His last—standing in the Temple in the presence of all the people and those who had been taught to regard the Pharisees and scribes as their teachers and patterns of piety: "Woe unto you, scribes and Pharisees, hypocrites—Woe unto you, ye blind guides—ye fools and blind—Woe unto you scribes—Woe unto you, thou blind Pharisee—ye serpents, ye generation of vipers, how can ye escape the damnation of hell?"

Curses and blessings go together. Love incarnate can curse a sinner. Love incarnate can damn a sinner. And if Love incarnate can curse and damn a sinner, it can do it for all eternity.

O Eternity! let thy ages tramp, thy cycles roll, but thou canst not crumble or scar the walls of Hell or rust and break its locks or silver the hair of God, who has sworn by His eternal self that the sinner shall die. The pendulum of thy horologe over the gates of woe vibrates through all eons and says "forever and ever"—"forever and ever"—"forever and ever"—its sounding bell striking off the centuries, the ages—the cycles. The appalling monotony of its pendulum—going—going—going—repeating still, "forever and ever"—"forever and ever"—"forever and ever."

O Eternity! God has wound up thy clock, and it will never run down—and its tickings and beatings are heard by all the lost—"forever and ever"—"forever and ever"—"forever and ever."

God being my judge, I would die to save you this day.

DOLPHUS PRICE
1919-

ABOUT THE MAN:

Evangelist Dolphus L. Price is a man with a God-blessed ministry. July, 1989, he celebrated his seventieth birthday and his fiftieth year in the ministry. He has held several pastorates, one of the most notable being the Brent Baptist Church in Pensacola, Florida. While pastoring this thriving church, he established a strong Christian school—one of the first in the nation—long before the Christian school movement became popular.

Dr. Price pastored and engaged in revival meetings at the same time. But calls for his service in revivals became so frequent that he entered full-time evangelistic work in 1950, and was there for many profitable years before re-entering the pastorate. He is once again a full-time evangelist and goes out regularly to minister worldwide.

Speaking of his decision to enter evangelism in 1950, he said, "It was at the first Sword of the Lord Conference on Evangelism that I surrendered my life to the Lord to use me as an evangelist, if that were His will for me. I went back to our home in Decatur, Alabama, rented a tent and began a meeting in a small adjoining town. In six days we saw 119 professions of faith and several rededications. Our ministry was never the same after that conference."

Evangelist Price was trained at Howard College, Moody Bible Institute, Bob Jones University, Tennessee Temple Schools, and Southeastern Baptist Theological Seminary.

He was one of the founders of Baptist International Missions Incorporated.

Dr. Price is a fiery preacher, who delivers a serious message with eloquence and pathos. His sermons are at once enthralling and convicting.

X.

Hell — a Place for the Lost

DOLPHUS PRICE

(Preached at Franklin Road Baptist Church, Murfreesboro, Tennessee, on March 15, 1972)

"There was a certain rich man, which was clothed in purple and fine linen, and fared sumptuously every day: And there was a certain beggar named Lazarus, which was laid at his gate, full of sores, And desiring to be fed with the crumbs which fell from the rich man's table: moreover the dogs came and licked his sores. And it came to pass, that the beggar died, and was carried by the angels into Abraham's bosom: the rich man also died, and was buried; And in hell he lift up his eyes, being in torments, and seeth Abraham afar off, and Lazarus in his bosom. And he cried and said, Father Abraham, have mercy on me, and send Lazarus, that he may dip the tip of his finger in water, and cool my tongue; for I am tormented in this flame. But Abraham said, Son, remember that thou in thy lifetime receivedst thy good things, and likewise Lazarus evil things: but now he is comforted, and thou art tormented. And beside all this, between us and you there is a great gulf fixed: so that they which would pass from hence to you cannot; neither can they pass to us, that would come from thence. Then he said, I pray thee therefore, father, that thou wouldest send him to my father's house: For I have five brethren; that he may testify unto them, lest they also come into this place of torment. Abraham said unto him, They have Moses and the prophets; let them hear them. And he said, Nay, father Abraham: but if one went unto them from the dead, they will repent. And he said unto him, If they hear not Moses and the prophets, neither will they be persuaded, though one rose from the dead."— Luke 16:19-31.

Ladies and gentlemen, I talk tonight about something that, like a great black shadow, casts its engulfing shroud on the great majority of the race of mankind.

They say there are about 5 billion people now on the earth (1987). Of that number, it is estimated that some 1.2 billion are saved. Whether we can say that or not is rather doubtful. But let us suppose that 1.2 billion are saved. That means 3.8 billion people do not know God. That means that the vast majority of mankind is falling off into eternity like a vast stream. Oh, may the Holy Spirit of God help us to see this!

A battle is going on for the souls of men, a battle that is as real as any war ever fought. And it is being won. They claim that there are forty-nine heathen babies born to every person we win to Christ. Statisticians say that at the present rate of converts, by the year 2000 less than 2 percent of the population of the world will know anything about Jesus Christ.

In the islands of the sea, 50 million do not know about Jesus.

In Africa, 70 million have never heard the Gospel one time in spite of the decades of gospel witness and missionary activity.

So the long tentacles of death and Hell reach out, and the shadow lengthens as the days go by. And the population explosion continues. So they claim that by the year 2000, more than 7 billion people on the earth—twice as many as we have now—will be unsaved and on their way to an everlasting Devil's Hell.

Most of the people you meet on the street are not saved. The vast majority of the folks you work with at the plant are not saved. Most of those you will see, most of those you will get acquainted with in your lifetime, will not be born-again believers. Many in our church membership do not know the Son of God. Why do I say that? Because of their actions. The average person in the church has to be begged, cajoled, persuaded, implored and everything else to do whatever activities he has to do for the Son of God. It is a terrible, terrible commentary upon the Christian religion that so many have to be begged into service for the Son of God.

Second Corinthians 5:17 says, ". . . if any man be in Christ, he is a new creature: old things are passed away; behold, all things are become new." The standard was set by the Son of God for Christian living when He said, "If any man come to me, and hate not his father, and mother, and wife, and children, and brethren, and sisters, yea, and his own life also, he cannot be my disciple" (Luke 14:26). There is a terrible, desperate situation, not only in the world but in our churches, of lost people without God and without hope.

What do I mean when I talk about Hell? I mean that place God has prepared for the Devil and his angels. I am talking about the antithesis of Heaven.

Whatever Heaven is, then Hell is not.

If Heaven is a place of light, then Hell is a place of darkness.

If Heaven is a place of joy, then Hell is a place of sorrow.

If Heaven is a place of singing, then Hell will be a place of tears.

If Heaven is a place where friends will know each other and abide forever together and there will be no funeral train in the sky and there will be rejoicing and reunion and fellowship with the Son of God and singing of His praises forever, then Hell will be an awful, dismal land where darkness covers and souls walk up and down the fire-blasted corridors of the damned and cry, "Lost! lost! lost!" forever.

Hell is an awful land. It almost stupifies the imagination of the soul. You can hardly conceive what a place would be like which would be the absolute opposite of Heaven. When a man commits a sin against God Almighty, he has committed an infinite crime. I believe with all my soul that when God punishes the criminal, He punishes him commensurate with the crime, because if God is just and holy, then it would be impossible for Him to ameliorate the sentence. He said, "The soul that sinneth, it shall die" (Ezek. 18:4). He said He prepared Hell for the Devil and his angels. "Hell from beneath is moved for thee to meet thee at thy coming: it stirreth up the dead for thee" (Isa. 14:9).

And if God is going to make the place of the abode of the eternal criminals commensurate with their crimes, Hell must be an infinite place. So Hell is infinite.

It is infinite distance away from God. It is infinite despair. It is infinite horror. It is infinite in all its aspects. There isn't anything about it that isn't infinite because it is filled with those who will be suffering the infinite sanctions of the law and the penal sanctions of death and the judgment of God Almighty. And all the horrors the human mind ever conceived could not compare with that place called Hell.

Elbert Munsey was one of the greatest preachers of all time on eternal punishment. I heard Dr. John R. Rice say that when Munsey preached you could not change one single word in the sentence to make it mean more than he said already. He was fantastic. By the time he was five years of age, he was reading political speeches. I suppose he rang the bell concerning Unitarianism and No-Hellism as hard as anybody. His sermons are classics.

One day when he was sitting in his study musing about the matter of eternal punishment and trying to determine what he thought in his mind Hell might be, these are some of the things he said:

> It [Hell] may be a gloomy, desolate and barren world, whose rocks and mountains are tumbled into anarchy; where there are no blushing flowers, nodding trees, dewy vales, grassy slopes and running streams; and where there are no homes, no churches, no preaching, no morality, no religion, no friendships, no God. . . .
>
> Then the best Hell we can promise is a world of ugly ruins shrouded in Night's blackest pall, where no one of the damned has a friend, and filled with cursings and strifes, and where all ranks and sexes are herded in one promiscuous mob with foulest demons, and where every stinking cave is inhabited with fiend and gnashing ghost, and on whose black crags the ravens of despair sit and croak, and where God's eternal justice plies His burning whip and remorse lays on with his fiery thongs —the flashes of whip and thongs their only light, world without end.
>
> Or it may be some huge cavern hollowing out the center of some blasted, shattered and God-cursed planet in which the poison and stench of ages have gathered and, condensing, distill on the walls— dimly lighted by sulphurous torches held by grimacing and howling fiends and whose sickly flickerings render the darkness in all the windings, pits, chasms and corners but blacker; and where occasional blue flames breaking through the fissures overhead lick along the arches and bolts of thunder crash through the grottoes and roar along the labyrinths, in which lost men and fallen angels may be driven from the judgment seat, the ponderous gates closing and locking behind them—the key fastened to the girdle of God and the divine omnipotence installed as perpetual sentinel to guard the way.
>
> Or it may be an unquenchable lake of fire and brimstone. . . bubbles dancing on every wave and swell and bursting emit fumes and smoke threaded with serpent flames, in whose ascending volumes everlasting lightnings flash and cross. . . .
>
> (Chapter 4, *Eternal Retribution*)

Ladies and gentlemen, this man died when he was about forty-three. Another thing he said in one of his books is something that haunts me at night: "Eternal Hell and eternal separation from God is weightier than all the mountains of the world pressing down upon the human mind." The thought of being separated from God in a place like that weighs so heavily upon my mind that I cannot sleep at night.

O Eternity, parent of ages! We are born in the center of the circle, we live in the center of the circle, we die in the center of the circle, we will be in the center of the circle forever. And he who goes to Hell will be eternally separated from God.

O Eternity, the thought of thee troubles me at night so that I cannot sleep!

Somebody asked me the other day, "Brother Price, how is it you can preach so much all the time?"

There are several reasons. One is, I am preaching for my father who was never allowed to preach. My grandfather would have killed him had he preached. So when he died, I told him, "Daddy, as long as I am able to go, I will preach for both of us and ask God to divide the spoils with you."

There is another reason. One day yonder several years ago I was flying up to Indianapolis. High in the air I was reading the Greek text, the 16th chapter of the Gospel of Luke. All of the sudden some of those words there bombed me. I am sure the stewardess must have wondered what was the matter with that short, fat fellow over there crying so hard. The word *rich* got hold of me. The word *torment* isn't torment; it's *torture*. It got hold of me. The word *never* got hold of me. The word *forever* got hold of me. The fact that a man is still there crying right now, "O God, send somebody down here to touch the tip of his finger in water and cool my parched tongue that I may cease some from my pain"— that thought of a man crying forever there in the bosom of the damned got hold of my soul. I wept. It did something for my ministry.

At home I was pacing up and down the living room. My wife said, "Honey, what's the matter? Don't you love to be home?"

I said, "Yes, I love to be home. Please forgive me. I preach so much now that when I am not preaching, I feel guilty."

Souls are on their way to Hell. Men are damned forever without the Son of God. Some of you have children who are likely to be in Hell soon, if you don't get them saved. I have looked into the face of too many people whom I have witnessed to, then had to bury that poor soul.

I heard a mother say some time ago, as she looked down into the face of her husband in a casket who had not been to church in fifty years, "Goodby, Sweetheart, goodby forever!" Oh, he had been dealt with, prayed for, witnessed to. Then she said to me, "Brother Price, I will never see my darling again! We will be forever separated! I am saved and he was lost!"

I have seen enough of that to last me a lifetime. The thought of souls being separated from God and snapped out in a moment without God and without hope, to burn in everlasting fire, troubles my soul.

I do not understand how it is that you have to beg Sunday school teachers, deacons and other Christians to visit, to pray, to work. Oh, that God would give us one glimpse into that awful abyss of the damned and let us hear the cries of the lost one time, then we would know!

You say, "Preacher, you talk with so many metaphors and adjectives and that sort of thing. What does the Bible say?" The Word of God says, "The wicked shall be turned into hell, and all the nations that forget God" (Ps. 9:17). "Hell from beneath is moved for thee to meet thee at thy coming: it stirreth up the dead [rapha—giants] for thee" (Isa. 14:9).

If I read the Word of God right, this means there will be a reception committee for every soul that dies outside the Son of God. It means that when a man dies, there will be a reception committee of the most hideous creatures you have ever seen, because if angels in Heaven are beautiful, then those creatures in Hell must be grotesque characters of God's creation. Of all the grotesque, contorted creatures you have ever seen, those demon spirits must be the worst because they have the antithesis of angels.

Sometimes we say about a little baby, "She is an angelic little creature." The highest compliment we can pay a woman is, "She is as beautiful as an angel."

My friends, whatever Heaven is, Hell is not. There will be no beauty or symmetry or accord or harmony in Hell; it will be all discord. Inhabitants of Hell must be awful! God says,

"Hell from beneath is moved for thee to meet thee at thy coming: it stirreth up the dead for thee."—Isa. 14:9.

"And fear not them which kill the body, but are not able to kill the soul: but rather fear him which is able to destroy both soul and body in hell."—Matt. 10:28.

"And if thy hand offend thee, cut it off: it is better for thee to enter into life maimed, than having two hands to go into hell, into the fire that never shall be quenched: Where their worm dieth not, and the fire is not quenched. And if thy foot offend thee, cut it off: it is better for thee to enter halt into life, than having two feet to be cast into hell, into

the fire that never shall be quenched: Where their worm dieth not, and the fire is not quenched. And if thine eye offend thee, pluck it out: it is better for thee to enter into the kingdom of God with one eye, than having two eyes to be cast into hell fire: Where their worm dieth not, and the fire is not quenched."—Mark 9:43-48.

Jesus said, "If your eye were to keep you from being saved, it would be better for you to rip it out of its socket. Take your hand and chop it off; take your leg and cut it off."

One time Rev. Waite, a pastor in Anderson, Alabama, and I went visiting. He said, "Preacher, I want us to go see a certain old man. He has a wonderful testimony. I want him to tell you about it."

When we got out to his place, this man was sitting up in a rocking chair and his peg leg was off to the right. He was whipping that old leg with a riding crop.

We walked up and my preacher friend said, "Hi, brother. I want you to meet our evangelist and tell him your story."

The old gentleman smiled, then tears began to run down his cheeks as he related his experience.

> Years ago Brother Waite used to come to my place and say to me, "Sir, I want you to be saved." I would say to him, "Not now. I don't have time. No, no. I am having too much fun. Furthermore, I know what will happen to me. If I join your church—that was my way of expressing it then—I won't be able to dance. And if I have to give up dancing, I'll just go to Hell."
>
> But one night coming in from Birmingham with a load of vegetables, I turned into a big curve that turns into the city and lost control of the truck. It spun over and crushed my legs. I was unconscious. When I woke up in the hospital, they were discussing which leg they could probably save. They were going to have to take one of them and they thought maybe they could patch up my left leg. They took off one leg.
>
> While I was in the hospital, God told me how close my life had come to being snuffed out, how close death was to me, how close eternity was. This preacher came in to see me. I received Jesus Christ as my Saviour.
>
> Brother Price, I lost my leg. But if I hadn't lost that old leg and if I didn't have a peg leg here today, I would probably be in Hell because I loved to dance so well and loved the wild life. I would never have given it up.

Ladies and gentlemen, that is exactly what Jesus said. Hell is so awful and being separated from God so terrible that no matter what it costs, it would be well worth the price in order for you to be saved. There is nothing in all of life that is worth one moment in Hell.

The Bible says:

"And to you who are troubled rest with us, when the Lord Jesus shall be revealed from heaven with his mighty angels, In flaming fire taking vengeance on them that know not God, and that obey not the gospel of our Lord Jesus Christ: Who shall be punished with everlasting destruction from the presence of the Lord, and from the glory of his power."—II Thess. 1:7-9.

"If he turn not, he will whet his sword; he hath bent his bow, and made it ready. He hath also prepared for him the instruments of death; he ordaineth his arrows against the persecutors."—Ps. 7:12,13.

You say, "Brother Price, you talk a great deal about what the Bible says and what other people say about this matter of Hell." I haven't said nearly as much as could be said. Jesus preached more about Hell than He did about Heaven.

A lady came to me some time ago and said, "Preacher, why don't you preach like Jesus? Why don't you preach on love like He did on the mount, the Beatitudes, etc.?"

I turned over there and read some things to her. You know, the Lord Jesus Christ said, "Ye serpents, ye generation of vipers, how can ye escape the damnation of hell?" (Matt. 23:33). That is pretty strong preaching, wouldn't you say?

Jesus preached more about Hell than He did about Heaven; more about Hell than He did about life; more about Hell than He did about death; more about Hell than He did about anything that He preached in this world. Why? Because He knew that He could look into Hell any moment He chose. He was all the time conscious of it. He knew there were multitudes there screaming and crying and writhing in their pain and lost forever and forever.

First of all, we could say that every Scripture agrees with the fact that Hell is a literal place. It isn't just a land of miasma. It isn't just some Never-Never land where people suffer in the agony of despair and blackness. It is that—but more. Hell is a place of literal fire, a place where souls burn forever and are never consumed. Hell is a place where they cry forever, where the lonely despair forever. Night is never broken by a star or the sun. They are there forever and forever. Hell is a place of eternal fire.

Years ago when a bomb was dropped on the great city of Hiroshima, Japan, some 130,000 souls disappeared from the face of the earth. But that bomb only exerted ten percent of its potential.

I talked with some folks in the University of Washington some time ago, and one of the men who programs the computer for the army said, "Preacher, today we have in our hands an instrument that can destroy the world in one stroke." Of course, God has put a damper on that thing. I believe it will happen exactly the way the Word of God says it will happen.

That atomic bomb that took 130,000 people out of one city in a flash was discovered by man. The one who made it is God. Whatever is created is less than the Creator. We have just discovered the energy that flows from the hand of God, that energy that was set forth the day He created the world, when He spoke and stars went out into space.

In every square inch of the surface of our sun, 500,000 horsepower units of energy are emitting all the time. And our sun is not the brightest star. Centaurus is 3.9 times brighter than our sun. Out yonder in the Milky Way, that blob of light that spans the heavens, there are stars that are one thousand times brighter than our sun. The Milky Way is made up of billions of galaxies of stars. Out beyond the Milky Way, if you were to travel at the speed of light, you would travel five billion years out to the next series of stars.

You say, "Preacher, how fast would that be, and how far would it be?" Oh, it scares me every time I think about it. You see, light travels at the rate of 186,000 miles per second. Multiply that times 60, times 24, times 365 1/4, times 5 billion, and you will know how far it would be. That is farther than you or I can comprehend.

Mr. Clark of the space agency says, "We believe there are stars there, from what we have been able to experiment with light proceeding from some source, that must be at least one million times brighter than our sun." These are created by the hand of God when He flung them from His flaming fingertips and put them in their elliptic orb. He did it simply by the word of His power.

And my friend, then God Almighty, the inimitable, illimitable God, the infinite God, created a place called Hell. He created it as an infinite place of torture for those who would reject His Son. Hell is a place of torture. Hell is the place of the lost.

Some years ago when I was pastor in Rossville, Georgia, word got out about six o'clock one evening than an eleven-year-old boy was lost in the woods. He had the mind of a three-year-old. It was a frosty, awfully cold night. A lady called. "Brother Price, Charlie is lost. Would you help us get somebody to look for him?"

I made a few phone calls. Shortly we had thirty men ready to go out in the zero weather to beat the bushes to look for that little boy. We decided if we hadn't found him by three o'clock in the morning we would meet at Lakeview Drive and Cloud Springs Road.

Three o'clock came. The men began to straggle in from different places. No one had seen him, nor heard a sound. Seeing the men were tired, I said, "Fellows, it would be good if we had some coffee and cake."

When we got home, Mom had gotten the two large coffee urns from the church and had made several gallons of coffee. She had cake. The fellows ate and relaxed. Directly one said, "Preacher, we are awfully tired. Don't you think we could rest the balance of the night and take up the hunt in the morning?"

I said, "I'll tell you what let's do. Everybody go home and rest a couple or three hours and be back here about six o'clock. Then we will take up the hunt again."

About the time the fellows began to put their overcoats and their caps on, down in the hollow below our house we heard the voice of a woman calling, "Charlie, Charlie!" That mother was out in the blackness of the night by herself.

I didn't have to say another word to those men. Every last one got his coat on, zipped it up and put his cap on and we went right back out and hunted the rest of the night.

Thank God, we found him unharmed about eight o'clock the next morning. He had at least sense enough to crawl under some old boards and paper and refuge in an abandoned barn.

But down yonder in a place called Hell on an abandoned island of despair, where no light ever shines, no friends ever come, where hope is gone and despair is forever, where the blanket of despair has been thrown over the door and the chains of everlasting night bind the doors forever—on that island men are crying, "Lost! lost! lost!" They are beyond God's mercy, beyond God's help. Lost forever!

O mother and daddy, Sunday school teacher, church worker, the most important thing in this world is rescuing fallen souls! Oh, I hope and pray to God there is not a Christian worker in this house or a preacher or anybody who is so careless that you have gotten to the place where you can't cry when you think about Hell.

Some go about their routine work day by day as if it were some professional thing. Oh, Jesus left us here for a purpose, and that purpose must have been to win souls to Christ. His work would have been a lot better had everybody gone on to Heaven when they got saved. We wouldn't have made a fool out of Christianity like we so often have. If the church weren't God-oriented and divine, it would have died a thousand years ago. Mankind, with his carelessness, coldness and ignorance, would never have kept it going. God Almighty had to do it.

I once heard Dr. Lee Roberson say, "I don't care what the rest of you folks do. Some of you are saying that I am getting old. I am older, but I am not going to let up. Until the day I die, I will be going."

I am not worried about whiskey. I am not worried about getting drunk. I am not worried about being immoral. I am not concerned about some other overt sins like shooting dice or dancing or drinking. I believe I have grown up a little bit more than that. But what I am scared of is becoming a cold, lackadaisical, professional Christian. I want my heart to stay hot. When I pray, I don't want it to be just a perfunctory prayer to God. I want to have a burdened heart over the lost.

Hell is a place for the lost. Hell is a place of memory.

Some time ago in Chattanooga a man went down to the local police station, put his pistol down on the desk and said to the desk sergeant, "Arrest me, sir."

"What do you mean?"

"Fifteen years ago I murdered a man in this town. Nobody knew I did it. I was never apprehended. I have been out in the West going from farm to farm, place to place, doing manual labor but not staying anywhere very long. I can't stand it any longer. When someone walks up behind me quickly, I think it is the police. When I hear dogs barking, I think it is the police. When a horn blows behind me, I think it is the police. When the telephone rings, I think it is the police. When somebody knocks on the door, I think it is the police. The thought that I killed that man troubles me. I can't stand it any longer. Lock me up!"

Memory is like the tiger that sits at the corner of every turn. You can't forget. There are some people in this house tonight who have done some heinous, wicked things, and you would do anything under God's Heaven to erase it from your mind, but you can't.

When I was little, a wicked fellow used to get a bunch of us kids off and tell us filthy stories. Those stories hang on the walls of my mind like pictures in an art gallery. Would to God that I could forget them. God can forget, but I can't.

How long will memory last? Take me to some far-flung cemetery in an infinite field, show me the tombstone of God Almighty and the day He died, then I will tell you how long memory will last. And that poor rich man down in Hell tonight is being reminded, "Son, remember! Son, remember! Son, remember!"

Durwood Williams and I were standing in front of the Union Gospel Mission several years ago. A fellow came along. Williams said to him, "We'll let you come in for the service. After that, you get a bath and we'll give you a good supper and you will have a place to sleep for the night."

This fellow said, "Sleep? I haven't slept in five years. I have gotten a catnap, but I don't sleep. Every time I get asleep, I can see the last man I murdered." (That man had killed five people. He had taken a knife and cut the last one's throat, and the man drowned in his own blood.) "I can hear the gurgling sound now every time I close my eyes. I don't care if I never sleep again."

Memory is a horrible thing. And those poor souls in Hell remember the times they could have been saved but weren't. They will be there forever!

Not only that, but Hell is a place of tears.

Some years ago when I was pastor of Brent Baptist Church, we had a program on Saturday morning called "Boys and Girls for Jesus."

One morning while headed toward downtown I saw a man being pulled down from an electric power pole. They were slapping him, jerking him, yanking him and doing whatever they could. I wanted to give some assistance, but a police officer motioned me on.

We drove on to the radio station WCOA and put on our children's program. After finishing, the announcer in the room raised one finger. I knew what that meant. I picked up the phone, pushed station No. 1 and said, "Hello."

On the other end was a hysterical voice. I said, "Who is this?"

I could hardly hear the lady. Finally she said, "This is Leita."

"Leita Cantrell?"

"Yes."

"Leita, what's the matter?"

"Brother Price, daddy. . . ."

I said, "What has happened to daddy?"

"He was electrocuted."

"Where?"

"Jordan Street."

"How long ago?"

"Several minutes ago. I've been trying to get through to you. But Brother Price, they have taken him to Sacred Heart Hospital. Will you go?"

I said, "Leita, as fast as I can."

One week before I had gotten down on my knees in that man's living room, opened the Word of God, prayed with him and asked him to be saved, but he refused. His family didn't know, but I knew what the real problem was. He was fooling around with another man's wife and having a high time, and he didn't want to give that up. The night before, Leita Cantrell had stayed in the bedroom with him until one-thirty in the morning pleading with her daddy to be saved. She said, "Daddy, I know something is wrong. I don't know what it is, but I have a sincere, earnest feeling that you had better get saved tonight."

He pushed her aside and went on to his work. That morning when he slipped that hot stick across the wires, he pushed it a little too far, and the long rubber gloves didn't quite cover the field of magnetic force from that 2300 volts of electricity, and it broke every bone in his body. He was the one I saw being dragged down the pole.

I got somebody to take my load of children back to the church, and I put my automobile in the street. I broke the speed law, hoping a police officer would stop me. I blew the horn as loud as I could and raced through red lights and around corners. I knew a man's eternal soul hung in the balance.

When I got to the Sacred Heart Hospital, I left the motor running and rushed to the emergency door. One of the Catholic nuns said, "Are you Mr. Price?"

"I am."

"Mr. Cantrell died about twenty minutes ago."

I asked, "Where is the family?"

"We have just now gotten them out. They are so broken up. We sent them home."

I went to the home. There sitting on the front steps of the house was Leita Cantrell, a fine little girl in our church who had been so faithful to the house of God. When I walked up to her and put my hand on top of her head, she said, "Pastor, daddy's in Hell! Daddy's in Hell! Daddy's in Hell!"

The other day up in Pekin, Illinois, a little fourteen-year-old girl came up to me and said, "Preacher, I want you to pray for mommy and daddy."

I said, "I will. What are their names?"

She told me and I wrote them down on a card. I said, "Where do they live?"

She said, "Preacher, they are not living. Mommy and daddy were killed three weeks ago in a car wreck. And, Brother Price, they weren't saved. Will you pray for my mommy and daddy?"

What was I going to tell her? I don't know what you would have done, but I said, "Sweetheart, it's too late. No amount of prayer will help mommy and daddy now. You will just have to ask God to help you to get over it, and He will. But I hope you will never get over the thought that people are lost, Honey."

Too late! I could have prayed until I stained the walls with my breath, but that wouldn't have helped. I could have prayed until I had a heart attack, but that wouldn't have helped. We could have burned every candle and said every rosary, but that wouldn't have helped. Too late! Too late!

Let's bow our heads and pray.

PRAYER: Father, I pray that tonight Thy blessed Holy Spirit will take this stumbling, stammering message. Father, the truth of it is sharper than a sword. O God, the long shadows of death hang like a cloud over our home. Father, if somebody told me three years ago that one of my boys wouldn't be living tonight, I wouldn't have believed it, but he is gone. Sometimes, O God, in the night I listen for the footfalls that never come; listen for the voice that never speaks. He is gone. His destiny is settled forever.

O God, who will be next? Maybe somebody out of this crowd, we do not know. O Lord God in Heaven, help us tonight. Help the lost ones in the service tonight to run quickly to Jesus. Help Christians, O God, who are playing church. Maybe they have been criticizing or griping about the things around this church. Maybe they have been complaining to God about little physical troubles. God, forgive us now. O God in Heaven, I pray Thee that You will do something to our church. Lord, breathe on us tonight. Open our eyes that we may see. God in Heaven, I pray this for Jesus' sake. Amen.

JOE HENRY HANKINS
1889-1967

ABOUT THE MAN:

"He was a weeping prophet" is the way Dr. Hankins was characterized by those who knew him best—one of the 20th century's great soul-winning preachers.

BUT—Hankins preached sharply, strongly against sin. Would to God we had more men of his mettle in a ministry today that has largely been given over to namby-pamby, mealy-mouthed silence when it comes to strong preaching against sin.

Dr. John R. Rice wrote of him: *"His method and manifest spiritual power would remind one of D. L. Moody. He has the keen, scholarly, analytical mind of an R. A. Torrey, and the love and compassion of souls of a Wilbur Chapman."*

Hankins was born in Arkansas and saved as a youth. he graduated from high school in Pine Bluff, then from Quachita Baptist College. He held pastorates in Pine Bluff, Arkansas; in Whitewright, Greenville and Childress, Texas. His last and most productive pastorate was the First Baptist Church, Little Rock, Arkansas. There, in less than five years, 1,799 additions by letter, 1,144 by baptism—an average of 227 baptisms a year—made a total of 2,943 members added to the church. Sunday school spiralled to nearly 1,400; membership mushroomed to 3,200 despite a deletion of 882 to revise the rolls.

In 1942, Hankins gave up the pastorate for full-time evangelism.

In 1967, Dr. Hankins passed on to the Heaven he loved to preach about. Be sure that he was greeted by a thronging host of redeemed souls—saved under his Spirit-filled ministry.

XI.

Who Cares if a Sinner Goes to Hell?

JOE HENRY HANKINS

(Sermon preached in 1946 at Central Baptist Church, Chicago)

"The Lord is not slack concerning his promise, as some men count slackness; but is longsuffering to us-ward, not willing that any should perish, but that all should come to repentance."—II Pet. 3:9.

"As I live, saith the Lord God, I have no pleasure in the death of the wicked; but that the wicked turn from his way and live: turn ye, turn ye from your evil ways; for why will ye die. . . ?"—Ezek. 33:11.

"And the Spirit and the bride say, Come. And let him that heareth say, Come. And let him that is athirst come. And whosoever will, let him take the water of life freely."—Rev. 22:17.

"Come unto me, all ye that labour and are heavy laden, and I will give you rest."—Matt. 11:28.

". . . him that cometh to me I will in no wise cast out."—John 6:37.

"Likewise, I say unto you, there is joy in the presence of the angels of God over one sinner that repenteth."—Luke 15:10.

"I pray thee therefore, father, that thou wouldst send him to my father's house: For I have five brethren; that he may testify unto them, lest they also come into this place of torment."—Luke 16:27,28.

I have taken several texts tonight so as to give you some idea of the persistence of the call of God and the longing of His heart for the salvation of lost men everywhere.

Beginning the very day that man sinned, until the last chapter of Revelation, the call of God rings to a lost world as He pleads, calls, warns and invites lost men to return to God and be saved from their sins.

From the day that Adam and Eve sinned, God has been seeking those who are lost. It is God who makes the first move. We are told that "there is none that understandeth, there is none that seeketh after God. They are all gone out of the way, they are together become unprofitable; there is none that doeth good, no, not one" (Rom. 3:11,12).

Thank God for a loving, compassionate, seeking God! When Jesus came He announced, "The Son of man is come to seek and to save that which was lost" (Luke 19:10).

Some think God is too good to send a person to Hell. God is good, but if any of you go to Hell, you go over the love of God, over the pleadings of God, over the warnings of God, over the wooing of the Holy Spirit. You will go to Hell over the Word of God, over the cross of Calvary. You will go to Hell over the pleadings of friends and loved ones, over the preaching of the Gospel, over the prayers of mother and father, over the ministry of the church of the Lord Jesus Christ. Yes, God has done everything possible to keep you out of Hell. But if you will not repent of your sins, if you will not heed the call of God, then there is nothing left for Him to do but to send you, with your sins, to that awful place of torment.

Yes, God is good, or He would never have given us Jesus. "For God so loved the world, that he gave his only begotten Son, that whosoever believeth in him should not perish, but have everlasting life." Many times the unsaved feel that nobody cares. When they are beaten down by Satan, when they become discouraged and many times broken by sin and nobody has sought them out, they sometimes feel as David felt: "I looked on my right hand, and beheld, but there was no man that would know me: refuge failed me: no man cared for my soul" (Ps. 142:4).

But I say to any unsaved person here tonight: many more people care than you realize. Oh, if we who are saved could look on the records of Heaven and see how many prayed for us before we were saved! If we could just know how many there are who care!

I. GOD THE FATHER CARES

But above all of that, there are others who care. Heading the list is God the Father. Listen to the words of Peter: "The Lord is not slack concerning his promise, as some men count slackness; but is longsuffering to us-ward, not willing that any should perish, but that all should come to repentance" (II Pet. 3:9).

Hear the call of God even in the Garden of Eden. Read how the first sinning parents hide themselves behind the trees in the garden and how God comes down from Heaven and walks through the garden, calling, "Adam! Adam! where art thou?"

Look through the pages of the Old Testament—to say nothing of the New—and see how many times you hear the call of God to a lost world. Someone has said the invitation, the plea, the call of God to the lost occurs more than nineteen hundred times in the pages of this blessed Book. Then that must mean that He is not willing that any should go to Hell.

"As I live, saith the Lord God, I have no pleasure in the death of the wicked; but that the wicked turn from his way and live."

Then He said, "Turn ye, turn ye from your evil ways; for why will ye die?" (Ezek. 33:11).

Again we hear Him saying, "All day long I have stretched forth my hands unto a disobedient and gainsaying people" (Rom. 10:21).

And again, "Look unto me, and be ye saved, all the ends of the earth: for I am God, and there is none else" (Isa. 45:22).

Listen again, "Let the wicked forsake his way, and the unrighteous man his thoughts: and let him return unto the Lord, and he will have mercy upon him; and to our God, for he will abundantly pardon" (Isa. 55:7).

And again, "Ho, every one that thirsteth, come ye to the waters, and he that hath no money; come ye, buy, and eat; yea, come, buy wine and milk without money and without price. Wherefore do ye spend money for that which is not bread? and your labour for that which satisfieth not? hearken diligently unto me, and eat ye that which is good, and let your soul delight itself in fatness" (Isa. 55:1,2).

Oh, how the heart of the heavenly Father yearns over a lost world! How He pleads! How He draws! How He calls! None of the redeemed of God will ever know how much He cares until we are at Home with Him.

II. THE HOLY SPIRIT CARES

Listen to another call. The Holy Spirit, the blessed third Person of the Trinity, cares. "And the Spirit and the bride say, Come"—the last invitation in the Bible. Jesus is speaking to the Apostle John, and He seems to be saying, "John, before you close the book, let us make one more call. And in this last call we will put everything in it. Let the Holy Spirit say, Come, for that is His business in the world."

Jesus said, "When he [the Holy Spirit] is come, he will reprove the world of sin, and of righteousness, and of judgment" (John 16:8).

In the mercy, in the grace, in the infinite wisdom and plan of God, He sent the Holy Spirit into the world; and the Spirit's primary purpose is to convict the world of sin and to call sinners to repentance.

Let me say this: When Jesus made that promise of the Holy Spirit and stated His mission of convicting the world of sin, of righteousness and of judgment, He preceded that statement by saying, 'When the Spirit is come unto you [the people of God], then He will do this work in a lost world and in the hearts of sinners.'

It scares me when I read that statement, for it means that in order for the Holy Spirit to do that indispensable work of convicting a lost world, in order for the Holy Spirit to woo and draw a lost world to God, He must first have a channel through which He can work. And that channel is the redeemed of God, when the Holy Spirit comes upon us.

Jesus said in John 6:44, "No man can come to me, except the Father which hath sent me draw him." That drawing power is the Holy Spirit. But oh, as children of God, think of the responsibility that rests upon us! He cannot draw except as He has channels through which to work, when He has come upon us! But the Holy Spirit is here. He is calling. He is knocking at the door of lost souls. He is wooing, pleading. In every way that the Holy Spirit can approach a heart, He does it.

Many of us have had this experience. When we are in sin or wandering away from God, we wake suddenly in the wee hours of the night. We can't go back to sleep. And in the stillness of the night we begin to ask ourselves, *What is it all about? Where am I going from here? What about my relationship to God?* Maybe we try to dismiss it from our minds, but it keeps hammering away at our hearts. What is it? The blessed Holy Spirit reaching for a soul.

Or perhaps you have sat by a mother's bedside as she went out to be with God. A wayward son or daughter was there, and mother looked up through those dimming eyes to say, "Son, meet mother in Heaven," or, "Daughter, meet mother in Heaven." Oh, how it gripped your heart! What was it? The Holy Spirit knocking at your heart's door.

Maybe you sat in a service such as this. The preaching or singing got hold of your heart. The still small voice said, *I ought to get right with God. I ought to quit the way I have been going. I ought to turn away from this.* Something grappled at your heartstrings that day.

The Holy Spirit is not willing that any should perish, and He is doing His utmost, with every means that He can lay His hand on, to stop that soul in its downward plunge and turn those feet Heavenward.

III. GOD'S SON CARES

Then there is the Son of God. Listen: "Come unto me, all ye that labour and are heavy laden, and I will give you rest." If you will read the account of the three years' ministry of our Lord and read the words which fell from His lips, as recorded in the four Gospels, you can never doubt how Jesus cares.

Look at Him as He sits on the curb of Jacob's well one day, tired and hungry. A broken, wretched, filthy, degraded sinner comes that way. So anxious is the Lord to reach that soul with salvation that He forgets all about His physical appetite and the fatigue of His tired body. When His disciples return with food bought at a nearby village and offer Him to eat, He says He is not hungry. They are astonished because they knew how hungry He was before they left, and so tired that He could not walk up to the village with them. They insist, "Master, eat." Jesus answers, "I have meat to eat that ye know not of." He went after a soul with such earnestness, with such love, with such compassion that, in the intensity of that hour, He lost His hunger for food.

Look at Him again in the early morning in the Temple when the Pharisees drag a poor unfortunate woman out to expose her in her shame. Jesus stoops down and writes on the ground with His finger. After awhile, when her accusers have all gone, Jesus looks at her and asks, "Woman, where are those thine accusers? hath no man condemned thee?" She answers, "No man, Lord." Then Jesus says, "Neither do I condemn thee: go, and sin no more." Men said, "Stone her"; Jesus said, "Save her."

Yes, so much does the Lord care that He left Heaven's glory, emptied Himself and became of no reputation, took upon Himself the form of a servant and became obedient unto death, even the death of the cross. Yes, He went all the way to Calvary and there shed the last drop of His blood, there dipped His soul in Hell, there made His soul an offering for sin, that any who will might be saved.

So great was His love, so much did He care, that even in the midst of His agony He could look down from the cross upon those who were crucifying Him, railing at Him, mocking and jeering Him, and pray, "Father, forgive them; for they know not what they do."

Yes, so much was His concern that He could forget about His own suffering to answer the heartbroken cry of a dying thief on the cross by His side and to say to that poor soul, "To day shalt thou be with me in paradise."

Oh, if you go to Hell, you go over the greatest love this world has ever known; you go in spite of the greatest effort that has ever been made in this universe, relative to anything God had anything to do with—that is, God's effort through Jesus Christ to reach a lost world.

IV. THE LOST IN HELL CARE

Not only do God the Father, God the Holy Spirit and God the blessed Son care, but the lost in Hell care.

You may be surprised to hear me say this, but when Jesus told that story of the rich man in Hell, He told us about his cry for mercy. And when he was informed that he was beyond reach of mercy, now his next cry was, "I pray thee therefore, father, that thou wouldest send him to my father's house: For I have five brethren; that he may testify unto them, lest they also come into this place of torment."

Abraham said, "They have Moses and the prophets; let them hear them."

But this man was not satisfied with that: 'Nay, father Abraham: but if one went unto them from the dead, and told them about Hell, surely they will repent. Won't you let Lazarus go and tell them to repent of their sins and not to come to this place!'

If the lost in Hell could speak while I am preaching, I think they would say, "Preacher, stop them some way! Preacher, warn them somehow! Preacher, tell them not to come to this place!"

Yes, my friends, every soul in Hell is interested in the salvation of the lost upon the earth.

V. THE SAVED IN GLORY CARE

But more than that; the saved in Glory care. Listen to Jesus' precious words: "Likewise, I say unto you, there is joy in the presence of the angels of God over one sinner that repenteth."

Down in Arkansas we used to sing, "There is joy among the angels." But, not realizing it, we sing a lot of songs that are unscriptural. Many of you have sung, "Will there be any stars in my crown?" That is an unscriptural and misleading song. The Bible says nothing about stars in anybody's crown. In fact, there will be mighty few people who will even have a crown. Not all the saved will wear a crown. We sing, "We shall wear a crown in the new Jerusalem," but that too is unscriptural.

This song I mentioned, "There is joy among the angels," is not scriptural. Jesus says nothing about joy among angels. However, He does say, "There is joy in the presence of the angels."

In a measure, no doubt, angels do rejoice, but they do not know how to rejoice when a sinner is saved because they have never been lost. The angels are ministering spirits, sent forth to minister to those who are saved; so their dealings are with saved people.

But there is a crowd yonder in Glory who know what it means to be lost, and they now know how to rejoice when a sinner comes to God. They are the redeemed of God who have trod the way before us, who have been saved and are now in Glory.

You ask, "Do those in Heaven know what is going on down here on the earth?" I believe they do. If not, then what did Paul mean in chapter 12 of Hebrews in that opening verse? After he has called the roll of the Heroes of Faith in chapter 11, starting with Abel, he comes across the centuries telling how the Lord by faith stopped the mouths of lions, quenched the violence of fire, how they lived and fought and suffered; then he said, "Seeing we also are compassed about [completely surrounded] with so great a cloud of witnesses, let us lay aside every weight, and the sin which doth so easily beset us, and let us run with patience the race that is set before us" (Heb. 12:1).

The whole figure is of a Roman arena. We who are here now are on the race course. The race set before us means the marked-out path into which the runner must stay or be disqualified. The Roman arena was a complete circle, with the race course in the middle. And in the grandstands around it, tier upon tier, were the spectators.

Paul said that we are completely surrounded by a veritable cloud of spectators—those who have gone before—and they are looking down upon us. That makes serving the Lord the most romantic thing in all the world!

When I preach the Gospel and stand in this pulpit, or when I plead with a sinner to give his heart to Christ, the greatest thing in the world is to be conscious that I am linked up with the plan of the ages and I have just taken up where those who ran the race before me laid down; now they are looking down upon me as I continue in the task they laid down.

I used to be number four man in the relay race, the hardest place on the team. Why? Because if number one fails, it throws number two and number three behind, and that throws number four behind. If number two fails to make up what number one lost, then number three is handicapped and number four has to make up for all three in front of him. Each man makes the race around the course and passes on to the next one an article that he holds in his hand; the next man grabs it and—away he goes!

One day somebody laid down a task he had been doing for God, somebody finished the course; I have taken it up and am making another lap in the race. Now Paul said, "All around us, like a cloud, they are looking down upon us." Oh, what an incentive to do our dead level best for God!

On the tenth day of December my mother went home to Heaven. Naturally, she thought I was the greatest preacher in all the world. She would get up from her sickbed to hear me preach. For the last ten years of her life she was sick so much of the time, but when I was in reach of her, she never missed a sermon. Now every time I go to the pulpit, I think she hears every word, and that thought thrills me through and through!

The saints of the ages are looking down upon us. There is joy in the presence of the angels of God when a sinner is saved. That crowd of spectators are not only looking down upon us, but they are pulling for us.

I used to play football. My college crowd out yonder in the grandstand would yell, "We want a touchdown! We want a touchdown!" It would thrill us from our toes to the top of our heads as they yelled for their team, as they pulled for us out yonder. That made us do our dead level best, giving every ounce of energy we had.

And when I think how another crowd is pulling for us, how interested they are in the salvation of sinners, I tell you, the most glorious thing on earth is to have a part in God's business. No wonder David said, "I had rather be a doorkeeper in the house of my God, than to dwell in the tents of wickedness" (Ps. 84:10). There is no little job for God, no little job in the service of the Lord.

One day when I was in my study, a man knocked at my door. I bade him enter. Nervously he asked for help. That was in the days of the Depression. "This is the first time I have ever had to ask for help," he apologized.

I am a pretty good judge of people. I can tell when one is on the level. Immediately I felt this man was sincere. So I reached in my pocket and gave him what he asked. When he started out I said, "I am doing this for you in the name of Jesus, my Lord."

That man stopped dead still, turned around, looked at me and said, "That is the first time anybody ever said anything like that to me in my life."

I asked, "Are you a Christian?"

"No, sir. But you never saw anybody want to be any more than I do. Five years ago my precious mother died, and as I sat by her bedside and held her hand, the last words she said were, 'Jake, promise me that you will meet me in Heaven.' I promised her I would. Preacher, for five years I have been doing everything I know to do to be saved. I have mourned over my sins. I have prayed, I have cried, I have begged God to save me. But somehow it seems I can't be saved."

I said, "Listen, fellow! God sent you here today to answer that mother's prayer. Sit down and I can tell you how to be saved."

I took my Bible and showed him the simple, beautiful plan of salvation in Jesus Christ. "Now," I said, "get down on your knees and let's pray."

I got down beside him and put my arm around him as he slipped his around me, and in just a few minutes he began to pray aloud. I waited until he had finished praying; then I prayed. And there on our knees he confessed his sins to God.

I said, "Tell the Lord you will trust Him and that you will receive by faith His promise that to 'as many as received him, to them gave he power to become the sons of God, even to them that believe on his name.'"

He said, "Lord Jesus, the best I know how, I am receiving You by faith."

When he said that, he threw both arms around me and said, "O preacher, it is done! I am saved!"

As he started to leave, he turned around, took me by the hand and said, "Preacher, I may never see you again in this world, and I don't know how to thank you for what you have done for me—but when you get to Heaven, my old mother up there will know how to thank you!"

I said, "Fellow, right now your mother is leading the shouting in Glory!"

Yes, there is joy in Heaven over one sinner who repents. He is not willing that any should perish.

Let me remind you again that a loving God is calling you. The Holy Spirit, the third Person of the Trinity, is seeking, calling, knocking, wooing, convicting and trying to lead you into salvation in Jesus Christ. The blessed Son of God, who died on Calvary's cross, is still standing over a lost world with outstretched arms as He did over Jerusalem, and many times I think I can all but see the tears again raining down His blessed cheeks as He says to a lost world, "Come unto me, all ye that labour and are heavy laden, and I will give you rest."

VI. THE DEVIL ALONE WANTS YOU IN HELL

The lost in Hell are urging lost souls here, "Don't come to this place!" The saved in Glory are pulling for your salvation tonight.

The truth is, only one being in the universe wants you to go to Hell and that is the Devil. And if you go, it will be because you listened to him and turned down or ignored all these other calls, all these other pleas from loving hearts in Heaven and on earth. You will go to Hell in spite of all that they all can do. Oh, don't listen to the Devil! Don't go to Hell!

Yonder in Little Rock one morning a man sat on the back pew in the church who had been coming to the services for a long time. I knew he was under conviction and wanted to be saved. So that morning when he failed to respond to the call, I went back at the close of the service, took him by the hand and said, "Jerry, why didn't you come this morning?"

He stood there trembling. "Brother Hankins, I don't know. I can't describe what goes on inside when you make the call. It seems my heart will pound out of my bosom. I want to come. It seems something pulls me so that I just must come. Then when I start, it seems as if a heavy hand grabs me and holds me in my tracks."

"Jerry, that pull at your heart's string so that your heart almost pounds out of your bosom, that something that grapples with your heart until you can hardly resist running down the aisle—that is God trying to draw you by the Holy Spirit through the Gospel and the prayers of God's people, unto salvation."

Then I said, "Do you know what the heavy hand is, Jerry?"

"I guess it is the Devil."

"Jerry, you don't have to guess. When that conflict is taking place inside, it is the battle of one of the greatest forces in the universe for that soul of yours. The Devil knows that the minute you break loose and turn to Christ, you are lost to him forever, and he is not going to give you up easily. The trouble with you, Jerry, is that you have been listening to the Devil instead of Christ."

He reached over, took me by the hand and said, "Brother Hankins, I have listened to the Devil for the last time! I am coming to Jesus!"

The Devil is the only one in the universe that wants you to go to Hell.

Surely you care about your soul. Won't you repent of your sins and trust Christ to save you? He says, "Let him that is athirst come. And whosoever will, let him take the water of life freely" (Rev. 22:17). He says, "Him that cometh to me, I will in no wise cast out" (John 6:37).

Will you trust Him?

R. A. TORREY
1856-1928

ABOUT THE MAN:

Torrey grew up in a wealthy home, attended Yale University and Divinity School, and studied abroad. During his early student days at Yale, young Torrey became an agnostic and a heavy drinker. But even during the days of his "wild life," he was strangely aware of a conviction that some day he was to preach the Gospel. At the end of his senior year in college, he was saved.

While at Yale Divinity School, he came under the influence of D. L. Moody. Little did Moody know the mighty forces he was setting in motion in stirring young R. A. Torrey to service!

After Moody died, Torrey took on the world-girdling revival campaigns in Australia, New Zealand, England and America.

Like many another giant for God, Torrey shone best, furthest and brightest as a personal soul winner. This one man led 100,000 to Christ in a revival that circled the globe!

Dr. Torrey's education was obtained in the best schools and universities of higher learning. Fearless, quick, imaginative and scholarly, he was a tough opponent to meet in debate. He was recognized as a great scholar, yet his ministry was marked by simplicity.

It was because of his outstanding scholastic ability and evangelistic fervor that Moody handpicked Torrey to become superintendent of his infant Moody Bible Institute. In 1912, Torrey became dean of BIOLA, where he served until 1924, pastoring the Church of the Open Door in Los Angeles from 1915-1924.

Torrey's books have probably reached more people indirectly and helped more people to understand the Bible and to have power to win souls, than the writings of any other man since the Apostle Paul, with the possible exceptions of Spurgeon and Rice. Torrey was a great Bible teacher, but most of all he was filled with the Holy Spirit.

He greatly influenced the life of Dr. John R. Rice.

XII.

God's Blockades on the Road to Hell

R. A. TORREY

My subject tonight is "God's Blockades on the Road to Hell." I have two texts. The first text is II Peter 3:9:

"The Lord is not slack concerning his promise, as some men count slackness; but is longsuffering to us-ward, not willing that any should perish, but that all should come to repentance."

Our second text is John 3:16:

"For God so loved the world, that he gave his only begotten Son, that whosoever believeth in him should not perish, but have everlasting life."

We saw last night and the night before the certainty that there is a Hell and what an awful place Hell is. We saw that Hell is a place of extreme and unceasing bodily suffering; that it is a place of anguish because of haunting, tormenting memories and of unceasing remorse. We saw that it is a place of insatiable and tormenting appetite and desire. We saw that it is a place of unutterable and everlasting shame and contempt. We saw that it is a place of the vilest and most repulsive and most degrading companionships. And we saw that Hell is a world utterly without hope.

But the passages of Scripture I have just read declare that nobody needs to go to Hell, that it is not the will of God that one single man, woman or child should go to that appalling place; that "the Lord is not willing that any should perish, but that all should come to repentance"; that "God so loved the world, that he gave his only begotten Son, that *whosoever* believeth in him *should not perish* but have everlasting life."

God has done, and is doing today, everything in His power to keep men and women out of Hell. If any man or woman in this audience tonight goes to Hell, it will be of your own deliberate choice. It is not God's intention or desire that you should go to Hell, no matter how wicked or unworthy you may have been. God has made the greatest sacrifice in His power to keep you from going there; and God has filled the road to Hell full of obstacles to prevent men and women from going that way. He has blockaded the road to Hell that men and women might turn out from that road, which in their mad folly they are now traveling, into that road that leads to a glorious Heaven. And every really sensible person here will turn back tonight if you have not turned back already.

No man or woman in this audience can go to Hell without surmounting the obstacles which God, in His infinite love, has put in the way of your going there. You must deliberately climb over these obstacles that God in His infinite love has put in the path to Hell if you get there at all. If any man or woman in this audience tonight is lost, it will not be God's fault; it will be no one's fault but your own. God does not wish you to be lost. God longs to have you saved.

We are told distinctly in God's own Word in I Timothy 2:3,4, that "God our Saviour would have all men to be saved, and come to the knowledge of the truth." God is doing everything in His power to bring you to repentance and to bring you to a knowledge of the truth. Of course, if you will not repent, He cannot save you. Of course, if you refuse to come to the knowledge of the truth and shut your eyes to the truth, there is no hope of your salvation. But that will be your own fault.

As Solomon put it many centuries ago, "The way of transgressors is hard" (Prov. 13:15). A great many people are saying today, "The Christian life is so hard." It is not. Christ's "yoke is easy," and His "burden is light" (Matt. 11:30). Experience teaches us that God tells the exact truth when He says, "The way of transgressors is hard" (Prov. 13:15). That path, the path that leads to Hell, is full of obstacles and you cannot continue in it without surmounting one obstacle after another.

I speak to you tonight about some of the obstacles that God has put in the path of sin and eternal ruin.

The first obstacle with which God has blockaded the road to Hell is

The Bible

You cannot get very far in the path of sin without finding the Bible in your way. The Bible is one of the greatest hindrances to sin in the world. With its warnings and with its invitations; with its descriptions of the character and consequences of sin; with its representations of the beauty and the reward of righteousness; with its wonderful pictures of God and of God's love—the Bible is a great obstacle to man's continuance in sin. It is a part, a very important part, of God's blockades on the road to Hell.

The Bible makes men uneasy in sin. They are determined to continue in sin, and the Bible makes them very uneasy in sin. So they hate the Bible because it makes it hard for them to continue in the path that they are determined to continue in, the path which ends in Hell. Men will give you a great many reasons why they object to the Bible, but in ninety-nine cases out of a hundred, if you should trace their objections to the Bible to their real source, you would find that men hate the Bible because it makes them so uneasy in their sins.

Men sometimes say to me, "I object to the Bible because of its filthy stories." But their real objection is not to the filthy stories, of which there are none, but to the uneasiness the Bible causes them in their own filthy lives.

There is not one single filthy story in the Bible. There are stories of sin; stories of the most disgusting sins; stories that speak of sin in all its unvarnished ugliness; stories that put sin in its true colors; stories that make sin hideous; but men's objection to the alleged filthy stories is because the Bible makes them uneasy in their own filthy lives. The Bible makes it hard for you to go on in sin, so you hate it.

The brilliant agnostic Colonel Robert Ingersoll, one of the bitterest enemies the Bible ever had, very frankly said himself on the lecture platform in Chicago when I lived there, that he did not object to the obscene stories in Rabelais (one of the vilest writers that France ever produced), because they were told with an exquisite humor; but that he objected to the obscene stories in the Bible because there was not "a touch of humor" in them. In other words, he did not object to the obscene, but he wanted the obscene to be made funny. But the Bible, thank God, never makes the unclean funny. It makes it hateful; shows it as it really is and makes it hard for men to continue in the unclean.

Therefore, men hate it.

How often a man has been turned back from the path of sin by a single verse from the Bible. Hundreds upon hundreds have been turned out of the path of sin into the path of faith and eternal life by Romans 6:23, "The wages of sin is death; but the free gift of God is eternal life in Christ Jesus our Lord." Thousands have been turned out of the path of sin by Amos 4:12, "Prepare to meet thy God." Tens of thousands have been turned out of the path of sin to eternal life by one of our texts, John 3:16, "For God so loved the world, that he gave his only begotten Son, that whosoever believeth in him should not perish, but have everlasting life." And other thousands by John 6:37, "Him that cometh to me, I will in no wise cast out."

Some years ago a man came into our church in Chicago who had not been in a house of worship for fifteen or sixteen years. He was a rampant infidel. I don't know why he came in that night. I suppose because he saw the crowd coming and was curious to know what was going on.

In my sermon that night I quoted John 6:37, "Him that cometh to me, I will in no wise cast out." It went like an arrow into that man's heart.

When the meeting was over he got up with the crowd and went out and tried to forget that verse, but could not. It kept ringing in his ears, "Him that cometh to me, I will in no wise cast out."

He went to bed but could not sleep. Through the night these words of God kept ringing in his mind, "Him that cometh to me, I will in no wise cast out."

The next day it haunted him at the breakfast table and at work; all day long there was one constant thought ringing in his mind, "Him that cometh to me, I will in no wise cast out."

And it haunted him the next day and the next and the next, and for days and weeks that verse haunted him. But he was bound that he would not come to Christ.

He came back to the street where our church stood. He walked up and down on the sidewalk in front of the church, stamped his foot and cursed the text, but he could not get it out of his mind.

Six weeks passed by, and for six weeks that text haunted him. Then one night he came into our prayer meeting, stood up and said, "Men and women, I was here six weeks ago and heard your minister preach on the text, 'Him that cometh to me, I will in no wise cast out.'" (He was mistaken. That was not my text. I simply quoted the passage in

my sermon. But this verse so impressed him that he thought it was my
text.) "I tried to forget it, but it haunted me night and day. It haunted
me at my meals, it haunted me at my work.

"I came back here and walked up and down and stamped on the
sidewalk in front of your church and said, 'D_____ that text!' but I cannot get rid of it. I have come back tonight to accept the Lord Jesus Christ.
Please pray for me."

We did, and he was saved. One single sentence from God's Word,
one part of a verse, turned him out of the path of unbelief and sin and
ruin, the path that leads to an eternal Hell, into the path of faith and
eternal life.

The second obstacle that God has put in the path of sin is

A Mother's Holy Influence and Teaching

How many there are here tonight who are not as yet Christians, who
have tried even to be infidels, tried to plunge down into the deepest
depths of sin; but your mother's holy influence and Christian teaching
won't let you go the way you wish to.

Sometimes it is only years afterward that a mother's teaching does
its work.

A young man in America who had a godly mother but who went
wrong, went out to Colorado in the silver mining days. He worked in
the mines during the day and gambled during the night, as so many
miners do. But he spent more money gambling than he made in the
mine. One night as he sat at the gaming table he lost his last cent. Then
he took some of his employer's money that he had with him and lost
that. He felt that he was a ruined man.

He arose from the gaming table, went out into the mountains, drew
his revolver, cocked it, held it to his temple and was about to pull the
trigger. Just then a word that his mother had spoken to him years before
came to him, "My son, if you are ever in trouble, think of God." And
there, standing in the cold moonlight with a revolver pressed against
his temple and his finger upon the trigger, he remembered what his
mother had said and dropped the revolver. He dropped on his knees
and cried out to God and was saved. Turned out of the path of perdition into the path of eternal life by a mother's teaching.

A third obstacle that God has put in the path of sin, the path that
leads to eternal ruin and an endless Hell, is

A Mother's Prayers

In the desperate hardness of our hearts we often trample the teachings and memory of our mother's holy influence under foot, but we find it exceedingly hard to get over a mother's prayers. Often at the last moment a man is saved by his mother's prayers.

I had in my church in Chicago a man who stood once outside the tabernacle in the old days with a pitcher of beer in his hand and, as the men came out of the meeting, offered them a free drink. The same man would often come in to the after meetings to disturb the workers and inquirers. He was a hard and desperate man, much feared even by the wicked men of Chicago; but he had a praying mother over in Scotland.

One night when he went home from the meeting where he had caused trouble, in the middle of the night, in answer to the prayers of this godly mother way over in Scotland, he was awakened and saved without getting out of bed. A mother's prayers had proved an insurmountable obstacle to his desperate determination to continue in sin and be eternally lost.

I stand here tonight a saved man instead of being in the other world and utterly lost, because when I was rushing headlong in the path of sin and ruin, my mother's prayers arose and I could not get over them.

I used to think that nobody had anything to do with my salvation, no living being; for I never, before my conversion, heard a sermon that made any very deep impression upon me, and no one ever spoke to me intelligently about accepting Jesus Christ; but I was awakened in the middle of the night and saved all alone by myself. I had gone to bed with no more thought of becoming a Christian than I had of jumping over the moon. In the middle of the night I awakened in an awful horror, jumped out of bed and hurried to my washstand. I opened the drawer to take out of it the instrument that would put an end to my miserable life, but something came upon me as I stood by that open drawer. So I dropped on my knees right there and surrendered to God.

As I say, I thought no man or woman had anything to do with it. But afterwards it came to me that a woman had something to do with it—my mother 427 miles away was praying that I would become a minister of the Gospel. And though I had gotten over sermons, arguments, churches and everything else, I could not get over my mother's prayers.

Do you know why some of you are not in Hell tonight? I will tell you why. Your mother's prayers have kept you out.

A fourth obstacle that God has put in the path of sin, the path that leads to Hell, is

The Sermons We Hear

How many thousands and tens of thousands and hundreds of thousands of men and women have been turned back from sin to God by the sermons they have heard. Some people think in these days that sermons are a waste of time. No indeed. A true sermon, preached in the power of the Holy Ghost, is one of the mightiest powers for God and for righteousness.

A few days ago a man said to me, "I am glad that you are going to speak on 'God's Blockades on the Road to Hell.' It was that sermon that you preached the night that I decided to accept Christ in Zanesville, Ohio."

That night, as I sat upon the platform before beginning my sermon, the leading minister of Zanesville called to my attention a man sitting in the front row. "If that man could be converted, it would pay for your coming to Zanesville, even if there were not another person converted."

This man was a graduate of the Law Department of Michigan University, a man of good parts and promise. He belonged to one of the leading families of Zanesville, but he had gone utterly wrong and was at that particular time in very serious complications because of his sinful life. But that very night when the sermon was ended on the same subject upon which I am preaching to you tonight, he arose and accepted Christ and made a public confession of his acceptance of Christ. He afterwards went to Africa as a foreign missionary and is now an ordained Presbyterian minister. No doubt he is in this audience tonight.

Sometimes a sermon does its work years after it is preached. In my first pastorate I preached one night on "The Parable of the Ten Virgins." One member of my congregation was very much on my heart in connection with that sermon, so I prayed before going to the church that she might be saved. And I thought I had assurance that she would be saved by that sermon.

When I preached and gave the invitation, I fully expected to see her rise, but she made no sign. I went home greatly puzzled, not knowing what to make of it. I said to myself, *I prayed for and fully expected* her conversion, but she is still unsaved. I don't know what to make of it.

Years passed. I had gone to another pastorate. Someone wrote me that this woman had been converted. I revisited the place and called upon her. I said, "I am very glad to hear you have been converted." She replied, "Would you like to know how I was converted?" I said I would. Then she said, "Do you remember preaching a sermon years ago on the ten virgins? I could not get it out of my mind. I felt I must take Christ that night, but I wouldn't. That sermon followed me, and I was converted years afterward."

She was converted by the sermon that I was sure she was going to be converted by, but I did not see it for years.

Many years after that, when Mr. Alexander and I were holding meetings in the big armory in Philadelphia, this woman, who happened to be there, saw the notice of the meeting and came, but the armory was packed. Not a seat was left except on the platform with the ministers. She begged to be admitted, and finally they gave her a seat on the platform.

It so happened that that night I read for my Scripture lesson the parable of the ten virgins. The next day this woman called at our home in Philadelphia and told me how she had heard me the night before, how difficult she had found it to get a seat and how she had been given a seat on the ministers' platform.

I said to her, "Did you notice what passage of Scripture I read last night?"

"Did I?" she exclaimed. "Why, when you read the passage, I almost jumped out of my seat!"

A boy of ten once heard John Farrel preach on the text, "If any man love not the Lord Jesus Christ, let him be anathema" (I Cor. 16:22). The boy was not converted. He lived to be ninety-six years of age and still was unconverted. But one day this old man of ninety-six sat in a chair in the sunlight and got to thinking of his past. The memory of that sermon came to his mind, so he said to himself, *The preacher said, "If any man love not the Lord Jesus Christ, let him be anathema, accursed." I don't love the Lord Jesus, so I am under a curse.* And sitting there he accepted the Lord Jesus Christ—saved by a sermon heard eighty-six years before!

Another obstacle that God has put in the path of sin, that leads to ruin and an eternal Hell, is

A Sunday School Teacher's Influence and Teaching

Many here tonight were brought to Jesus Christ by the influence and teaching and prayers of a faithful Sunday school teacher. Let me say to you that a Sunday school teacher who is faithful is one of God's best instruments on earth for the salvation of the perishing.

In the first Sunday school that Mr. Moody had in Chicago, there was a class of very unruly girls. Nobody could manage them. As a rule, boys are far harder to manage than girls, but when girls are bad, they are far harder to manage than boys.

Mr. Moody tried teacher after teacher, but everyone failed with that class. Finally he found a young man who did manage them. One day this young man came into the store where Mr. Moody worked (before Mr. Moody went out of business) and said, "Mr. Moody"; and as he said it he burst into tears.

Mr. Moody replied, "What is the matter?"

"Oh," the young man replied, "the doctor says I have consumption and must go to California at once, or die." He sobbed as if his heart would break.

Mr. Moody tried to comfort him. "You have no reason to feel so bad about that. You probably won't die; you may get well out there in California. Even if you do die, you have nothing to be afraid of, for you are a Christian."

"Oh," he said, "it is not that, Mr. Moody. I am perfectly willing to die. I am not afraid to die, but here I have had this Sunday school class all these years, and not one of them is saved. And I am going off to leave them, every one unsaved," and he sobbed like a child.

Mr. Moody replied, "Oh, we can fix that. I will get a carriage, and we will drive around and visit them one by one, and you can lead them to Christ."

He got a carriage and took that pale teacher around to the homes of the girls, and he talked with them about Christ until he was so tired that he had to be taken home. The next day they went out again; and they went out every day until every one of those young women but one was saved.

The night before he was to leave for California they all met for a prayer meeting. One after another led in prayer, and at last the one unsaved girl in the whole company broke down and led in prayer, too, then accepted Christ.

The young man left by a very early train the next morning, and Mr. Moody went down to the station to see him off. As they were waiting for the train, one by one the girls dropped in without any pre-arrangement, until every one of the young women was there. He spoke a few words of farewell to them, and as the train pulled out of the station, he stood upon the back platform of the car with his finger pointing Heavenward, telling his Sunday school class to meet him in Heaven.

The sixth obstacle that God has thrown in the path of sin, that leads to ruin and to an eternal Hell, is

A Kind Word or Act

A lady friend of mine was standing in a window looking out on Bleecker Street in New York. A man who had gone into the depths through drink came down the street. He had once been a man of high social standing and of political influence; he had once been the mayor of one of our largest southern cities. But drink had brought him down until now he was a penniless drunkard on the streets of New York.

He had made up his mind to commit suicide that night and was then on his way to the river to drown himself. But going down Bleecker Street he thought, *I have spent a lot of money in that saloon, and I certainly can stand the man off for one more drink before I die.* He went in, asked for a drink and told the man he had no money to pay for it.

Instead of giving him the drink, the man came around from behind the bar, caught hold of him and kicked him into the gutter. My friend, looking out of the window, saw the poor wretch picking himself up out of the gutter. She crossed over and helped him arise, and with her handkerchief wiped the mud off his clothing and said, "Come over in there [pointing across the street]. It is bright and warm there, and you will be welcome." The poor wretch went over and sat down behind the stove.

Soon the people commenced to come in, and the meeting began. One after another gave their testimony of the saving power of Jesus Christ. The lady who had brought him in sang very sweetly and told the story of how she too had been saved.

When the meeting was over, that lady came to speak to him about his soul. His heart was deeply touched, and he accepted Christ that night.

He was a man of considerable ability and soon got a position, then a better one, and finally was made manager of one of the largest publishing houses in New York City.

One day, after he was up in the world again, he came to my friend and said, "I have some friends down at the hotel, and I want you to meet them."

She went with him to the hotel; and after introducing her to a fine-looking, middle-aged woman and another fine-looking young lady, he said, "This is my wife and daughter." They were beautiful and refined, cultured ladies whom he had left when he had drifted to New York and gone down to the very verge of Hell. But a kind act and word of invitation to accept Christ had turned him out of the path that leads to perdition, to an eternal Hell, into the path that leads to endless glory, when he was within one step of Hell.

Oh, let each of us who are already saved go out as missionaries of God's grace and block the path of sinful men and women with kindly deeds and words of love, and thus turn them into the path of righteousness and of faith in Jesus Christ, the path that leads to life eternal.

Another obstacle that God puts in the path of sin and ruin, that leads to an eternal Hell, is

The Holy Spirit and His Work

You and I have experienced it time and time again. When right in the midst of a carousal, a strange feeling has come in, an unrest and dissatisfaction with the life you are living, a longing for something better, memories of home, church, mother, the Bible and God. What did it mean? The Holy Spirit was doing His work in your heart.

A man in England was connected with one of its noble families. He himself was not a nobleman, but his uncle was an Earl and childless, and this man was the heir to the title and the estate.

But this uncle became so disgusted with the wild career of his nephew that he married late in life and had an heir, so this man lost the earldom. He was a thoroughgoing worldling. In one year he made a proposal of marriage to eighteen different women and was accepted by every one of them—but married none of them. He was a wild, reckless spendthrift.

One day, with another desperate companion of like mind, he rode at breakneck speed through the narrow street of an English village where there was a sudden turn at the end and where it meant almost certain accident, if not death, for men to ride through as they did. When they reached the corner, he made the turn successfully, but his companion was thrown and killed. Still he went on in his wild career. He married and had a son. This son had grown to manhood. Still he pursued his godless career.

One night he was playing cards at a table in his hunting lodge in Scotland, playing with his own son. As he sat there playing cards, suddenly the voice of God's Spirit spoke in his heart. An awful sense of misery overwhelmed him. He thought he was going to die.

He sprang up from the table, threw down his cards, rushed to his room and flung himself on his bed. The maid came in to make a fire. A great longing came into his heart to get up and kneel down and pray, but he thought, *I cannot do it with someone in the room.* But his misery became so great that he did arise, fall on his knees and cry out to God for mercy. He cried to God for Christ's sake to forgive his sins; and God heard him and did save him right then and there.

That man was Brownlow North who did such a great work for God in Ireland and Scotland in 1859 and 1860.

Last night while you were in some den of wickedness, there came into your heart a sense of self-disgust, a longing for something better, a calling to a purer life. What was it? God's Spirit.

As you sit here in this place tonight, there is a strange stirring in your heart right now; you are saying to yourself while I am speaking, *I wonder if I had better not become a Christian tonight.* You have almost reached the determination to stand up and accept Christ as soon as I give out the invitation. What is it? God is sending His Spirit into your heart to blockade the road to Hell.

Listen to God's Spirit tonight. Yield to the Spirit of God and accept Jesus Christ tonight. That act means eternal life and eternal glory; to say "no" to God's Spirit means an eternal Hell.

There is one other obstacle that God has put in the path of sin, the road that leads to an eternal Hell, and that is

The Cross of Christ

No man can get very far down the path of sin and ruin before he sees looming before him a cross. On that cross there hangs a Man, a Divine Man, the Son of Man and the Son of God. Oh, look at Him as He hangs there with the nails in His hands and feet. What agony there is in His face! What suffering racks that body. See the blood stains upon that back. See the blood on His face that flows from the wounds where the crown of thorns has pierced His brow. Those lips are moving. Listen—what is He saying? "It is for you that I suffer all this. I am bearing all this for you. I am dying for you. I am being wounded for your transgressions, bruised for your iniquities, the chastisement of your peace is upon Me."

Oh, men and women, listen! In the pathway of every man and every woman here tonight stands the cross with Christ upon it, and if you go out of this auditorium to continue in sin, you must needs go over the cross and trample under foot the crucified form of the Son of God. Is your love for sin so great that you are willing to do that? Are you so dead to every appeal to reason and to gratitude that you are willing to do that?

I heard once of a godly old man who had a worthless son. That son was far more anxious to make money than he was for honor or right or anything else. He determined to go into that infamous business in which there is much money but which no self-respecting man will undertake—the liquor business. Any man who is willing to coin money out of rum selling, whether legalized or bootlegging, is willing to coin money out of the tears of brokenhearted wives, out of the groans and sighs of drunkards' sons and daughters, out of the hearts' blood of their fellowmen, for this infernal rum traffic is sending thousands every year to premature graves.

Well, this man of whom I speak was so far lost to self-respect that he was going to open a saloon. His father was ashamed and nearly brokenhearted. He pled with his boy: "My son, you bear an honored name which has never been disgraced before. Don't disgrace it now by putting it up over a saloon." But the son was so bent on money-making that he would not listen to his father's voice.

The day came for the opening of the saloon. The father was about the first one on hand. He stood outside the door of the saloon, and he stepped up to every man that approached the door and told him of the misery that came from strong drink and warned of the consequences of entering such a place as that. One after another turned away.

The son wondered why he had no customers. When he looked out of the window to see if he could find the reason, he saw his father outside turning his customers away.

In great anger he came outside and said, "Father, go home! You are ruining my business."

The father replied, "I cannot help it, my boy. I won't have my name dishonored by this business. And if you are bent on going on with it, I will stand here and warn every man that approaches not to enter your door."

Finally the son lost control of himself and struck his aged father.

The father turned to him without the least anger and said, "My son, strike me if you will; kill me if you will, but no man shall enter your saloon unless he goes over my dead body."

Oh, men and women, listen! No man or woman here tonight will ever enter Hell unless you go over the dead body of Jesus Christ. No man or woman here will go out of this place tonight, refusing to accept Christ, without trampling under foot the form of Him who was crucified on the cross of Calvary for you; without trampling under foot the One who was wounded for your transgressions and bruised for your iniquities and upon whom the chastisement of your peace was laid.

Oh, men and women! In His wonderful love to you, God has piled mountain high the obstacles that lie in the path of sin that you are so persistently pursuing and that ends in an everlasting Hell. Don't try longer to surmount those obstacles. Turn back tonight. Yield to God. Turn out of the path of unbelief that leads to an eternal Hell and turn into the path that leads to eternal glory by accepting Jesus Christ as your personal Saviour.

(From the book, *Soul-Winning Sermons,* Vol. II.)

TOM MALONE
1915-

ABOUT THE MAN:

Tom Malone was converted and called to preach at the same moment! At an old-fashioned bench, the preacher took his tear-stained Bible and showed Tom Malone how to be saved. He accepted Christ then and there. Arising from his knees in the Isbell Methodist Church near Russellville, Alabama, he shook the circuit pastor's hand; and this bashful nineteen-year-old farm boy announced: "I know the Lord wants me to be a preacher."

Backward, bashful and broke, yet Tom borrowed five dollars, took what he could in a cardboard suitcase and left for Cleveland, Tennessee. Immediately upon arrival at Bob Jones College, Malone heard a truth that totally dominated his life and labors for the Lord ever after—soul winning!

That day he won his first soul! The green-as-grass Tom, a new convert himself, knew nothing of soul-winning approaches or techniques. He simply asked the sinner, "Are you a Christian?" No. In a few minutes that young man became Malone's first convert.

Since that day, countless have been his experiences in personal evangelism.

Mark it down: Malone began soul winning his first week in Bible college. And he has never lost *the thirst* for it, *the thrill* in it, nor *the task* of it since. Pastoring churches, administrating schools, preaching across the nation have not deterred Tom Malone from this mainline ministry.

It is doubtful if young Malone ever dreamed of becoming the man he is today. He is now Doctor Tom Malone, is renowned in fundamental circles for his wise leadership and great preaching, is pastor of the large Emmanuel Baptist Church of Pontiac, Michigan, Founder and President of Midwestern Baptist Schools, and is eagerly sought as speaker in large Bible conferences from coast to coast.

Dr. John R. Rice often said that Dr. Tom Malone may be the greatest gospel preacher in all the world today!

XIII.

There Is a Hell

TOM MALONE

"And if thy right eye offend thee, pluck it out, and cast it from thee: for it is profitable for thee that one of thy members should perish, and not that thy whole body should be cast into hell."—Matt. 5:29.

Hell is an awful fact. Jesus said that there is a Hell. If one were to go through just the book of Matthew and read what Jesus said about Hell and contemplate His many statements about it, it would revolutionize his heart, thoughts and ministry. It would make greater soul winners out of every layman and greater preachers out of us who are called to preach the Word of God. It would also bring about a great revival.

A young lady came to us several years ago before the mid-week prayer meeting and said, "Brother Tom, I have been praying that God would give me a passion for souls and do something for me tonight."

"What do you want God to do for you?" I asked.

"I would like for Him to impress upon my heart afresh and anew the fact of an awful Hell where sinners shall be separated forever from God and Christian loved ones if they continue to reject Jesus Christ."

That night at a mid-week prayer meeting and Bible study, where about 200 had met together to fellowship, a visiting preacher in my church stood up and said, "Men and women, tonight I have been led of God's Spirit to speak on the subject of Hell." I had never before heard such a red-hot sermon on that subject. The young lady came at the close of the service and said, "God has done something for me tonight, and I doubt that I shall ever be the same."

For several years I observed her life and work in the church. And it is true—she was never the same. Time and time again she walked down the aisle leading some sinner by the hand, a man or a woman or a boy or a girl whom she had witnessed to and won for Jesus and whose soul had been saved from Hell through her prayers, her tears and her consecrated life.

Yes, Christians need to read again and again what Jesus said about Hell. It must be an awful place for Jesus to use such strong language. He said, *"If thy right hand offend thee, cut it off, and cast it from thee."* It would be better to go through life one-handed than it would to have two hands in this life and then go to Hell. He said, *"If thy right eye offend thee, pluck it out, and cast it from thee."* It would be better to be one-eyed than to go through life with two good eyes and lose your soul and go to Hell forever.

Now Jesus is good authority. You say, "I believe what Jesus said." But do you? No one can ever say he believes the words of Jesus and deny that there is a Hell, a lake of fire burning with brimstone, where the beast, the false prophet are, and every sinner is separated from God, alienated from His grace and mercy forever throughout all eternity.

Five statements seem to come forth on the subject of Hell as I read what Jesus said about it.

I. THE FACT OF HELL

Jesus says there is a Hell. Bible writers teach it. The Word of God, beyond any shadow of a doubt, teaches that there is a place of eternal torment for Christ-rejecters.

Now there are many who do not believe in Hell. Recently someone in my acquaintance who was living in sin and without God, committed suicide. That person evidently did not believe in Hell. How could one commit suicide, murder his own soul and go out into eternity unprepared if he really believed there was an eternal Hell?

People who persist in sin, continue in their wickedness, continue to harden their hearts against God, must not really believe in Hell. If they did, they would not pursue a path that they know will inevitably lead their soul to Hell.

I fear many Christians do not really believe with a deep-down conviction in their hearts that there is a Hell. How can a Christian believe there is a Hell and never shed one tear over the lost? How can a Christian really believe there is a Hell and not try to win one soul for Jesus Christ?

Many preachers, I feel, take this matter very lightly, look over it and do not preach on it very much. Why? Is it because they, deep down in their hearts, do not believe in a Hell as the Bible teaches it?

Someone might say, "Well, there is so much confusion on the subject. There are different terms used. The Bible speaks of Hell, and it speaks of a lake of fire. What is the difference?" The difference is the same difference between a jail and a penitentiary.

Revelation, chapter 20, teaches that on the judgment day death and Hell shall give up their dead. Death shall give up the body, Hell shall give up the spirit, and the unsaved shall stand at the judgment bar and face the Judge of all the earth. Then they shall receive their eternal punishment and penalty and be assigned, not to a jail but to a penitentiary, which is the lake of fire.

One who violates the law today and is taken into custody is placed in jail only until his judgment is set. This is exactly the way God deals with sinners. Hell today is merely the jail. Later the lake of fire will be an eternal penitentiary. God does not judge people yet, because all the score has not been added up. The results of their evil deeds have not yet come in. The final tabulation on all their wicked influence is still being accumulated. But God will assign them to the penitentiary on judgment day.

A few days ago I was in the hospital visiting an unsaved lady. We gave her the Gospel and did all we could do. When we were about to decide there was no more to be said and we should leave the matter up to this person, a thought occurred: *This lady may die! And if she dies as she is now, she is forever lost.* The Spirit of God seemed to say to us, "Hang on. Keep trying. Keep pleading. Keep praying."

We reached out our hand and asked the lady to shake our hand if she would trust Christ. One in a hospital bed in the same room looked at us as if we were a fool. This seemed to embarrass the lost one. It did embarrass us. But a soul was at stake.

Finally the lady looked at me and said:

> Brother Tom, I have a five-year-old boy. The other night when the tornadoes were coming through this section, my little boy got down on his knees and prayed this simple childlike prayer:
> "Dear God, don't let the tornadoes come through and kill people, because if the people who are unsaved would get killed, they will go to Hell. My mother is not saved. My mother would go to Hell if she gets killed. O God, don't let people go to Hell."

Brother Tom, I have never been able to get that little childlike prayer off my mind. I will accept Christ now. I will be saved now.

She gripped my hand while her tears fell and while I thanked God that another precious soul had escaped the eternal fires of an everlasting Hell.

II. JESUS TAUGHT THAT HELL IS ETERNAL

In Matthew 25:41 Jesus said these words, *"Depart from me, ye cursed, into everlasting fire, prepared for the devil and his angels."* Jesus said that Hell was a place of everlasting fire.

In verse 46 He said, *"And these shall go away into everlasting punishment: but the righteous into life eternal."* Jesus taught that the Hell of a sinner and the punishment of a sinner are everlasting.

Some try to teach annihilation, saying that Hell is not eternal, but the Bible does not teach that. It says Hell, or the lake of fire, has no end, that the smoke of their torment will ascend up forever and forever.

The word used for *eternal* in relationship to the sinner's Hell is the same word used for *eternal* in relationship to the Christian's everlasting life. If Hell is not eternal, neither is the spiritual life of the child of God. How absurd, how foolish, for one to say that Hell is not eternal when Jesus taught that it was!

Some say, "It isn't right for a sinner to suffer throughout all eternity for a short life of sin."

In the upper peninsula of the state of Michigan, a man murdered a beautiful young schoolteacher twenty-one years old, with no cause, no reason, except the sin in his wicked heart. He attacked and murdered an innocent young girl. That man was sentenced to life in prison.

Now, with one sudden blow of a club, in a second's time, he took a life. You say it is wrong for that man to suffer all the rest of his life for what he did in one second. I say it is not wrong. He got what was coming to him. He deserved life in prison. In fact, he deserved worse. He is fortunate that he did not get the greater punishment—the death penalty.

A man can commit enough sin in a short lifetime, commit enough sin even in one second, to outrage an infinite and holy God. And it is commensurate with God's holiness and justice to let a sinner suffer forever in Hell for the sins of a lifetime.

The fact of the matter is, the sin that damns the soul is the sin of unbelief. God's Word says, *"He that believeth on him is not condemned: but he that believeth not is condemned already, because he hath not believed in the name of the only begotten Son of God."*

Sin is an awful thing. Men in this generation have come to look upon it lightly. But sin is a violation of God's law. Sin is a coming short of His glory. Sin is an antagonism against His will. Sin is the depravity of the human heart. Sin outrages and enrages a holy God. Sin must and will be punished. And sinners who reject God's Son will suffer for it forever.

III. HELL, A PLACE OF AWFUL REMORSE

Jesus clearly taught this in Luke 16 where He gave the record of the rich man in Hell being in torments. There when he begged for water and for someone to be sent to his five lost brothers, Abraham said to him, *"Son, remember that thou in thy lifetime receivedst thy good things,"* Abraham referred him back to his lifetime and said, *"Son, remember."* Hell will be a place of awful memory.

While visiting in the Holy Land, as our guide pointed to a deep valley running north and south in Jerusalem, known in Bible times as the Valley of Hinnom or the Valley of Gehenna, he said, "This is Hell."

In a sense, he was correct; for this is the valley Jesus used to illustrate Hell a number of times in the New Testament. In fact, one of the Greek words used in the New Testament for *Hell* is *gehenna*. Out of the twelve times it is used, Jesus Himself used it eleven times. He spoke of Hell as being a place where the fire is not quenched and where the worm dieth not. Some students believe that when Jesus said, ". . . where their worm dieth not . . .," He perhaps was referring to the memory of the unsaved in Hell.

This Valley of Hinnom in the Old Testament times was used by at least two of the more wicked kings of the children of Israel as a place of worship to the false god Molech. Here human sacrifices were made, and here the garbage of the city was dumped. Fires burned there continually. Jesus used this as an illustration of Hell, "where their worm dieth not" and where one's memory will never die.

Man will remember. It could easily be true that he will remember every sermon he heard preached, every prayer prayed in his behalf, every invitation he heard sung. If the only hell a sinner had was the hell of memory, it would still be awful.

I think of Agrippa who said to the Apostle Paul, *"Almost thou persuadest me to be a Christian."* In a burning infernal Hell, today he screams and cries, "Almost! Almost! I was nearly saved! I could have escaped all this and gone to Heaven, but I would not believe!"

I think of the lost thief and his awful memory—when in Hell he cries out, "I was almost saved! So near was I to Jesus that I could hear the dripping blood and the agonizing groans of His suffering. Yet I railed upon Him and would not trust Him!"

Memory! I think of the memory of wicked sinners who went on hardening their hearts and are in Hell today. Hell will be a place of awful remorse.

IV. JESUS TAUGHT THAT HELL IS A PLACE OF AWFUL ASSOCIATIONS

In Revelation 21:8 is what we might call the Roll Call of Hell: *"But the fearful, and unbelieving, and the abominable, and murderers, and whoremongers, and sorcerers, and idolaters, and all liars, shall have their part in the lake which burneth with fire and brimstone: which is the second death."*

Here we read of eight different classes of sinners who will be there. What an awful association! Read it. Notice it. If you are lost and you go to Hell, these are the people you will spend eternity with. This will be your crowd. These will be your associates.

I recently read of a young lady who, having graduated from college, went home for the summer. The first week at home she, with her Christian parents, attended a revival campaign. Her parents had prayed that she might be saved. Throughout the meeting she was under conviction but would not trust the Lord.

Following the revival, she was making a trip with her father on the train. He stepped out of the car for a moment; and when he came back, he found her in tears.

She said, "Daddy, let's get out of here. Let's go into the smoker."

"No, darling, it's filled with smoke and men. You don't want to go in there."

"Oh," she said, "but daddy, we must get out of here!"

He followed her into the smoker. As he lifted up the window on the train to let some fresh air in, she said, "O daddy, while you were gone, the men back in the other car used such vulgar language that it shocked my modesty. They are such terrible men!" Having said that, she dropped her head on her father's shoulder and began to cry.

He said, "Darling, unless you get saved, these are the kind of people you are going to spend eternity with in Hell."

"Daddy, I don't want to go with that crowd. I want to be a Christian," she said. And she trusted Christ as her personal Saviour.

Dear friend, the broad road that leads to Hell is filled with wicked people—the fearful, the unbelieving, the abominable, the murderers, the whoremongers, the sorcerers, the idolaters and all liars. This is the association you will have forever in the lake of fire which burneth with brimstone. May God help you to think on your way and to realize that you are in the wrong crowd and on the wrong road.

V. THE BIBLE TEACHES IT IS EASY TO GO TO HELL

All you have to do to go to Hell is do nothing. All you have to do is to drift downstream, take the road of least resistance and follow the crowd.

Jesus clearly taught that there are two roads of life—a narrow road that leads to life everlasting and only a few find it; and a broad road that leads to destruction and many travel therein.

The broad road is an easy road. It is the road of popularity. It is the road of worldly pleasure. It is the road of evil companions. It is the road of ease. It is the road of luxury. It is the road of sin and lust. It is easy to go to Hell—just follow the crowd. And the Bible says most people are going there.

It is the few who are on the narrow road that leads to life everlasting.

Some years ago I read where an old preacher told of how he stood one day on the banks of the Niagara River a little above the Niagara Falls and saw an eagle floating down the Niagara on the body of a dead, frozen lamb. As the eagle floated along on the dead carcass, the old preacher said to himself, *Eagle, if you are going to go, go now. If you stay on that lamb, your feet will become frozen. In a moment when you seek to fly away, you will find that it is too late, and over the falls you will go to destruction.*

The eagle remained on the frozen body and floated on lazily toward the falls. The preacher put his hands to his mouth and shouted, "Go away, old eagle! If you ever expect to escape, go now!" But the eagle did not hear, of course, and in a moment the preacher saw him disappear over the falls and go to his death, standing on the brink, as it were, of eternity.

In the closing of this age of grace nearing the coming of the Lord, approaching the day of God's awful judgment, I cry to you, "Come now into the ark of safety! Leave your sins! Come to Jesus Christ and trust Him."

May God help you to decide for Jesus now.

> Loved ones will weep o'er my silent face,
> Dear ones will clasp me in sad embrace,
> Shadows and darkness will fill the place,
>   Five minutes after I die.
>
> Faces that sorrow I will not see,
> Voices that murmur will not reach me,
> But where, oh, where will my spirit be
>   Five minutes after I die?
>
> Quickly the years of my life have flown,
> Gathering treasures I thought my own,
> There I must reap from the seed I have sown
>   Five minutes after I die.
>
> Naught to repair the good I lack,
> Fixed to the goal of my chosen track,
> No room to repent; no turning back,
>   Five minutes after I die.
>
> Now I can stifle convictions stirred,
> Now I can silence the Voice oft heard,
> Then the fulfillment of God's sure Word,
>   Five minutes after I die.
>
> Mated for aye with my chosen throng,
> Long is eternity, O so long,
> Then woe is me if my soul be wrong,
>   Five minutes after I die.
>
> Oh, what a fool — hard the word, but true
> Passing the Saviour with death in view,
> Doing a deed I can ne'er undo
>   Five minutes after I die.
>
> If I am flinging a fortune away,
> If I am wasting salvation's day,
> "Just is my sentence," my soul shall say,
>   Five minutes after I die.
>
> God help you to choose! your eternal state
> Depends on your choice, you dare not wait;
> You must choose now; it will be too late
>   Five minutes after you die.

—Author Unknown

XIV.

Why Good People Go to Hell

FRED BROWN

(Preached at Landmark Baptist Temple, Cincinnati, 1971)

In this parable we will soon read, these two men represent to me the attitudes of heart with which people go to church on Sunday morning.

There are about 22 million people in church in America this morning; there will be about 2 million tonight and about 750,000 on Wednesday night. And there are two attitudes of heart with which people go to church, even in churches like this one and mine in Chattanooga.

Some people go saying, "Well, I got everything I need. . . ." and they go just to grace the audience with their august presence. They feel a need for nothing; they are as good or better than anybody else.

If you go to church feeling that way, you will come away just like you went. You will get nothing. But if you go realizing your shortcomings and expecting a blessing, then you will get it.

If you come in here spiritually proud, you will go out the same way. But if you come in here as a suppliant, as one who feels his need, you will go away blessed.

Now in this 18th chapter of Luke we read:

"And he [Jesus] *spake this parable unto certain which trusted in themselves that they were righteous, and despised others:* [They kind of looked down their noses on everybody else.] *Two men went up into the temple to pray* [Someone has facetiously said that one went to pray and one went to brag.]; *the one a Pharisee. . . ."*

Nobody, in any age, of any sect, was better than the Pharisee of Christ's day, morally speaking. So straight-laced were these that they leaned over backwards. They had 613 different laws and prohibitions which they heaped upon themselves to show their ability to keep the law. I mean, they stood in a class by themselves. They represented the very highest achievement of man in the flesh.

"...*and the other a publican.*"

The publican of Christ's day was at the bottom of the totem pole of humanity. One could have scoured the earth and not come up with a bigger rascal. They were renegade Jews sold out to collect the excess taxes imposed upon their own people by a foreign power, leaders of the grosser sinners. The very best and the very worst you can imagine went up to the Temple to pray.

"*The Pharisee stood and prayed thus with himself, God,* [He started out fine, but that is the last time God is mentioned. From there on he began to lift up perpendicular pronouns] *I thank thee, that I am not as other men are, extortioners, unjust, adulterers. . . .* "

He wasn't any of these things; he was telling the truth. Evidently praying with his eyes open, he looked around over the crowd, and seeing some who were guilty of these things, he was calling their number. Can't you see these old sinners in the audience begin to turn red and duck their heads? He had been reading somebody's mail! Boy, he was hitting some right on the head in that prayer! Then he looked over and saw the publican.

"*. . . or even as this publican. I fast twice in the week. I give tithes of all that I possess.*"

Quite a prayer, wasn't it? Five perpendicular pronouns. Exactly the same number the Devil lifted up when he tried to take God's place on the throne, in the 14th chapter of Isaiah—five I's.

"*And the publican, standing afar off, would not lift up so much as his eyes unto heaven, but smote upon his breast, saying, God be merciful to me a sinner.*"

Then Jesus said something that must have thrown that crowd into a tizzy:

"*I tell you, this man went down to his house justified rather than the other: for every one that exalteth himself shall be abased; and he that humbleth himself shall be exalted.*"

My! He dropped a bomb on that crowd! This is contrary to all human thinking. Everybody thinks good folks go to Heaven and bad folks go to Hell. But Jesus is saying that the bad man went to Heaven and the good man went to Hell. That really must have been a shock.

WHAT A GOOD MAN THE PHARISEE WAS!

Now, it won't strain me at all to prove that this good man in this parable is better than anybody I am preaching to this morning—I won't even have to work up a sweat! How good was this good man?

First, the Pharisee could thank God he wasn't an adulterer.

You say, "You don't intend to insinuate . . .?" No, I don't. "Well, do you mean to imply . . .?" Nothing. I'm not implying anything about you, just stating the fact that this man could look right up into the face of God and declare that as far as this dirty word is concerned, he was innocent.

But before you start to jump to any conclusions or make any decisions about yourself, let me remind you that the Lord Jesus interpreted that word in the New Testament. He said that anybody who thought an evil thought was as guilty as if he had committed the deed.

Now, with all the rottenness loose in this world today, with the billions being spent on pornography, drugs, dirty movies, filthy books and with every other avenue of communication being directed in this direction to pollute and to drag the minds of people into the gutters and into the streets of the cities of this nation, how many under the onslaught of this filth today can stand up, look God in the face and say, "I have never had a dirty thought"? How many could?

But even if you could honestly say that, it wouldn't save you. This man could say it—and he went to Hell. So it takes more than purity of life to get one into Heaven.

And those who think they are saved simply because they are moral in character had better think again. I see people trying to go to Heaven the way this Pharisee tried to go, who don't have any morals. How in the name of Heaven do they expect to make it **without** morals, when this fellow didn't make it **with** morals!

Now a Christian ought to be pure in his life. You should keep your mind out of the gutter. You should fill it so full of the Word of God and thoughts of Christ that you don't have time for the filth of this world. But if all you have to boast of is that you are clean morally, you just don't have enough, brother, sister. Here was a moral man who went to Hell.

Then, the Pharisee was honest in business. He wasn't an extortioner.
He didn't misrepresent his products. He didn't put shavings in his corn-
flakes, nor sawdust in his coffee, nor sand in his sugar. When he weighed
out a pound, it was a pound; when he measured off a yard, it was a
yard. And he didn't weigh his thumb with every piece of meat he put
on the scales. When he worked for a man, he gave him an honest day's
work. He didn't hide out on the boss, nor goof off. When he paid an
employee, he gave him an honest day's wages.

This fellow, this Pharisee, could look back over his life, look everybody
in the face and say, "I am level with all men. I have nothing to be
ashamed of. I have treated others as I would like them to treat me."

Could you make such a boast this morning? Have you always truthful-
ly represented things you sold? Have you always given an honest day's
work and never once goofed off, never once hid out on the boss? Have
you always given back change when you were given too much? Can
you say that in all your dealings throughout all your life, "I don't have
one blot on my conscience"? This man could. Yet he went to Hell.

So this idea of being saved by the Golden Rule is just for the birds.
This man lived up to the Golden Rule—and perished. No one is saved
by the Golden Rule.

Now a Christian ought to be honest, so honest that he would suffer
himself to be defrauded before he would defraud a person. But if all
one has to boast of is that he has been honest, then he just doesn't
have enough to boast about, because they won't get him to Heaven.

This Pharisee had absolute integrity in his business according to Jesus'
words here. He was highly respected. When he walked down the street,
everyone in the community could look at him and say: "My! If my son
would just grow up to be a fine, upstanding, religious, honest man like
that, how happy I would be!"

Some folks think they are going to Heaven because they have a good
reputation before their families, or in the community. You know, you
can be voted the community's citizen most likely to succeed; you can
win the loving cup; everyone can think well of you, applaud you, pin
medals on you—and still go to Hell.

You are not saved by what people think about you but what God
thinks about you. And God looks down beneath the veneer of outward
appearance and sees a black, sinful heart. You can fool everybody in
the world except God. So you are not saved by your reputation. This
man had a great reputation—but he was lost.

This Pharisee could find nothing wrong with himself. He went off in a corner, set himself there, walked away and left himself sitting there and went over to the other corner and stood there and examined himself. (That's a pretty good trick if you can do it!) He stood there looking at himself. And the more he looked, the more impressed he became with himself. *"Well, look at me! Why, do you know, I don't know anybody exactly like me!"* He got so carried away with himself that finally he drew a line and put everybody in the world on one side of it and himself on the other and said, "I thank God I'm not like anybody!" He thought he was the only one in the world!

What does that prove? That he examined himself.

You will always come out with a record like that if you examine yourself. Big men and prominent women all over this nation walk down aisles, stand in front, look up at me with big, wide-eyed innocence; and when I ask, "Are you ready to confess your sins?" this is the answer:

"Well, I have never done anything wrong."

"You mean you are not a sinner?"

"No, sir. I'm all right."

"Go back to your seat then. You are too good to be saved."

If you are not a sinner, you can't get saved. Jesus didn't die to save good folks. He died to save bad folks. He didn't come to call the righteous to repentance, but sinners. "They that are whole need not a physician; but they that are sick" (Luke 5:31). And if you don't qualify as a Hell-deserving sinner, you don't even qualify as a candidate for salvation. Since you are too good to go to Heaven, then you will just have to go to Hell.

And the reason this Pharisee didn't find anything wrong was because he examined himself. Had he allowed the Spirit of God to take the searching Scriptures and focus them into his black heart, he wouldn't have come out bragging about one thing.

When God does the searching, He knocks all the brag out. Not one iota of brag is left when one has been searched of God. When He turns His truth into our black hearts, we come out, not bragging about what we are, how good we are, but with a cry for the mercy of God.

This man was religious—not Christian but religious. Everybody has religion, even atheists like Madalyn Murray, who started a church for atheists. They even now have a Dial-a-Prayer for atheists: you dial a number and nobody answers! Religion is a cloak you put on or take off. Many put it on on a Sunday morning—the only time during the week they do. Many go to church Sunday morning so stiff and starchy, if you bent them an inch they would break. They think being good is being pious.

I am afraid of pious people. Every time I meet such a one and shake his hand, I want to count my fingers when I get my hand back. It is a pose, an outward thing.

This Pharisee was religious. Oh, was he! More religious than anybody here. So religious was he that he never missed prayer meeting. Now a Christian ought to be in prayer meeting. Christianity certainly ought to take you there. He never missed. If he wasn't called on for something, he volunteered. Standing up so all could hear him, he would pray the longest, most eloquent prayer.

Not only that; he fasted. Did you ever fast? This was the fastest faster in Jerusalem! He would fast at the drop of a hat.

Long about forty days before Easter, America breaks out in a religious rash and scratches it with something called Lent. The night before Lent begins, they go out on a binge. That is what Mardi Gras is for. After lapping up enough sin to last for forty days, they have a forty-day hangover. Then by the time Lent is over, they are about ready to jump back into the middle of it again. During that time they quit doing something they shouldn't be doing all the rest of the year anyhow, and they call that fasting!

A fellow asked me once, "What are you giving up for Lent this year?" I said, "Lent! What are you giving up?"

If you don't fast at least twice a week, then you are not in it with this fellow. This Pharisee fasted twice a week and let everybody know what he was doing.

Not only that; he brought one-tenth of everything he received and put it on the collection plate every Sunday.

Take this man and stand him up in front of eighty-five percent of the congregations in this nation and say, "Look, folks, we have a man who wants to come into our fellowship today. He is as clean as a hound's tooth, as honest as the days are long. He has a great reputation before his neighbors. He is one who fasts and tithes and prays. He wants to unite with us. How many of you will vote to receive him?" Eighty-five percent of the churches in this nation, on that recommendation, would vote him in without a dissenting vote. Because he is so much better than the average church member, they would be ashamed not to vote for him.

But when he got through with all his performance and walked away, the Lord Jesus said, "Unjustified!"

Here is man's top achievement. This is the very best you can do in the flesh. Nobody ever rose to a higher height than this in the flesh. But after man has put on his best act, God writes, "Unjustified!" over the best that any human being can do apart from Jesus Christ.

And everybody in this land this morning who goes in the church depending on what he is or what he has done or on his record, and walks out still depending on that, is going to hear, as he walks out of the door of whatever place of worship he is in, a condemnation of God ringing in his soul—"Unjustified!" Because you just don't make it that way.

THE LAW IS NOT A WAY TO BE SAVED; IT IS A "SCHOOLMASTER TO BRING US TO CHRIST"

You say, "Well, why was he lost?" Because he was trying to be saved by an impossible method. Man can't get saved just any way he wants to get saved. He has to get saved the way God says to get saved. This Pharisee was trying to be saved by keeping the law. Nobody ever got saved keeping the law, and nobody ever will. The law wasn't given for folks to be saved by the keeping of it. You say, "Nobody ever got saved by keeping the law?"

No.

"Nobody ever will?"

NO!

"Well, why?"

Because nobody ever did, and nobody ever will keep it. A very simple reason. You can't be saved by keeping something you didn't keep, can you?

You say, "Well, did God give the law?"

Yes.

"Did He ask folks to keep it?"

Yes.

"Well, did He know they couldn't keep it?"

Yes.

"But He gave it to folks who couldn't keep it and asked them to keep it knowing they couldn't keep it?"

Yes.

"Well, isn't that somewhat of a mockery?"

No. God doesn't mock people.

The law is a necessity. God had to give us the law to reveal to us the rotten sinners we are. We would never have known it if God hadn't given us the law. The law wasn't given to be saved by keeping it; the law was given to show that you need saving.

Go into the bathroom and look into the mirror. You can see your face is dirty, but you can't wash your face with the mirror. Mirrors are not made to wash faces with. They are made to reveal the dirt.

Take your flashlight and go up to the attic, and if your attic is like mine, you can discover it is dirty. But you can't clean your attic with a flashlight. It just shows the dirt.

Take a plumb line, lay it down by the side of a building, and you will discover the building is out of plumb. But you can't straighten the building with a plumb line. That is not the purpose of plumb lines. They are just to show you whether the building is straight or not.

God gave us the law, not to be saved by, but to show us that we need saving. And you look into the law and discover the sinner that you are; then the law acts as a schoolmaster to bring you to Christ, who can save you.

Let me show you how impossible it is to be saved by keeping the law.

James says in 2:10 that, if we have broken any little bit of God's law, any small portion of it, any iota of God's law, we are guilty of how much of it? All of it! Is there anybody here this morning who has never broken one bit of God's law? Can you stand up this morning and say, "I am absolutely perfect. I have always done everything I should have done, and I have never in my life done anything I should not have done, and I am perfect. From the day of my birth till now I have lived perfect before God"? If so, stand up and let me look at you.

Then how much of the law are you guilty of? The most respectable, most virtuous, purest, kindest person in this audience this morning is just as condemned in God's sight as the biggest wino down here on skid row, because we are all under the condemnation of a broken law.

Suppose there is a ravine here 100 feet deep and 30 feet across. And this fine musician and I are on this side of this ravine and we want to cross it, but there is no bridge over it. I say to him, "I'll jump first." Did you ever try to jump thirty feet? I advise you not to do it unless you are badly scared.

Up till now nobody ever has jumped thirty feet. So, I get back; and in spite of the fact that nobody ever did it, I run and jump just as far as I can jump. I set a new world record—I jump 29 feet, 11 1/2 inches. (I jump 129 feet, 11 1/2 inches—29 feet, 11 1/2 inches across and 100 feet down!)

Undaunted by my failure, he gets back and runs as hard as he can run and jumps as far as he can jump, which is five feet. That might be a fair comparison of our respective athletic abilities! I don't know how much of an athlete he is. But since I'm telling it, I'll outjump the singer!

Now, I'm a lot better off than he is, am I not? No. We both are a mess at the bottom of the ravine!

And if you don't jump the whole distance, you might as well not jump an inch. And if you haven't kept all the law, you are just as guilty as if you had broken every one in the catalog.

You say, "But now wait a minute, preacher. We are not under law but under grace." Thank God for that! Well, what is God's standard of righteousness under grace? It is His own Son, the Lord Jesus Christ. I am not going to ask you the fool question this morning, "Who here thinks you are as good as Jesus Christ?" It would be sacrilegious to even think about it. But did you know that you have to be exactly as good as He is to get to Heaven? But when you stand yourself up against the sinless, spotless Son of God and see the best you are able to do is nothing but dirty old filthy rags and see yourself falling a million miles short of the perfection that is found in Christ, you say, "If that is what God expects of me, I can never make it." I know you can't. I know I can't.

Then it stands to reason that, if you ever stand accepted or approved before God, you can't stand accepted or approved in what you are or in what you have done. You have to get rid of those dirty old rags and come to Christ in confession of your guilt, be clothed upon with His righteousness and stand one day before God approved in the righteousness of Christ, or perish.

And if that old Pharisee had forgotten about all he had done and remembered what Somebody had done for him, and if he had been pleading the blood of Christ instead of his own good works, he would have walked out of that place justified. But since he walked out depending on what he was and what he had done, then God had to write over his whole accomplishment, "Unjustified!" And so He does with every person who tries to go to Heaven any other way except by the blood of Christ.

THE PUBLICAN, A PICTURE OF US ALL—SINNERS!

But the publican had nothing to brag about. I don't either. You don't either. The publican is the picture of all of us in reality. And until we put ourselves in that position, there will never be salvation for any of us. He wasn't bragging.

There is the Pharisee standing out there in the limelight stroking himself on the brow and comparing himself with everybody in the audience. No sinner ever got saved or ever will get saved comparing himself with anybody. As long as you are trying to find somebody worse than you, you will never get saved. Until you see yourself as the worst sinner, you will never get saved.

The Pharisee was standing out there stroking himself on the brow. But you don't get saved head first. The publican, standing out there beating himself on the chest, had his hand down here in the vicinity of the heart. You get saved heart-first. Get the Son of God in the heart, and He will straighten out the head.

The publican had nothing to brag about. He could only beg, "God, be merciful to me a sinner," pleading the blood on the mercy seat in the sky.

And the only hope of redemption for us is in what Christ did for us. And our only acceptance before God is through the merit of Christ.

The hardest people to win to Christ are good people, reputable people, self-righteous people. This group would rather go to Hell than to bow the old stubborn knee, bend the old stiff neck, admit they are lost and get down to business before God. Yes, some will go to Hell before they will acknowledge they are sinners.

I can win people at a rescue mission easier than I can win the self-righteous who are big wheels, put on a big show and make a reputation in the church, when they know in their hearts they are not saved. I can win skid-row bums easier than I can win self-righteous church members.

I preached at the LeTourneau plant in Toccoa, Georgia, for five days. On the closing day I gave an invitation to the morning shift. God broke things up. Those workers didn't go to the aisles to make their way up front; they climbed over backs of seats as they came falling on their faces around the front of that platform, crying out to God. Personal workers were kneeling with their Bibles, leading them to Christ. I saw twenty-five men kneeling there weeping and crying out to God.

While this was going on, a well-dressed, intelligent person from the office force walked along the side and stood over to one side, with his face buried in his hands. He was sobbing. I walked over to him during the invitation and asked, "What troubles you, sir?"

"It's awful!"

"What's awful?"

"It's just awful!"

"What's awful?"

"Well, you don't understand."

"I would if you would explain it to me. I catch on very well. What don't I understand?"

"These men all think I am a Christian."

"Well, are you?"

"No."

"Then get down here on your knees."

"Brother Brown, it isn't that easy."

"What's so hard about it?"

"O preacher, it's awful! I'm a member of the First Baptist Church at Toccoa, but that isn't the worst. I teach the men's Bible class there. If I get down on my knees in front of these men, before nightfall everybody in Toccoa will know I have been a hypocrite, and I can't stand them thinking that of me."

I asked, "Do you want to go on being a hypocrite?"

"No."

"Do you want to go to Hell on top of that?"

"No."

"Then don't you think it would be far more sensible to admit you have been one and quit being one and get saved and go to Heaven, than go to Hell and live with hypocrites forever?"

He said, "Yes."

I said, "Get down there, then."

He looked over where those men were kneeling, took a step or two, and finally his old stubborn knees buckled under him. He pitched on his face by the side of one of those workers. I got down beside him with my Bible and led to Jesus Christ the man who came very close to going to Hell because he had a reputation! He was a religionist.

I don't know what you are pretending. I don't know how many churches you belong to or how many ways you have been baptized.

But I know one thing: if you are not saved by faith in Jesus Christ, if you have never come as a Hell-deserving sinner and opened your heart to the Saviour and done business with God in reality by repenting of your sin and turning in faith to Christ, you need to come today and acknowledge that and get it settled before you leave this place. If you don't, when you walk out through that door, you are going to hear God say, "Unjustified!"

I don't know how you came in today, but I know how you can go out today. I wouldn't for the world walk through one of those doors until I could go out with assurance that I would hear the approbation of God ringing in my soul, "Justified!" which means, "Just as if I had never sinned."

Forget your reputation. Forget what people may think. Forget everything except whether or not you need Christ.

And if you have never done business with God, come on up here. Don't come up here empty and go away empty. Don't come up lost and go away lost. If you come up here this morning without a knowledge of Christ, for God's sake come to the Saviour this morning as the publican of old and say, "God, be merciful," and today receive the Saviour and walk out of this place saved, clothed in the righteousness of Christ, accepted in the Beloved for all eternity.

Be sure you know how you go out of here this morning. Be sure it is with Christ in your heart.

CHARLES HADDON SPURGEON
1835-1892

ABOUT THE MAN:

Many times it has been said that this was the greatest preacher this side of the Apostle Paul. He began preaching at the age of 16. At 25 he built London's famous Metropolitan Tabernacle, seating around 5,000. It was never large enough. Even when traveling he preached to 10,000 eager listeners a week. Crowds thronged to hear him as they came to hear John the Baptist by the River Jordan. The fire of God was on him as on the Prophet Elijah facing assembled Israel at Mount Carmel.

Royalty sat in his Tabernacle, as did washerwomen. Mr. Gladstone had him to dinner; and cabbies refused his fare, considering it an honor to drive for this "Prince of Preachers." To a housewife kneading bread, he would say, "Have you ever tried the Bread of life?" Many a carpenter was asked, "Have you ever tried to build a house on sand?"

He preached in all the principal cities of England, Scotland and Ireland. And although invited to the United States on several occasions, he was never able to visit this country.

HOW GREAT WAS HIS HEART: for preachers, so the Pastors' College was founded; for orphans, so the orphans' houses came to be; for people around the world, so his literature poured forth in an almost unmeasurable volume. He was a national voice; so every national issue affecting morals, religion or the poor had his interpretation, his counsel.

Oh, but his passion for souls! You can see it in every sermon.

Spurgeon published thousands of poems, tracts, sermons and songs.

HIS MESSAGE TO LOST SINNERS WILL LIVE AS LONG AS THE GOSPEL IS PREACHED.

XV.

Heaven and Hell

CHARLES H. SPURGEON

(Preached in the open air at Hackney, England, to 12,000 people)

". . . many shall come from the east and west, and shall sit down with Abraham, and Isaac, and Jacob, in the kingdom of heaven.

"But the children of the kingdom shall be cast out into outer darkness: there shall be weeping and gnashing of teeth."—Matt. 8:11,12.

My text has two parts. The first is very agreeable to my mind and gives me pleasure; the second is terrible in the extreme; but since they are both the truth, they must be preached.

I. THE PROMISE OF HEAVEN

Let us take the first part. Here is a *most glorious promise.*

". . . many shall come from the east and west, and shall sit down with Abraham, and Isaac, and Jacob, in the kingdom of heaven."

I like that because it tells me what Heaven is and gives me a beautiful picture of it. It says Heaven is a place where I shall sit down with Abraham and Isaac and Jacob.

1. A Land of Rest

What a sweet thought that is for the working man! He often wipes the hot sweat from his face and wonders whether there is a land where he shall have to toil no longer. He scarcely ever eats a mouthful of bread that is not moistened with the sweat of his brow. Often he comes home weary and flings himself upon his couch, perhaps too tired to sleep. He thinks, *Oh, is there no land where I can rest! Is there no place where I can sit, and for once let these weary limbs be still! Is there no land where I can be quiet!*

Yes, thou son of toil and labor,

**"There is a happy land
Far, far away—"**

where toil and labor are unknown. Beyond your blue welkin is a city
fair and bright. Its walls are jasper, and its light is brighter than the sun.
There "the weary are at rest, and the wicked cease from troubling."
Immortal spirits are yonder, who never wipe sweat from their brow,
for "they sow not, neither do they reap"; they have not to toil and labor.

**There on a green and flowery mount,
Their weary souls shall sit;
And with transporting joys recount
The labors of their feet.**

To my mind, one of the best views of Heaven is that *it is a land of
rest*—especially to the working man. Those who have not to work hard
think they will love Heaven as a place of service. That is very true. But
to the working man, to the man who toils with his brain or hands, it
must ever be a sweet thought that there is a land where we shall rest.

Soon this voice will never be strained again; soon these lungs will
never have to exert themselves beyond their power; soon this brain shall
not be racked for thought; but I shall sit at the banquet-table of God;
yea, I shall recline on the bosom of Abraham and be at ease forever!

Oh, weary sons and daughters of Adam, you will not have to drive
the ploughshare into the unthankful soil in Heaven! You will not need
to rise to daily toils before the sun hath risen and labor still when the
sun hath long ago gone to his rest; but ye shall be still, ye shall be quiet,
ye shall rest yourselves, for all are rich in Heaven, all are happy there,
all are peaceful.

Toil, trouble, travail and labor are words that cannot be spelled in
Heaven; they have no such things there, for they always rest.

2. The Blessed Company of Heaven

And mark the *good company they sit with.* Some think that in Heaven
we shall know nobody. But our text declares here that we "shall sit down
with Abraham, and Isaac, and Jacob." Then I am sure that we shall
be aware that they are Abraham and Isaac and Jacob.

I heard of a good woman who asked her husband when she was
dying, "My dear, do you think you will know me when you and I get
to Heaven?" "Shall I know you! Why, I have always known you while

I have been here, and do you think I shall have lesser knowledge when I get to Heaven!"

If we have known one another here, we shall know one another there.

I have dear departed friends up there, and it is always a sweet thought to me that when I shall put my foot upon the threshold of Heaven there will come my sisters and brothers to clasp me by the hand and say, "Yes, thou loved one, and thou art here!" Dear relatives who have been separated, you will meet again in Heaven.

One of you has lost a mother—she is gone above; and if you follow the track of Jesus, you shall meet her there. Methinks I see yet another coming to meet you at the door of Paradise; and though the ties of natural affection may be in a measure forgotten—if I may be allowed to use a figure—how blessed would she be as she turns to God and says, "Here am I, and the children whom thou hast given me."

We shall recognize our friends. Husband, you will know your wife again. Mother, you will know those dear babes of yours—you marked their features when they lay panting and gasping for breath. You know how you hung over their graves when the cold sod was sprinkled over them and it was said, "Earth to earth, dust to dust, and ashes to ashes." But ye shall hear those loved voices again; ye shall hear those sweet voices once more; ye shall yet know that those whom ye loved have been loved by God.

Would not that be a dreary Heaven for us to inhabit, where we should be alike unknowing and unknown? I would not care to go to such a Heaven as that. I believe that Heaven is a fellowship of the saints and that we shall know one another there.

I have often thought I should love to see Isaiah. As soon as I get to Heaven, methinks I would ask for him, because he spoke more of Jesus Christ than all the rest. I am sure I should want to search out good George Whitefield—he who so continually preached to the people and wore himself out with a more than seraphic zeal.

Oh yes! We shall have choice company in Heaven when we get there. There will be no distinction of learned and unlearned, clergy and laity; but we shall walk freely one among another; we shall feel that we are brethren; we shall "sit down with Abraham, and Isaac, and Jacob."

3. Multitudes to Be in Heaven

But my text hath a yet greater depth of sweetness, for it says that "*many* shall come . . . and shall sit down." Some narrowminded bigots think that Heaven will be a very small place where there will be a very few people who went to their chapel or their church.

I confess, I have no wish for a very small Heaven. I love to read in the Scriptures that there are many mansions in my Father's house.

How often do I hear people say, "Straight is the gate and narrow is the way, and few there be that find it. There will be very few in Heaven; most will be lost."

My friend, I differ from you. Do you think Christ will let the Devil have more in Hell than there will be in Heaven? God says "a number that no man can number will be saved"; He never says "a number that no man can number will be lost." A host beyond all count will get into Heaven.

What glad tidings for you and for me! For if there are so many to be saved, why should not I be saved? Why should not you? Why should not yon man, over there in the crowd, say, "Cannot I be among the multitude?" May not that poor woman there take heart and say, "Well, if there were but half a dozen saved, I might fear that I should not be one; but since many are to come, why should not I also be saved?"

Cheer up, disconsolate! Cheer up, son of mourning, child of sorrow. There is hope for thee still!

I can never know that any man is past God's grace. There be a few who have sinned that sin that is unto death, and God gives them up; but the vast host of mankind are yet within the reach of sovereign mercy—"and many of them shall come from the east and from the west, and shall sit down in the kingdom of heaven."

Look at my text again, and you will see where these people come from. They are to "come from the east and west."

The Jews said that they would all come from Palestine, every one of them, every man, woman and child; that there would not be one in Heaven who was not a Jew. And the Pharisees thought that, if they were not all Pharisees, they could not be saved.

But Jesus Christ said many will come from the east and from the west. There will be a multitude from that far-off land of China (we hope that the Gospel will yet be victorious in that land). There will be a multitude from this western land of England, from the western country beyond the sea in America, from the south in Australia, from the north in Canada, Siberia and Russia. From the uttermost parts of the earth there shall come many to sit down in the kingdom of God.

But I do not think this text is to be understood so much geographically as spiritually. When it says that they "shall come from the east and west," I think it does not refer to nations particularly, but to different kinds of people.

Now, "the east the west" signify those who are the very farthest off from religion; yet many of them will be saved and get to Heaven. There is a class of persons who will always be looked upon as hopeless. Many a time have I heard a man or woman say of such a one, "He cannot be saved: he is too abandoned. What is *he* good for? Ask *him* to go to a place of worship—he was drunk on Saturday night. What would be the use of reasoning with *him*? There is no hope for *him*. He is a hardened fellow. See what he has done these many years. What good will it be to speak to *him*?"

Now, hear this, ye who think your fellows worse than yourselves— ye who condemn others, whereas ye are often just as guilty: Jesus Christ says "many shall come from the east and west." There will be many in Heaven who were drunkards once. I believe, among that blood- bought throng, there are many who reeled in and out the tavern half their lifetime. But by the power of divine grace, they were able to dash the liquor cup to the ground. They renounced the riot of intoxication— fled away from it—and served God. Yes! Many will be in Heaven who were drunkards on earth. There will be many who were harlots: some of the most abandoned will be found there.

You remember the story of Whitefield's once saying that there would be some in Heaven who were "The Devil's castaways," some the Devil would hardly think good enough for him, yet whom Christ would save. Lady Huntingdon once gently hinted that such language was not quite proper. But just at the time there happened to be heard a ringing at the bell, and Whitefield went downstairs. Afterwards he came up and said, "Your ladyship, what do you think a poor woman had to say to me just now? She was a sad profligate, and she said, 'O Mr. Whitefield, when you were preaching, you told us that Christ would take in the Devil's castaways, and I am one of them,'" and that was the means of her salvation.

Shall anybody ever check us from preaching to the lowest of the low? I have been accused of getting all the rabble of London around me. God bless the rabble! "God save the rabble!" then say I.

But suppose they are "the rabble" who need the Gospel more than they do. We have lots of those who preach to ladies and gentlemen, and we want someone to preach to the rabble in these degenerate days. Oh, here is comfort for me, for many of the rabble are to come from the east and from the west!

What would you think if you were to see the difference between some who are in Heaven and some who shall be there? There might be found one whose hair hangs across his eyes, his locks matted. He looks horrible. His bloated eyes start from his face. He grins almost like an idiot. He has drunk away his very brain until life seems to have departed, so far as sense and being are concerned. Yet I would tell to you—that man is capable of salvation. And in a few years I might say, "Look up yonder! See that bright star? Discern you that man with a crown of pure gold upon his head? Notice that being clad in robes of sapphire and in garments of light? That is the self-same man who sat there a poor, benighted, almost idiotic being; yet sovereign grace and mercy have saved him!"

There are none except those who have sinned the unpardonable sin who are beyond God's mercy. Fetch me out the worst; still I would preach the Gospel to them. Fetch me out the vilest; still I would preach to them. I recollect my Master saying, "Go ye out into the highways and hedges, and compel them to come in, that my house may be filled."

". . . many shall come from the east and west, and shall sit down with Abraham, and Isaac, and Jacob, in the kingdom of heaven."

They shall come! They shall come! And naught in Heaven nor on earth nor in Hell can stop them from coming.

And now, thou chief of sinners, listen one moment while I call thee to Jesus. There is one person here tonight who thinks himself the worst soul that ever lived. There is one who says to himself, I do not deserve to be called to Christ, I am sure!

Soul! I call thee! Thou lost, most wretched outcast, this night, by authority given me of God, I call thee to come to my Saviour.

Some time ago, when I went into the county court to see what they were doing, I heard a man's name called out. Immediately the man said, "Make way! Make way! They call me!" And up he came.

Now I call the chief of sinners tonight. Let him say, "Make way! Make way, doubts! Make way, fears! Make way, sins! Christ calls me! And if Christ calls me, that is enough!"

I'll to His gracious feet approach
Whose sceptre mercy gives.
Perhaps He may command me, "Touch!"
And then the suppliant lives.

I can but perish if I go;
I am resolved to try,
For if I stay away, I know
I must forever die.

But should I die with mercies sought,
When I the King have tried,
That were to die, delightful thought!
As sinner never died.

Go and try my Saviour! If He casts you away after you have sought Him, tell it in the pit that Christ would not hear you. But *that* you shall never be allowed to do. It would dishonor the mercy of the covenant for God to cast away one penitent sinner; and it never shall be while it is written, ". . . many shall come from the east and west, and shall sit down with Abraham, and Isaac, and Jacob, in the kingdom of heaven."

II. BUT SOME WILL BE CAST OUT, MISSING HEAVEN

The second part of my text is heartbreaking. I could preach with great delight to myself from the first part; but here is a dreary task to my soul, because there are gloomy words here. But as I have told you, what is written in the Bible must be preached, whether it be gloomy or cheerful.

Some ministers never mention anything about Hell. I heard of a minister who once said to his congregation, "If you do not love the Lord Jesus Christ, you will be sent to that place which it is not polite to mention." He ought not to have been allowed to preach again if he could not use plain words.

Now, if I saw that house on fire over there, do you think I would stand and say, "I believe the operation of combustion is proceeding yonder"? No. I would call out, "Fire! Fire!" Then everybody would know what I meant.

So if the Bible says, "The children of the kingdom shall be cast out into outer darkness," am I to stand here and mince the matter at all? God forbid! We must speak the truth as it is written.

1. Some Externally Religious Will Be Cast Out

It is a terrible truth, for it says, *"The children of the kingdom* shall be cast out"! Now, who are those children? "The children of the kingdom" are those who are noted for the externals of piety but who have nothing of the internals of it. People whom you will see with their Bibles and hymnbooks marching off to chapel as religiously as possible, or going to church as devoutly and demurely as they can, looking as somber and serious as parish beadles and fancying that they are quite sure to be saved, though their hearts are not in the matter; nothing but their bodies—these are "the children of the kingdom." They have no grace, no life, no Christ, and they shall be cast into utter darkness.

2. Some Children of Godly Parents Will Be Cast Out

Again, these people are *the children of pious fathers and mothers*. Nothing touches a man's heart like talking about his mother.

I have heard of a swearing sailor whom nobody could manage, not even the police, who was always making some disturbance wherever he went. Once he went into a place of worship, and no one could keep him still. But a gentleman went up and said to him, "Jack, you had a mother once." With that the tears ran down his cheeks. He said, "Bless you, sir, I had; and I brought her gray hairs with sorrow to the grave, and a pretty fellow I am here tonight." He then sat down, quite sobered and subdued by the very mention of his mother.

And there are some of you—"children of the kingdom"—who can remember your mothers. Your mother took you on her knee and taught you early to pray. Your father tutored you in the ways of godliness. Yet you are here tonight without grace in your heart—without hope of Heaven. You are going downwards towards Hell as fast as your feet can carry you. Some of you have broken your poor mother's heart. Oh, if I could tell you what she has suffered for you when you have at night been indulging in your sin!

Do you know what your guilt will be, ye "children of the kingdom," if ye perish after a pious mother's prayers and tears have fallen upon you? I can conceive of no one entering Hell with a worse grace than the man who goes there with drops of his mother's tears on his head and with his father's prayers following him at his heels.

Some of you will inevitably endure this doom; some of you shall wake up one day and find yourselves in utter darkness, while your parents shall be up there in Heaven, looking down upon you with upbraiding eyes, seeming to say, "What! After all we did for you, all we said, are ye come to this?"

"Children of the kingdom," do not think that a pious mother can save you. Do not think, because your father was a member of such-and-such a church, that his godliness will save you.

I can suppose someone standing at Heaven's gate and demanding, "Let me in! Let me in!" What for? "Because my mother is in there." Your mother had nothing to do with you. If she was holy, she was holy for herself. If she was evil, she was evil for herself. "But my grandfather prayed for me!" That is no use. Did you pray for yourself? "No, I did not." Then grandfather's prayers and grandmother's prayers and father's and mother's prayers may be piled on the top of one another until they reach the stars, but they can never make a ladder for you to go to Heaven by.

You must seek God for yourself; or rather, God must seek you. You must have vital experience of godliness in your heart, or else you are lost, even though all your friends were in Heaven.

That was a dreadful dream which a pious mother once had and told to her children. She thought the judgment day was come. The great books were opened. They all stood before God. Jesus Christ said, "Separate the chaff from the wheat; put the goats on the left hand, and the sheep on the right." The mother dreamed that she and her children were standing just in the middle of the great assembly. And the angel came and said, "I must take the mother—she is a sheep: she must go to the right hand. The children are goats: they must go on to the left."

She thought as she went that her children clutched her and said, "Mother, can we part? Must we be separated?" She then put her arms around them and seemed to say, "My children, I would, if possible, take you with me." But in a moment the angel touched her. Her cheeks were dried; and now, overcoming natural affection, being rendered supernatural and sublime and resigned to God's will, she said, "My children, I taught you well. I trained you up. Yet you forsook the ways of God. Now all I have to say is Amen to your condemnation." Thereupon they were snatched away, and she saw them in perpetual torment while she was in Heaven.

Young man, what will you think, when the last day comes, to hear Christ say, "Depart, ye cursed!" and a voice just behind Him, saying, "Amen"? Upon inquiring whence came the voice, you find it was your mother.

Or, young woman, when thou art cast away into utter darkness, what

will you think to hear a voice saying, "Amen"? As you look, there sits
your father, his lips still moving with the solemn curse.

"Children of the kingdom," many penitent reprobates will enter
Heaven; publicans and sinners will get there; repenting drunkards and
swearers will be saved; but many of the "children of the kingdom" will
be cast out. Oh, to think that you who have been so well trained should
be lost, while many of the worst will be saved! It will be the Hell of hells
for you to look up and see there "poor Jack," the drunkard, lying in
Abraham's bosom, while you, who have had a pious mother, are cast
into Hell—simply because you would not believe on the Lord Jesus
Christ, but put His Gospel from you and lived and died without it! That
were the very sting of all—to see ourselves cast away, when the chief
of sinners finds salvation.

III. UNCONVERTED TO BE CAST INTO HELL

Now listen to me whilst I undertake the doleful task of telling you
what is to become of these "children of the kingdom." Jesus Christ says
they are to be 'cast into outer darkness where there is weeping and
gnashing of teeth.'

1. Forcibly Thrown Out

First, notice, they are to be *cast out.* They are not to *go*; but when
they come to Heaven's gates, they are to be *cast* out. As soon as
hypocrites arrive at the gates of Heaven, Justice will say, "There he
comes! He spurned a father's prayers and mocked a mother's tears.
He has forced his way downward against all the advantage mercy has
supplied. And now, there he comes! Gabriel, take the man."

The angel, binding you hand and foot, holds you one single moment
over the mouth of the chasm. He bids you look down—down—down.
There is no bottom; and you hear coming up from the abyss sullen
moans and hollow groans and screams of tortured ghosts. You quiver,
your bones melt like wax, and your marrow quakes within you.

Where is now thy might? Where thy boasting and bragging? Ye shriek
and cry, ye beg for mercy; but the angel, with one tremendous grasp,
seizes you fast, then hurls you down with the cry, "Away! Away!" Down
you go to the pit that is bottomless and roll forever downward—
downward—ne'er to find a resting place for the soles of your feet. Ye
shall be cast out.

2. The Outer Darkness of Hell

And *where are you to be cast to?* Ye are to be cast "into outer darkness"; ye are to be put in the place where there will be no hope. By "light" in Scripture we understand "hope"; you are to be put "into outer darkness," where there is no light—no hope.

Is there a man here who has no hope? I cannot suppose such a person.

One of you, perhaps, says, "I am thirty pounds in debt and shall be sold up by-and-by; but I have a hope that I may get a loan and so escape my difficulty."

Says another, "My business is ruined, but things may take a turn yet—I have a hope."

Says another, "I am in great distress, but I hope that God will provide for me."

Another says, "I am fifty pounds in debt; I am sorry for it; but I will set these strong hands to work and do my best to get out of it."

One of you thinks a friend is dying, but you have a hope that, perhaps, the fever may take a turn—that he may yet live.

But in Hell there is no hope. They have not even the hope of dying— the hope of being annihilated. They are forever—forever—forever— lost! On every chain in Hell is written "forever." In the fires, there blazes out "forever." Up above their heads, they read "forever." Their eyes are galled and their hearts are pained with the thought that it is "forever."

Oh, if I could tell you tonight that Hell would one day be burned out and that those who were lost might be saved, there would be a jubilee in Hell at the very thought of it. But it cannot be—it is *"forever"*— they are "cast into outer darkness."

3. "Weeping and Gnashing of Teeth"

But I want to get over this as quickly as I can; for who can bear to talk thus to his fellow-creatures?

What is it that the lost are doing? They are "weeping and gnashing their teeth." Do you gnash your teeth now? You would not do it except you were in pain and agony. Well, in Hell there is always gnashing of teeth. And do you know why?

There is one gnashing his teeth at his companion and muttering, "I was led into Hell by you! You led me astray! You taught me to drink the first time!" And the other gnashes his teeth and says, "What if I did?

You made me worse than I should have been in after times."

There is a child who looks at her mother and says, "Mother, you trained me up to vice." And the mother gnashes her teeth again at the child and says, "I have no pity for you, for you excelled me in it and led me into deeper sin."

Fathers gnash their teeth at their sons, and sons at their fathers.

And, methinks, if there are any who will have to gnash their teeth more than others, it will be seducers, when they see those whom they have led from the path of virtue and hear them saying, "Ah! We are glad you are in Hell with us! You deserve it, for you led us here!"

Have any of you tonight upon your consciences the fact that you have led others to the pit? Oh, may sovereign grace forgive you! "We have gone astray like lost sheep," said David. Now a lost sheep never goes astray alone, if it is one of a flock. I lately read of a sheep that leaped over the parapet of a bridge and was followed by every one of the flock. So, if one man goes astray, he leads others with him. Some of you will have to account for others' sins when you get to Hell, as well as your own sins.

Oh, what "weeping and gnashing of teeth" there will be in that pit!

4. Old and Young Alike in Danger of Hell

Now shut the black book. Who wants to say any more about it? I have warned you solemnly. I have told you of the wrath to come. The evening darkens, and the sun is setting. Ah! The evenings darken with some of you. I can see grayheaded men here. Are your gray hairs a crown of glory or a fool's cap to you? Are you on the very verge of Heaven, or are you tottering on the brink of your grave and sinking down to perdition?

Let me warn you, grayheaded men; your evening is coming. O poor, tottering grayhead, wilt thou take the last step into the pit? Let a young child step before thee and beg thee to consider. There is thy staff—it has nothing of earth to rest upon. Now, ere thou diest, bethink thyself this night; let seventy years of sin start up; let the ghosts of thy forgotten transgressions march before thine eyes. What wilt thou do with seventy wasted years to answer for—with seventy years of criminality to bring before God? God give thee grace this night to repent and to put thy trust in Jesus.

And you, middle-aged men, are not safe. The evening lowers with you, too. You may soon die.

A few mornings ago I was roused early from my bed by the request that I would hasten to see a dying man. I hurried off with all speed to see the poor creature; but when I reached the house, he was dead—a corpse. As I stood in the room, I thought, *Ah! that man little thought he should die so soon.* There were his wife and children and friends— they little thought he should die, for he was hale, strong and hearty but a few days before.

None of you have a lease on your lives. If you have, where is it? Go and see if you have it anywhere in your chest at home. No! Ye may die tomorrow. Let me therefore warn you by the mercy of God; let me speak to you as a brother may speak, for I love you, you know I do, and I would press the matter home to your hearts. Oh, to be amongst the many who shall be accepted in Christ—how blessed that will be! God has said that whosoever shall call on His name shall be saved. He casts out none that come unto Him through Christ.

And now, ye youths and maidens, one word with you. Perhaps you think that religion is not for you. "Let us be happy," say you. "Let us be merry and joyous." How long, young man, how long? "Till I am twenty-one." Are you sure that you will live until then? Let me tell you one thing. If you do live until that time, if you have no heart for God now, you will have none then.

Men do not get better if left alone. It is with them as with the garden: if you let it alone and permit weeds to grow, you will not expect to find it better in six months—but worse. Men talk as if they could repent when they like. It is the work of God to give us repentance. Some even say, "I shall turn to God on such-and-such a day." But if you felt aright, you would say, "I must run to God and ask Him to give me repentance now, lest I should die before I have found Jesus Christ my Saviour."

IV. CHRIST, THE ONLY ESCAPE FROM HELL, ONLY WAY TO HEAVEN

Now, one word in conclusion. I have told you of Heaven and Hell. What is the way, then, to escape from Hell and to be found in Heaven? I will now tell you my old tale again tonight. I recollect when I told it you before, a good friend in the crowd said, "Tell us something fresh, old fellow." Now really, in preaching ten times a week, we cannot always say things fresh. You have heard John Gough, and you know he tells his tales over again. I have nothing but the old Gospel.

"He that believeth and is baptized shall be saved." There is nothing here of works. It does not say, "He who is a good man shall be saved," but, "He who believes and is baptized shall be saved." Well, what is it to believe? It is to put your trust entirely upon Jesus.

Poor Peter once believed, and Jesus Christ said to him, "Come on, Peter, walk to Me on the water." Peter went stepping along on the tops of the waves without sinking. But when he looked down at the waves, he began to tremble, and down he went.

Now, poor sinner, Christ says, "Come on. Walk on your sins. Come to Me." And if you do, He will give you power. If you believe on Christ, you will be able to walk over your sins—to tread upon them and overcome them.

I can remember the time when my sins first stared me in the face. I thought myself the most accursed of all men. I had not committed any very great open transgressions against God; but I recollected that I had been well trained and tutored, and I thought my sins were thus greater than other people's. I cried to God to have mercy, and I feared that He would not pardon me.

Month after month I cried to God. He did not hear me, and I knew not what it was to be saved. Sometimes I was so weary of the world that I desired to die; but then I recollected that there was a worse world after this and that it would be an ill matter to rush before my Maker unprepared. At times I wickedly thought God a most heartless tyrant because He did not answer my prayer; then, at others, I thought, *I deserve His displeasure; if He sends me to Hell, He will be just.*

But I remember the hour when I stepped into a little place of worship and saw a tall, thin man step into the pulpit. I have never seen him from that day and probably never shall, until we meet in Heaven. He opened the Bible and read, with a feeble voice, "Look unto me, and be ye saved, all the ends of the earth: for I am God, and there is none else." Thought I, *I am one of the ends of the earth.* Then turning round and fixing his gaze on me, as if he knew me, the minister said, "Look! Look! Look!"

Why, I thought I had a great deal to *do,* but I found it was only to *look.* I thought I had a garment to spin out for myself, but I found that, if I looked, Christ would give me a garment.

Look, sinner—that is to be saved. 'Look unto him, all ye ends of the earth, and be saved.'

That is what the Jews did. When Moses held up the brazen serpent, he said, "Look!" and they looked. The serpent might be twisting round them, and they might be nearly dead; but they simply looked, and the moment they looked, the old serpent dropped off and they were healed.

Look to Jesus, sinner. None but Jesus can do helpless sinners good. There is a hymn we often sing, but which I do not think is quite right. It says,

> **Venture on Him, venture wholly;**
> **Let no other trust intrude.**

Now, it is no venture to trust in Christ, not in the least. He who trusts in Christ is quite secure.

I recollect that when dear John Hyatt was dying, Matthew Wilks said to him, in his usual tone, "Well, John, could you trust your soul in the hands of Jesus Christ now?" "Yes," said he, "a million! a million souls!"

I am sure that every Christian who has ever trusted in Christ can say amen to that. Trust in Him. He will never deceive you. My blessed Master will never cast you away.

May the blessed Spirit reveal to you your state! May He show you that you are dead, that you are lost, ruined. May He make you feel what a dreadful thing it would be to sink into Hell! May He take you as the angel did of old, and put His hand upon you and say, "Flee! flee! flee! Look to the mountain: look not behind thee; stay not in all the plain." And may we all meet in Heaven at last; and there we shall be happy forever.

Mr. Spurgeon added the following note to the published sermon:

P.S. This sermon was watered by many prayers of the faithful in Zion. The preacher did not intend it for publication; but seeing that it is now in print, he will not apologize for its faulty composition or rambling style; but instead thereof, he would beg the prayers of his readers that this feeble sermon may all the more exalt the honor of God, by the salvation of many who shall read it. "The excellency of the power is of God, and not of man."

For a complete list of books available from the Sword of the Lord, write to Sword of the Lord Publishers, P. O. Box 1099, Murfreesboro, Tennessee 37133.